ADVANCED LEARNER'S DICTIONARY *Of* INTERNET

ADVANCED LEARNER'S DICTIONARY

Of

INTERNET

Compiled & Edited by

A Team of Experts

ANMOL PUBLICATIONS PVT. LTD.

NEW DELHI - 110 002 (INDIA)

ANMOL PUBLICATIONS PVT. LTD.
4374/4B, Ansari Road, Daryaganj
New Delhi - 110 002

Advanced Learner's Dictionary of Internet

First Edition, 2000

ISBN 81-261-0468-6

PRINTED IN INDIA

Published by J.L. Kumar for Anmol Publications Pvt. Ltd., New Delhi and Printed at Mehra Offset Press, Delhi.

Preface

This *Advanced Learner's Dictionary of Internet* is basically designed for students and teachers as well. It is the result of a careful analysis of the needs of advanced level students and should be an invaluable aid in their day-to-day learning.

As it is extremely difficult to limit the contents of such a dictionary at 'Advanced' level standard, many headwords are included that are above this level and that may be of interest to Advanced Learners. A few headwords that are not strictly scientific are also included because of their common usage in everyday scientific terminology. It has been our aim to provide explanations that are easily understood, whilst maintaining academic standards.

We have tried to include the more important terms used at advanced level, but would welcome any comments regarding serious omissions or indeed about the content of any of the entries.

We would like to thank all the people who have cooperated in producing this dictionary. We are also grateful to many people who have given additional help and advice.

—Editors

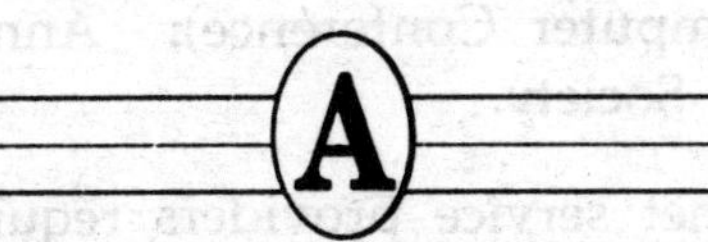

ABE (rhymes with *babe*): *A* DOS binary-to-ASCII conversion program for sending files via e-mail.

ABEND (*ab-end,* n): A computer crash (from "abnormal end" error message).

Ablative Pit: An indentation (pit) burnt into the surface of CD-ROM and WORM drives as a means of recording digital information. The absence or presence of the pit is detected during read operations and interpreted as binary 0 or 1.

Above Board: In an IBM or IBM compatible PC, a printed circuit board that contains additional RAM. The name "Above Board" is used since the board provides memory "above" the conventional Memory 640KB.

Absolute Address: This is a method of assigning an address to each location in computer memory, these usually relate to some fixed, designated part of RAM or ROM and are therefore referred to as absolute addresses, they are not dependant on the present location. In everyday life, a house number is an absolute address, it is not dependant on where you start looking for a particular house or Property. Compare this to "the third house on the right. This address is relative to the present address The phrase "absolute address" is also used in spreadsheet terminology. If a formula embedded in cell All reads AVERAGE (A1:A10) it averages the ten cells immediately above this (present) location (All), the cells to be averaged are addressed relative to the present address. If this formula is copied to address B11 it would read AVERAGE (Bl:B10). In absolute addressing the first formula may read AVERAGE($A$1:$A$10), the dollar signs are used to indicate that no matter where this formula is transferred it is always the cells A1 through A10 that are to be averaged.

Abstract: A short description of a document.

abstract syntax: A syntax (set of rules for properly formed commands) not limited to a single application or platform.

Abstract Syntax Notation One (ASNA.1): An OSI language used to encode Simple Network Management Protocol packets, part of the infrastructure of the Internet.

ACC (Australian Computer Conference): Annual conference of the Australian Computer Society.

acceptable use: Internet service providers require that all their users agree to some guidelines of acceptable use of Internet and Usenet resources. Acceptable use policies vary from provider to provider.

access (n): 1. A connection to the Internet; 2. A type of Internet connection (network access, dial-up access, etc.); 3. The ability to perform certain activities or read privileged information.

Access Control List (ACL): A site's table of services and hosts authorized to use those services.

Access privileges: Authorization for a specific level of access.

Access provider: An institution providing Internet access, such as a commercial service provider, university, or employer.

Access Time: The time taken from first request for data to that data appearing on the data bus. Access time to disk or is tape is largely determined by file size and the hardware device, whether or not the read/write head has to be repositioned and whether the data file occupies a favourable sequence of disk sectors, tape sections etc. Typical hard disk access times are in the 30-80ms range. In the case of RAM, the access time is largely a function of the type of RAM chips being used and the size of the file. Typical RAM access times are in the order of 100ns.

(v) 1. To connect to the Internet; 2. To connect to a site; 3. To open a file.

account (n): A form of access to a computer or network for a specific username and password, usually with a home directory, an e-mail inbox, and a set of access privileges.

Accumulator: A register which is used to store the results of intermediate or final calculations. An accumulator is an integral part of a microprocessor, forming a part of the ALU.

Accuracy: A measure of the closeness of a calculation to the real situation, that is, the truth, often a difficult item to define.

ACK (rhymes with *pack):* 1. Acknowledgment from a computer that a packet of data has been received and verified; 2. The mnemonic for ASCII 6.

ACM: Association for Computing Machinery.

active star: A network design (a way of arranging the devices themselves in a network) in which a central hub retransmits all network traffic.

AD *(ay-dee)*: Administrative Domain.

ADA: This is a high level language developed for the US Department of Defense during the 1970s. ADA is a structured language and was named after Augusta Ada, a 19th Century mathematician.

Addicted to Noise: A music magazine, featuring sound clips, on the Web at http:// www.addict.com/ATN/.

Add/Strip: A Macintosh shareware program that inserts or deletes carriage returns (ASCII 13) at the end of each line of a text file, for conversion between Macintosh and UNIX systems.

Address: This describes a location in memory. Addresses are usually referred to by using hexadecimal notation, for example an area of RAM may occupy addresses C000H-D00H.

address book: In some programs, a list of abbreviations for e-mail addresses.

Address Bus: A set of wires or printed circuit tracks that is used for specifying addresses within the computer and its peripherals.

address command: A UUCP extension that provides additional routing and confirmation options to the basic file-copying transaction that underlies UUCP.

Address Mapping Table (AMT): A table used to resolve physical addresses into logical addresses.

address mask: The portion of an IP address that identifies the network and subnet.

address resolution: Conversion of a physical address into a logical address.

Address Resolution Protocol (ARP): A TCP/IP protocol for converting physical addresses to logical addresses.

ADJ: (rhymes with *badge)* [Boolean operator] *Adjacent to.* A text search with ADJ between two words matches only documents in which those words are adjacent.

Administrative Domain (AD): The portion of a network overseen by a single administrator.

administrator: 1. A system administrator (someone who runs a network); 2. Someone who maintains the addresses and handles the administrative chores for a mailing list or other Internet discussion group.

administrivia: Information regarding the administration of a mailing list or moderated newsgroup, such as the announcement of a new moderator, posted to the list or group.

Advanced Program-to-Program Communications (APPC): An IBM peer-to-peer network protocol.

Advanced Research Projects Agency (ARPA): A U.S. Department of Defense agency that, along with universities and research facilities, created ARPAnet, the precursor of the Internet.

agent: 1. The process in client/server communication that handles negotiation between the client and the server; 2. A Simple Network Management Protocol program that monitors network traffic; 3. A program that performs some action on the behalf of a user without the direct oversight of the user.

AIR NFS: A Windows version of NFS (Network File System).

ALGOL: Acronym for ALGO-rithmic Language, a high level programming language developed, during the mid-1960s. ALGOL is a structured language and is regarded as a forerunner of other structured languages such as PASCAL.

Algorithm: A set of instructions that provide a solution to a given problem. Named after AI Khwarizmi, an Arab mathematician of the ninth century, author of many treatises on mathematics and algebra.

alias (n): 1. An abbreviation for an e-mail address stored in a mail program, allowing the user to type or select the shorter alias instead of the full address, 2. An alternate name for an Internet address.

ALL-IN-1: A VAX e-mail and conference program.

Alphanumeric: Any characters of the alphabet and the arabic numbers 0-9. This definition of alphanumeric is used to specify data types in a database. For example a database entry for "Employee Address" would usually include alphabetical characters and numbers and can therefore be categorised as an alphanumeric entry.

Alpha Test: Initial testing of a new product, usually performed in-house by the hardware-software developer.

alt.: A hierarchy of newsgroups in the Usenet mold but outside of Usenet proper, devoted to "alternative" topics. It is easier to create alt. groups than to create standard Usenet groups, and it's effectively impossible to remove them.

ALT Key: On IBM and IBM compatible PCs, a key that in combination with other keys invokes a particular action. The ALT key can also be used to generate any ASCII character on screen, for example ALT+65 (on the numeric key pad) produces ASCII character 65 (A). ALT+36 produces the dollar sign ($) etc.

alt.config: A newsgroup for the discussion of new newsgroup formation in the alternative newsgroup hierarchy. Although the alt. hierarchy was created in part to sidestep the consensus rules of Usenet, there is still a range of views about what new alt. newsgroups should be created, how they should be named, and whether they will be accepted and propagated by system administrators all over the Net.

alternative newsgroup hierarchy: 1. Any hierarchy of newsgroups in the Usenet mold but not, strictly speaking, part of Usenet; 2. The alt. hierarchy in particular.

Alt.fan group: A newsgroup devoted to a real-world or Net celebrity or villain.

alt.plastic.utensil.spork.spork.spork: One of several spork news-groups (a spork is a cross between a spoon and a fork). An example of improper use of a dot instead of a hyphen (plastic.utensil) and of a popular silly group ending.

alt.swedish.chef.bork.bork.bork: The original silly group with a *gag.gag.gag* ending.

ALU: Abbreviation for Arithmetic Logic Unit. This is part of the Central Processing Unit (CPU) and is involved in arithmetic operations, for example, A=B*(C+D/E) and logic calculations, for example, is X greater than Y.

America Online (AOL): [online service] info@aol.com, (800) 8276364. America Online added full Internet access in 1994. The resulting flood of new users, especially on Usenet, was greeted with dismay by many longtime users.

American National Standards Institute (ANSI): U.S. organisation that develops and promotes voluntary standards in a wide range of academic and research fields.

Amiga: A personal computer produced by Commodore, based on the Motorola 68000 microprocessor.

Amoeba: A silly name for Amiga

ampersand (&): In HTML (Web) documents, used with special codes to indicate special characters (the HTML code for an ampersand itself is *&)*

Amplitude: A measure of the waveform of a transmitted signal. The amplitude of a sine wave is measured from the highest point of the signal to the lowest.

Amplitude modulation: A transmission technique which uses changes in the amplitude of the signal to transmit information (voice, music or data).

analog (adj): Representing values as physical states and changes in values as changes in physical states. In a stereo, for example, a CD player converts the digital information encoded on the CD into an analog signal sent to the amplifier.

Analog Computer: A computer designed to respond to an infinite number of variations in signal, compared to a digital computer which responds to discrete off and on (binary 0 and 1) signals, Examples of analog computer usage include monitoring temperature, voltage and current readings in a power station. Each of these parameters can attain an infinite number of values, not just simply off and on. In many cases however, it is comparatively simple to convert analog signals to a coded binary signal, enabling digital computers to perform many tasks that were previously the domain of analog computers.

Analog Transmission: A method of transmitting data or information that uses an infinitely variable signal. Whereas digital transmission can only transmit off and on signals (binary 0 and 1), analog can transmit any designated value. Using photography as an example, in digital transmission it would be possible to transmit a black and white photograph, but only black and only white would be transmitted, whereas analog could transmit every possible shade of grey.

Anarchie *(anarchy)*: A Macintosh program that combines the functions of archie and FTP.

Anchor (n): An HTML tag that indicates a hypertext link or the destination of such a link.

And [Boolean operator]: *And.* A text search with AND between two words matches only documents containing both words.

AND Gate: A logic gate that has two or more inputs and one output. It is used to detect when two or more inputs are present. Two or more inputs must read 1 before the gate makes an output (1). The truth table for an AND gate is shown below.

Input A	Input B	Output
0	0	0
0	1	0
1	0	0
1	1	1

Andrew File System (AFS): A set of network protocols that makes remote files accessible as if they were local (as contrasted with being available via. FTP).

angle brackets: They surround return addresses in e-mail headers. In IRC channels, MUDs, and some e-mail and Usenet posts, angle brackets surround descriptions of actions or expressions for example, <looking over my left shoulder> or <groan>. Similarly, some use <grin> or <g>.

In UNIX, a right angle bracket redirects the output of a command into a file. A double right angle bracket (>>) appends the redirected output of a command to the end of a file.

Animation: Movement of graphics objects during a computer program.

annoybot (n): An IRC bot that pesters real users.

anon.penet.fi: The best known anonymous remailer service, info@anon.penet.fi.

anonymous FTP: The most common use of FTP, the Internet file transfer protocol. FTP sites that allow anonymous FTP don't require a password for access—you only have to log in as *anonymous* your e-mail address as a password (for their records).

anonymous remailer: A service that provides anonymity to users on the Net who wish to send mail and Usenet posts without their actual e-mail address and real name attached. Instead of sending mail or posting articles directly, users send them to the anonymous remailer, with special header lines indicating the ultimate destination and the pen name of the user.

ANSI: Abbreviation for American National Standards Institute, a powerful industry association of the USA. ANSI is active in negotiating and promoting industry standards, many of which have been adapted into international standards by CCITT and/or ISO. ANSI standards exist for many aspects of computer usage, for example programming language such as ANSI C and the ANSI defined Data Dictionary.

***.answers Moderated:** Usenet news groups dedicated to the posting of FAQs (frequently asked questions) and their answers.

any key: Some programs prompt you to continue by telling you to press any key. This means that any key you press will suffice to continue the process. There is no specific "Any" key.

AOL: The standard abbreviation for America Online, from aol.com, the subdomain and domain for that online service.

API *(ay-pee-eye)*: *Application* Programming Interface.

Apple: A personal computer, first produced in 1976, which is based on a Motorola microprocessor. Apple Corporation, the manufacturer of Apple Computers, was founded by Steve Jobs and Steve Wozniak, originally working out of a suburban garage.

AppleLink: Apple's online service for employees, developers, and industry people, @applelink apple.com; being phased out in favour of eWorld.

AppleTalk: Apple Computer protocol for data transmission/network connections.

application: A computer program that performs a specific function for the user, as contrasted on one hand with a document (which is a file created by an application) and on the other with a shell, environment, or operating system (all of which handle communication between the user and the computer itself).

application layer: The top (seventh) layer of the OSI Model.

Application Programming Interface (API): Software that controls communication between a program and a computer environment.

April Fool's jokes: Beware strange news or e-mail posted on April Ist.

.arc: A DOS file extension that indicates a compressed archive file.

archie: A client/server application that gives users access to databases that keep track of the contents of anonymous FTP *archives*—hence the name.

archie client: The archie program you run to get information from an archie server.

Archie for Nextstep: An archie client for the Nextstep operating system.

archie server: The archie program that houses a database listing the contents of anonymous FIT sites, in a searchable form, accessible to archie clients.

archie site: A computer with an archie server running on it.

Archive: (1) A secure storage area for disks and tapes. Many organisations archive their data off-site for security reasons (mainly fire risk). 2) An operating system or software application feature that allows data to be compressed into a disk/tape space saving format for archiving. Archived data cannot usually be used as a working copy, the data must be "dearchived" before it can be used by the original program.

archive file: A file that has been compressed or that contains a number of related files.

archive site: 1. An FTP site, a computer on the Internet that stores files; 2. Any repository of information accessible via the Net.

Are you on the Net?: This question usually means, "Do you have an e-mail address that can be reached from the Internet?"

Argument: A value that is passed to a program module each time the module is called by the main program. The use of arguments allows a module to perform programming tasks on similar, but not necessarily identical datasets.

ARMM: Dick Depew's Usenet robot (ARMM stood for *Automated Retroactive Minimal Moderation* intended to retroactively cancel anonymous posts and post follow-ups, it spun out of control instantly during its first run on March 31, 1993, posting, follow-ups to its own follow-ups, spamming several newsgroups, and crashing systems all over the Net. For more on this, see the Net.Legends.FAQ at gopher:/ / dixie.aiss.uiuc.edu:6969/11/urban.legends/ Net. Legends. FAQ.

ARPAnet *(are-pah-net)*: The predecessor to the Internet, established in the 1970s by ARPA, which demonstrated the utility of the TCP/IP protocols.

article: A Usenet newsgroup post, that is, a message posted publicly and available for reading by every subscriber to the newsgroup(s) it's been posted to.

Artificial Intelligence (AI): A field of computer science research aimed at understanding how the human mind thinks and creating intelligent machines that can learn from their experiences.

AS: Autonomous System.

asbestos: Usenet or e-mail posters expecting flames often speak of donning asbestos overalls or other protective gear.

ASCII (*askee*): American standard *code* for information interchange. ASCII is a standard character set that's been adopted by most computer systems around the world (usually extended for foreign alphabets and diacriticals).

ASCIlbetical order: A sorting order based on the ASCII character set that corresponds to English alphabetical order but sorts symbols and numbers before letters and uppercase letters before lowercase letters.

ASCII file: A file containing text only. ASCII files are easier and quicker to transfer than binary files.

ASCII file transfer: A method of file transfer by which an ASCII file is sent as a sequence of characters (letters, numbers, and symbols) instead of as a sequence of binary data (1s and 0s). When necessary, newline characters are changed by the filetransfer program.

ASCII font: A "font" created out of plain ASCII characters, usually found in sig blocks, often spelling out the writer's name.

ASCII graphic: A drawing composed of ASCII characters, such as an enormous medieval sword, an attempt to limn Bart Simpson, or a map of Australia.

AskERIC: An educational information service of the Educational Resources Information Center (ERIC), askeric@ricir.syr.edu.

aspect ratio: The proportion of height to width. Most computer displays have a 3 to 4 aspect ratio.

assigned numbers: Standard numbers for ports, sockets, and so on, established by the Internet Assigned Numbers Authority.

Association for Computing Machinery (ACM): An association of computer researchers and developers that serves as both a source of technical information and an umbrella group for numerous SIGs (Special Interest Groups).

asynchronous (adj): Not happening at the same time. The word is used both for data transmission and for human communication.

Asynchronous Transfer Mode (ATM): A standard for handling heavy network traffic at high speeds.

asynchronous transmission: A transmission method that uses start bits and stop bits to regulate the flow of data, as attachment opposed to synchronous transmission, which uses a clock signal.

AT commando *(ay-tee commands)*: Hayescompatible modem commands, most of which begin with AT (for "attention"), such as *ATZ*, which resets a modem's factory initialization (the basic settings for the modem when it was created).

Athene: An online fiction magazine available at ftp://quartz.rutgers.edu/.

ATM: Asynchronous Transfer Mode.

attach: To send a document along with an e-mail message.

attached file: A file sent with an e-mail message.

attachment: A file sent with an e-mail message.

Attachment Unit Interface (AUI): A universal Ethernet device that connects to a transceiver.

attribute (n): A setting associated with a file that indicates whether the file is a *system file* (a protected file created by the operating system and not to be tampered with), a hid*den file* (one that won't show up in normal file listings), or an *archive file* (one that has been grouped out of many and/or compressed) and who can read it.

attribution: The portion of a Usenet follow-up post that identifies the author of a quoted text (from previous posts). Be very careful to attribute a quotation to the correct author, or face the ire of whomever you are misquoting. (When America Online first made Usenet available to its members, its newsreader software contained a bug that seemed to attribute the text of a follow-up to the author of the preceding post, which annoyed oldbies to no end.)

authentication: Verification of the identity of the sender of a message.

automagically (adv): Happening automatically and so smoothly that the process appears to be magic.

Autonomous System (AS): A set of routers overseen by a common administrator, using the same protocol.

autoselect (v): In Usenet kill files, to select automatically—the opposite of to kill (to mark as already having been read). A kill file comprises instructions to search for certain key words and then either kill or autoselect the articles containing those words.

A/UX: Apple's UNIX clone for the Macintosh.

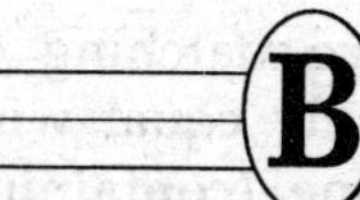

back: The command in paging programs, gopher clients, newsreaders, and Web browsers to back up one screenful or return to the previous menu choice or link.

backbone: A large, fast network connecting other networks. The National Science Foundation maintains one of the largest backbones in the United States, NSFnet.

backbone cabal: A now-defunct group of large-site administrators who set in place most of the procedures for Usenet newsgroup creation and orche-strated the Great Renaming of the Usenet hierarchy.

back door: A security loophole that a programmer to evade restrictions and enter an otherwise secure system. If a back door remains after the software is released, it becomes a security risk.

background: In a multitasking computer environment, any processes that take place out of sight or with lower priority than the main process are said to take place in the background.

backslash: The \ character, often found above the Enter key on keyboards. In DOS paths, it separates directories and subdirectories; in UNIX, it precedes switches (command-line arguments).

backspace (v): To use the Backspace key to move a cursor to the left and in the process delete characters on a computer screen.

Backspace key: A key found directly above the Enter key on most computer keyboards, often used to erase characters to the left of the cursor.

Use of the Backspace key in terminal emulations that don't support it sometimes leaves the original text on-screen, followed by one ^ H character for every time Backspace is pressed. This results in the digital equivalent of an unzipped fly.

Bad Thing: Something generally or widely accepted to be bad. Racism is a Bad Thing. So is spamming Usenet.

balanced line: A cable containing electrically equal wires such as a twisted-pair cable.

balun *(bal-un, n)*: An impedance-matching device that connects a balanced line (containing electrically equal wires), such as a twisted-pair cable, to an unbalanced line (containing electrically unequal wires), such as a coaxial cable.

bandwidth (n): Literally, the speed at which data can be transmitted across a medium. Also used colloquially through-out the Internet to refer to the speed or capacity of a network connection or network resources in general, something almost everyone at some time or another is accused of wasting.

If you post a uuencoded binary file containing a 9xl2 24-bit image to a talk newsgroup, you're definitely wasting bandwidth. But even if you have a sig block of over four lines, if you include too much quoted text in your follow-up post, or if you continue a flame war, you too may be accused of wasting bandwidth.

bandwidth hog: A user or process that consumes more than his, her, or its fair share of bandwidth.

bang (n): An exclamation point. It precedes each site in a UUCP mail path. In some UNIX programs, it enables the user to shell out.

bang path: A UUCP mail path that specifies every site along the way from the sender to the receiver. Although it is rarely necessary any longer to specify the route your mail will take (there are many interchangeable routes on the Internet), mail headers still sometimes include the entire bang path back to the sender.

bar: A popular dummy variable used by programmers in place of specific terms, such as the dummy mail address foo@ bar.baz.

barfic (n): An ugly ASCII graphic.

barney: 1. A dummy variable used by programmers in examples in combination with fred; 2. A large, purple, talking dinosaur who is praised and excoriated in various Usenet newsgroups.

Bart Simpson: A popular subject of ASCII graphics in big, ugly sig blocks.

baseband (adj): Signal transmission that uses the entire bandwidth of the medium, the method used by most LANs.

BASIC: A programming language invented at Dartmouth College in the 1960s as a teaching language. Many feel it teaches bad programming habits.

Basic Encoding Rules (BER): A technique for encoding data (preparing data for transmission) defined in ASN.1 (Abstract Syntax Notation One).

Basic Rate Interface (BRI): An ISDN (Integrated Services Digital Network) service that connects LANs (local area networks) via 64 kps data channels.

batch (adj): 1. Noninteractive, handed without interaction, as *in batch mode;* 2. All at once, or in a bunch, as in *batch printing.*

baud *(bawd)*: Usually confused with bits per second (bps), baud is technically the number of times per second that your modem changes the signal it sends through the phone lines.

baz: A popular dummy variable used by programmers in examples in place of specific terms, such as the dummy mail address foo@bar.baz.

bboard: A BBS. Newbies often refer to, Usenet newsgroups as bboards.

BBS: A *bulletin board system,* communications software that runs on a PC a enables users to log in via modem, check messages, communicate in topic groups, engage in real time chats, and (sometimes) access the Internet.

bcc: *Blind carbon copy.* Borrowed from the world of paper memos, the blind carbon copy list is a list of additional recipients of an e-mail message whose names and addresses will not appear in the header.

beam (v): 1. To transfer a file to someone (from *Star Trek* and other science fiction); 2. To wish someone well via e-mail.

beige toaster: A derogatory term for a Macintosh.

Berkeley Internet Name Domain (BIND): UNIX name server software developed and distributed by the University of California at Berkeley.

Berkeley Software Distribution (BSD): A version of UNIX developed and distributed by the University of California at Berkeley.

beta *(bay-ta)*: Prerelease software made available to a small group of testers (often called *beta testers)* in the "real world" to put it through its paces and identify any bugs or design flaws that did not show up when it was tested by the developers before being shipped commercially.

B1FF: Also called B1FF. A prototypical newbie on Usenet, looking for k00l warez kool is B1FF-speak for cool, warez-pronounced *wares,* from software-means pirated game software). He posts in all caps, substitutes numbers for letters, uses exclamation marks liberally, and has a huge sig block-all of which are marks of a BBS culture of the 1980s populated mainly by teenage boys.

big-endian (adj): 1. A storage format in which the most significant byte has the lowest address, as opposed to littleendian; 2. The way Internet addresses arc written in the United Kingdom starting with domain, then subdomain then site (the opposite of the standard order on the rest of the Internet).

bigot: Someone who believes beyond all rational discussion that one particular type of computer is the best (or the worst),

big red switch: Sometimes abbreviated BRS, the on/off switch on a computer or any crucial toggle switch that when switched off, will shut clown the system.

big seven: The seven top-level Usenet hierarchies (also known as traditional newsgroup *hierarchies): comp., misc.,* news., rec., sci., soc., and talk.

binaries newsgroup: A Usenet newsgroup dedicated to the posting of uuencoded binary files, often .gif or .jpg image files. Some sites won't carry binaries newsgroups because their uuencoded binaries consume so much bandwidth (and storage space on the news site computers).

binary: 1. Base 2, a numerical system using two digits: 0 and *1* (compare with *decimal-base* 10, a numerical system using 10 digits: 0 through 9); 2. A binary file.

binary data: Computer information stored in the form of O and Is (most program files and image files, as well as some documents, are stored as binary data).

binary file: A file that contains more than simple text, such as an image file, a sound file, or a program file (as opposed to an ASCII file, which contains text only.) It may be copied literally, bit for bit, or it will be corrupted.

Binary Synchronous Control (Bisync): An IBM protocol for controlling communications in synchronous environments.

binary file transfer: A file transfer in which every bit of the file is copied exactly as is (as opposed to a text is transferred to whatever format the receiving machine prefers).

BinHex: A Macintosh program that converts binary files to ASCII files so that they may be transmitted via-e-mail

BIOSIS/FS: A database of biological and biomedical research available through h OCLC (Online Computer Learning Center).

Birds of a Feather (BOF): An ad hoc discussion group on a conference program.

bis: In modem standards, an enhancement to the standard, but not a completely new standard. V.32bis is an improvement on V.32, for example.

bisymchronous (adj): Communication in which the sending and receiving takes place at the same time.

bit: A binary digit, the smallest unit of computer information, transmitted as a single on or off pulse symbolized by 1 or 0.

bit bucket: 1. An imaginary place where extra bits land when they "fall off a register" the computer equivalent of forgetting to "carry the 1" during addition, 2. The computer equivalent of the circular file, or the place where all lost socks and pencils go.

bitnet.: A hierarchy in the Usenet mold populated by newsgroups gated to BITNET listserv mailing lists.

BITNET: *Because Its* Time *Network, a* huge network distinct from the Internet but fully connected to it, used largely for e-mail and listserv mailing lists.

bits per second (bps): A measurement of the speed of a medium, meaning the number of bits that can pass through the medium in one second.

bitty box: A derogatory term for a personal computer, from the workstation or mainframe point of view.

biz.: A hierarchy in the Usenet mold dedicated to commercial and business communication. Advertising is explicitly permitted in the biz. hierarchy.

black hole: The place where missing e-mail messages or Usenet posts are said to have disappeared to

block (n): A standard unit of data the size varies from system to, system) measured in terms of storage or transmission.

bogometer *(boe-gom-i-ter)*: A mythical device that measures bogosity or bogon flux.

bogon *(boe-gon,)*: A mythical basic particle of bogosity,

bogon filter: A mythical device that can limit the flow of bogons.

bogon flux: A mythical measurement of the strength of a field of bogons.

bogosity (boe-goss-i-ty): The extent to which something is bogus

bogus (adj): 1. Lame, stupid, false, useless; 2. Fake.

bogus newsgroup: Silly or joke-named Usenet-style newsgroups created by pranksters with the necessary access privileges.

boink (n): A party at which participants of a Usenet newsgroup meet in the flesh.

bomb (v): To crash, to suffer from an unrecoverable error.

bookmark: In gopher clients and Web browsers, a reference to a menu or page to which you might want to return later, In gopher clients, bookmarks appear together on a gopher menu.

Boolean operator: One of several conjunctions used to limit or specify a search criterion (from George Boole, nineteenth-century English mathematician).

Operator	What it specifies
ADJ	The terms on either side of the operator must appear adjacent to each other in the source text.

AND The terms on either side of the operator must both appear in the source text.

NAND The term before the operator must appear in the source text, and the term that appears after the operator must not.

NOT The term appearing after the operator must not appear in the source text.

OR One of the terms on either side of the operator must appear in the source text,

XOR Only One, but not both, of the terms on either side of the operator must appear in the source text

Boolean operators may be combined with parentheses if necessary to clarify the order of application.

Boolean search: A method of searching a database or text in which Boolean operators are used to limit and specify the search criterion.

boot (v): To start or restart a computer, o technically, to load and start the operating system. The term comes from the expression "lifting oneself by one's bootstraps", because the computer kernel must write remainder of the startup code itself each time the computer is booted.

Bootstrap Protocol (BOOTP): A protocol for booting diskless nodes on a network.

Border Gateway Protocol (BGP): An exterior gateway protocol based on the External Gateway Protocol used by NSFnet.

'bot: A robotic entity on the Net that automatically performs some function that people usually do. Many IRC channels are kept open by semipermanent 'bots that stay connected just as real users might. In the past, people have spammed Usenet by employing 'bots to automatically post (robopost) reams of redundant text.

bounce (v): E-mail that fails to reach its destination and returns to the sender is said to have bounced.

bounce message: A message from a mailer daemon indicating that it cannot find the recipient of an e-mail message and is returning it to the sender.

bozo filter: A kill file. It allows you to filter out the bozos whose Usenet posts you don't wish to, see.

brain dump (n): An undifferentiated mass of information, often in response to a simple question (by analogy from core dump, screen dump, etc.).

brain-dead (adj): 1. Completely broken, nonfunctional, usually said of hardware or software; 2. Ridiculously inappropriate, said of an approach to a problem.

branch (n): 1. An intermediate part of a logical tree, somewhere between the root and a leaf, 2. A participant in a tape tree who receives copies of a tape from her parent and makes copies for her children (who may themselves be branches or leaves).

bridge: A device that connects two net work components (such as zones) that use same protocols.

brief (adj): An operating mode for some systems and applications in which the prompts and reports of activities are abbreviated or skipped altogether.

broadband (adj): Signal transmission that can carry multiple signals at once, each on separate channels, each taking up a portion of the bandwidth.

broadcast (n): A transmission sent to all hosts or clients at once, such as "System going down in 10 minutes. Please finish up"

broadcast storm: The confusion and possible network break-down that occurs when a faulty packet is broadcast, generating multiple incorrect packets in response, ad infinitum.

brouter *(brow-ter)*: A device that combines the functions of a bridge and a router, controlling transmission from one network component to, another (as a bridge) and from the network to the Internet (as a router).

browse: To skim an information resource on the Net, such as Usenet, gopherspace, or the Web.

browser: A client program used to, view Web documents

btoa *(bee-to-ay)*: A UNIX program that converts binary files to ASCII files.

BUAF (bee-you-ay- eff): *Big, ugly ASCII front* Character sets made from ASCII characters, often generated by special programs and often used to spell out names in sig blocks.

BUAG *(bee-you-ay-gee)*: *Big, ugly ASCII* graphic. Large, often crude drawing composed of ASCII characters, such as a map of Australia, a medieval sword, the U.S.S. *Enterprise* etc., often appearing in a sig block.

buffer (n): A memory location that stores a certain amount of data or text until it can be processed or displayed. A screen's display *buffer is* the amount of text you can scroll back to, review. If your computer or connection freezes and you type repeatedly until each keypress results in a beep, then you have overflowed your *keyboard buffer*.

bug (n): A flaw in a program (from the expression "working the bugs out"). Also, jokingly defined as an undocumented feature.

bugg (adj): Said of software, unstable, unreliable, full of bugs.

bundle (v): To group packets of data into, a single cell for transmission over a cell switching: network.

Bunyip: The company formed by the people who invented archie.

burble (v): To flame at a very low level of competence or clarity.

bus (n): An electronic pathway or connector.

bus topology: *Also daisy chain* a network architecture in which all nodes are connected to a single cable.

buzz word: Also stop word, a.word so common that it is useless to search for it (such as and, *address, record,* and so on). Most searchable databases have lists of buzz words and filter them out during searches.

by hand (adv): Executed step-by-step by a human being, instead of automatically by a computer process.

byte: A binary "word" (unit of meaning), usually consisting of eight bits.

***bzzzzt*, wrong:** A rejoinder to an incorrect Usenet post, alluding to radio and TV quiz shows in which a timer buzzes when a contestant answers incorrectly.

C

C: A high-level programming language developed by Bell Telephone Company in 1965. This is a very powerful language, being versatile, efficient and productive.

cable: A sheathed length of wires used to transmit signals from device to device.

Cache: A special area of primary memory set aside to be used as a temporary store for programs, parts of programs or data. Cache is pronounced cashay or caysh, from the French word cachier-to hide. Cache memory is usually quite small (typically 64KB on a PC that may have 4MB of RAM and 80MB of hard disk storage) and has very high access speeds. It is used to raise the overall processing speed of a computer. Information that will be required frequently or within the next few instruction cycles are loaded into cache memory for subsequent access by the CPU. Since the required information is in cache memory and not on hard disk or floppy disk, the access time is much reduced. Because of its high access speed, cache memory is expensive and requires special control circuitry.

Cache Controller: Electronic circuitry that controls' read/ write operations to cache memory. The controller may be a chip or discrete components.

Call for Votes: (CFV) A stage in the Usenet newsgroup creation process, after the Request for Discussion (RFD).

Camera-Ready Artwork: Printed material that is ready for photographing at commercial printing premises. Once photographed the camera-ready artwork image is then used to make the printing plates.

Campus-Wide Information Server (CWIS): The information system for a college or university, usually including schedules, announcements, job listings, bulletin boards, calendars, and so on.

cancel: On Usenet, to delete an article after you've posted it. It takes a while for the article to vanish everywhere, as the cancel message has to catch up with the propagating article.

canonical 1: Deriving from an official source. In Star Trek newsgroups, facts that come from any of the television series or movies is considered canonical; 2. Prototypical, to programers.

Canned Program: A commercial software package that is available for sale to the public or ready for use by a particular organisation.:

Caps Lock Key: A key on a computer keyboard that provides access to upper case letters (a-z becomes A-Z) but not the "second function" of any other key. Compare this to the Shift Key which affects alphabetic characters and the "second function" of other keys.

capture (v): To save text as it scrolls across the screen. Captured text can be read white offline.

card: A printed circuit board, added to a computer to enable it to control an additional device.

Card Reader: An electro-mechanical device that reads data from a sequence of paper cards. The cards have a series of pre-perforated tabs which can be removed to form a pattern recognisable by the card reader. The card reader converts each pattern into machine code for use by the processor. Card readers are infrequently used today as the cards are prone to user error, easily destroyed and generally not reusable. As well the card readers themselves, being largely mechanical, were often the source of computer breakdowns.

caret: The ^character. Indicates an exponent (for example, x^2 means x^2, that is, x *squared).*

The caret is also used in e-mail and Usenet posts to underscore and emphasize text on the preceding line, as shown in the example at the top of the page.

careware: A form of shareware in which the creator of the software requests that payment be made to a charity.

carpetbagger: Someone who comes to the Internet looking to, make a quick profit in what they consider to be a ripe, undeveloped territory (borrowed from the American Reconstruction period's pejorative term for Northerners looking to make a quick buck off the war-torn South).

carriage return: A character that moves the cursor back to the beginning of a line (ASCII 13), usually starting a new line in combination with a line feed character.

carrier: A signal constantly transmitted by a modem over a phone line as a reference for the modem on the other end of the line. When a line is disconnected, some modems will report "no carrier."

Carrier Signal: In data communications, a signal: established on the transmission medium for modulation by data signals.

carrier detect: The notice that a modem has identified the carrier signal from another modem over a phone connection.

Carrier Sense Multiple Access (CSMA): A protocol that enables multiple devices to transmit on the same channel, by "listening" for the sounds of other devices and only transmitting when the line is clear.

Carder Sense Multiple Access with Collision Avoidance (CSMA/CA): A version of CSMA in which devices can detect impending collisions and avoid them.

Carrier Sense Multiple Access with Collision Detection (CSMA/CD): A version of CSMA in which devices can detect collisions as they occur and resend the corrupted signal.

Cartridge Tape: This is a magnetic tape, about 8mm wide, which is housed in a plastic cover approximately 12cm x 12cm. Cartridges are used mostly on mainframe computers, and provide compact data storage (sequential access) and easy loading. They are often used as a back-up system and typically offer up to 2000MB storage. Cartridge tapes used on personal computers have capacities in the 60-100MB range.

cascade: A series of one-line follow-up posts, each a play on the previous one. Each post contains all of the previous ones leading up to the latest change, usually in ever-shortening lines, due to the rows of >'s (or sometimes other characters) automatically inserted by newsreader positing commands to indicate an inclusion from a previous post.

case-insensitive: Not distinguishing between upper and lowercase characters. In a case-insensitive search, *Internet, internet,* and INTERNET all match the same key word.

The DOS and Macintosh operating system are case-insensitive, as are e-mail addresses UNIX, on the other hand, is case-sensitive.

case-sensitive: Distinguishing between upper and lowercase characters. To a case-sensitive program, *Peter,* PETER, *peter,* and *PeTeR* all mean different things.

UNIX is case-sensitive; DOS and Macintoshes are not. E-mail addresses are not case-sensitive.

Cassette Tape: A magnetic tape housed in a plastic cover, used mostly on early personal computers and on some mainframe computers to store boot information. Cassette tapes used on computers are, in general, audio cassettes.

cat: A UNIX command (short for *catenate* from *concatenate)* that can pour the contents of one file into another or dump the contents onto the screen.

catch up: When reading news, to mark all the articles in a newsgroup as read, to clean the slate.

Cathode Ray Tube: The technical name for the screen of a computer monitor. This name originated through the use of "cathode rays" (electron beams) in the monitor. Cathode rays strike phosphor beads on the monitor screen, thereby producing the appropriate image. Usually abbreviated to CRT.

cc: A list of additional recipients for an e-mail message in the header of the message (from carbon copy, a carrier from office-memo shorthand). Most e-mail programs enable the sender to add address to the cc: list

CCITT: Abbreviation for Consultative Committee on International Telegraphy and Telephony. This is an international standards organisation based in Paris, and is a member of the International Telecommunications Union. CCITT negotiates international standards for many aspects of communications.

cd: A UNIX and DOS command meaning *change directory.*

CD-ROM: Abbreviation for Compact Disk-Read Only Memory, this is secondary storage that uses optical (laser) techniques to read\write data. CDROM has a reasonably fast access time and vast storage capability. Compare this to hard disk access times and storage capability.

Cell: A data entry point on a spreadsheet. A cell occurs at the intersection of every row and column.

cell-switching: A variation on X.25 packet-switching protocol in which data is bundled into equal-sized cells.

Cello: An integrated Web browser and general Internet tool (gopher, WAIS, Usenet, mail) for Windows. Available by anonymous FTP from ftp.law. cornell.edu.

censorship: The public spaces of the Internet (such as Usenet newsgroups, IRC, and so on) are largely free from censorship and can be noisy and childish at times. Online services, however, take more responsibility for the contents of their networks and may therefore place some restrictions on what can be written in public or even in private.

Centred Text: Text that is centred within the text block. A technique often used with headings.

central processing unit (CPU): The heart of a computer, the part that does the "thinking."

CERN European Particle Physics Laboratory *(surf-net)*: (The acronym CERN comes from an earlier French title of the Lab: *Conseil Europeen pour la Recherche Nucleaire)* The creators of the World Wide Web and the first (text-based) Web browser, www. You can reach CERN on the Web at http://www. cern.ch/.

CERT: Computer Emergency Response Team.

Chain Printer: A line printer that has its character set embedded on a metal chain. The chain is moved horizontally at high speed whilst a series of hammers make contact with the band, transferring the image onto the paper. Characters are printed seemingly at random across the paper, the printer detects when a particular character is at the right position at the right time, and words are not necessarily printed consecutively from left to right.

Chameleon NFS: Socket, TCP/IP, and Internet tools software for Windows, made by NetManage. Information is available on the Web at http://www.netmanage.com/.

Chameleon Sampler: A free collection of socket, TCP/IP, and Internet tools available via FTP from ftp.netmanage.com, in the pub/demos/sampler directory, in a self-extracting archive file called sampler.exe.

channel (n): 1. The path along which one device sends a signal to another, meaning a physical cable or wire or an assigned frequency of a physical channel; 2. An IRC topic area.

channel hopping: On IRC, jumping around from channel (definition 2) to channel.

channel op: A privileged user of an IRC channel, able to kick antisocial participants.

Character: Any alphanumeric (A-z, a-z, 0-9), facet of syntax (! ? ' etc), mathematical operator (= + * /) or graphics symbol. Characters are represented in computer memory by a series of bits.

Character Generator: Software embedded in ROM that will generate characters on-screen (using pixels) or on a print medium.

character-based: Said of a computer, operating system, environment, or terminal emulation, displaying screens composed entirely of characters (as opposed to graphical images) and accepting input only in the form of characters (as opposed to mouse clicks).

character-based interface: A computer front end which displays only characters on the screen—no graphics, no icons, no mouse pointer, etc. Many dial-up Internet connections are to UNIX boxes with character-based interfaces.

character length: A terminal emulation setting that determines the number of bits in a character (usually seven or eight). ASCII characters require seven bits per byte (one byte per character); binary transfers may require eight bits per character.

character string: A string of characters that must be handled as text, not as numeric data.

Character Sets: Combinations of characters grouped together by software and hardware engineers for specific purposes. For example, the "Roman" character set would contain all the characters necessary to generate a text file in any of the latin languages. A "mathematical" character set would contain all of the symbols necessary for intricate mathematical formulae and calculus. Not all characters are supported by all computer software and hardware.:

Characters Per Second: A measure of printer, scanner or typist speed, usually abbreviated to cps.

charter: The founding document of a Usenet newsgroup, it defines what constitutes on-topic and off-topic discussion, and establishes whether the newsgroup is moderated or not.

chat (n): 1. Synchronous (happening in real time, like a phone conversation, unlike an e-mail exchange), line-by-line communicatior with another user over a network; 2. The chat program itself, nov largely superseded by the IRC program.

cheapernet: Slang for the "thin" Ethernet specification, generally usec in offices.

checksum: An error-checking method in which the sending and receiving modems both sum up the bytes in a data packet and compare the totals.

chmod *(see-aitch-mode)*: The UNIX command for changing the read-write permissions of a file (from *change mode).*

choad (n): Slang for penis, popularized by the denizens of alt.tasteless.

Church of the SubGenius: A half-serious antireligion founded by the Rev. Ivan Stang and blending the principles of Discordianism with '50s advertising clipart images and mindnumbing homilies. SubGenii can be found in the Usenet newsgroup alt.slack and elsewhere on the Net, often talking about the deity Bob (sometimes BoB).

CIA World Factbook: A source of basic information on every country in the world, reachable by WAIS at world-factbook.src; also, one of the books made available for free by Project Gutenberg.

cipher (n): A code that involves character-for-character substitution (as contrasted with word-for-word substitution or other schemes), a simple example of which is rot13.

circuit: A channel carrying an electrical current between two devices.

circuit board: A computer card holding printed circuits.

circuit-switched network: A network arrangement in which each node is connected to the next via a dedicated line.

Circular Reference: On a spreadsheet this is a formula embedded in a cell that uses its own address as part of the formula. For example the formula in cell AK36 might read =sum(AK15:AK36). This formula will soon produce a very large number as it Is constantly adding itself to itself.

clari: The Usenet-style news-group hierarchy dedicated to ClariNet news items.

ClariNet: An online news service analogous to newspaper wire services. If your service provider gets a ClariNet newsfeed, then the news is part of your overhead cost. Otherwise, you can get ClariNet news by direct subscription. For information, send e-mail to info@clarinet.com.

CLASS: Cooperative Library Agency for Systems and Services.

clear channel: A 64 kps channel with its entire bandwidth available for transmission.

Clearinghouse for Networked Information Discovery and Retrieval (CNIDR): An organization supporting research and cooperation relating to information resources on the Internet (such as WAIS, gopher, archie, and the Web) and ways to search and retrieve information from them. They distribute free-WAIS, a free version of WAIS. CNIDR can be reached on the Web at http://cnidr.org/welcome.html.

client: An application or computer that communicates with and requests information from a server. In conventional networking, client usually refers to a computer; for Internet client/server applications, client usually refers to a program.

client/server: 1. A method of distributing information or files in which a central server application archives (stores) the files and makes them available to requests from client applications; 2. A LAN architecture, in which files and other resources are kept on a central server computer and individuals interact with the network through client computers.

ent/server application: A network application that functions with a central server as a repository of information and clients that communicate with the server arid request information on behalf of individual users.

Clip Art: A graphics file, often provided as part of a graphics software application, that includes many items of computer generated artwork. The user can select a piece of clip for later use.

Clipboard: Part of a software application that allows the user to make notes, often unrelated, whilst using another package. Clipboards usually produce ASCII text files and can store graphics files.

Clipper Chip: A U.S. government sponsored encryption standard that telecommunications industries will be encouraged to adopt when it becomes final, according to pending proposals. The Clipper Chip includes a back door that would allow government agencies to eavesdrop on communication encrypted with the chip The government would need a court order use the decryption keys, otherwise kept in escrow.)

Opponent of the Clipper Chip are suspicious: government following its own rules and believe that any individual or company should have access to the best encryption technology available, not just government approved encryption.

clobber: Kill, delete, erase.

Clock: 1) The internal timing function of the CPU. High clock speeds are usually synonymous with high processing capability. Clock speeds are measured in megahertz (millions of cycles per second). The symbol MHz is also used, for example, an Intel 80386 microprocessor may easily attain speeds of 25MHz. Whilst clock speed gives an indication of processing speed there are other factors involved in completing a task quickly. These include hardware considerations and the use of memory management techniques.

Clock speeds have been rising steadily and many computer professionals wonder if there is a limit to be reached, and whether any further increases will be meaningless in the majority of applications.

Clock: 2) The timing device found in many computers, providing time and date on demand via the operating system. Most use a small battery to keep running when power is removed from the computer. The clock is often located on a small circuit board or directly on the motherboard. Utility software provides a means of updating the clock, either for times or dates.

close (v): To hang up a telnet, FTP, or other remote connection.

clueless newbie: A derogatory term for a beginner who POSTS IN ALL CAPS or betrays some ignorance of the Net. We were all clueless newbies once.

Coalition for Networked Information (CNI): A coalition of libraries and research organizations dedicated to the sharing of information over computer networks.

coax (co-ax): Slang for coaxial cable.

coaxial cable (co-axial): Cable containing two conductors, one inside the other, used for broadband and baseband networks, as well as for cable TV.

code (n): Computer program contents. (v) To write or edit a computer program.

cognitive dissident: The vocation, coined by Electronic Frontier Foundation cofounder John Barlow, for those who challenge the status quo in cyberspace.

Coke machine: At one time or another, there have been many soda machines on the Internet. This usually means that some device monitors the machine, keeping track of how many cans of soda are in each slot and possibly how long they've been there (i.e., how cold they are). This device then updates an information file that can usually be fingered from anywhere on the Internet. To see such a readout for yourself", try fingering drink@drink.csh.rit. edu.

cold boot (v): To start a computer that's completely off.

collision: What happens two devices try to: use the same channel at the same time.

colon: In URLs, a colon (:) appears after the protocol name., In e-mail and Usenet posts, colon sometimes indicate included text.

Colorado Alliance of Research: Libraries (CARL): An alliance of seven libraries that contribute to a database containing abstracts of thousands of journals. For more information, send e-mai[l] to help@carl.org.

.com: The Internet domain dedicated to commercial entities, generally in the United states.

comm: Communications (sometimes spelled com), usually in the context of communications software, a communications port on a computer, and so on.

comma: In Usenet newsreaders, you can often cross-post your article to several newsgroups simply by listing them one after another, separated by commas(,). Likewise, in most mail programs, you may list several e-mail recipients the same way, separated by commas.

command line: A single line of text, with a Prompt, often at the bottom of the screen, where the user may enter commands directly. DOS and UNIX are command-line operating systems; Macintosh, Windows, and X Window are graphical environments that do not automatically make a command-line available.

command-line interface: A front end that allows or forces the user to memorize and type commands at a prompt, as opposed to one that allows or forces the user to click graphical elements and select commands from pull-down menus.

command mode: A program mode in which you can enter commands. In vi, the UNIX text editor, users start off in command mode and will be frustrated if they try to start typing text. First, they must switch to insert mode.

commercial access provider: A service provider that charges for access to the Internet, as opposed to employers, universities, and free-nets, which provide access for free.

Commercial Internet Exchange (CIE or CIX): An organization of service providers that represents the interest in making commercial transactions acceptable and secure over the Internet. For more information, send e-mail to info@cix.org.

communications program.: A program that operates a modem and provides terminal emulation so that the user can log in to and communicate with a remote computer.

Communications Terminal Protocol (CTERM): Part of DECnet's virtual terminal service (protocols that allow a user to emulate a different terminal type) specifications.

comp: A Usenet hierarchy devoted to computers.

Compact Pro: A Macintosh shareware compression program. Files compressed with Compact Pro have a*.cpt* extension.

COM port: The communications port on a computer. On PCs, it's a serial port.

compress (v): The squish a file in order to save disk storage space. (n) A UNIX compression program.

compression: A method of squishing a file in order to save disk storage space or the amount of squishing.

Compu$erve (CI$): A mildly derogatory name for CompuServe that refers to its expensive connect time fees.

CompuServe Information Manager (CIM): A program that provides a graphical interface (or front end) for CompuServe, available for both Macintosh and Windows.

Computer Emergency Response Team (CERT): A network-security task force available round-the-clock to assist Internet users with security problems. For more information, send e-mail to cert@cert.org or call their 24-hour hotline, (412) 268-7090.

computer geek: Someone who enjoys messing around with a computer, not necessarily as a programmer or at the same level of sophistication as a hacker. This is riot necessarily a derogatory term. It depends on the context and the company.

computer-mediated communication: Any form of communication aided and abetted by computers, including, but not limited to, e-mail, chat, and conferencing.

Computer Professionals for Social Responsibility (CPSR): An organization of computer professionals concerned with the computers might have on society. Originally formed to discuss the connections between computer research and the nuclear arms race, it now also addresses such issues as privacy, the role of the computer m the workplace, and research priorities in the coming century.

Computer + Science Network (CSNET): A computer-science research network that merged with BITNET to create the Corporation for Research and Educational Networking (CREN).

conductor: A particular type of wire, such as copper.

conferencing (adj): Said of software that enables many users to engage in a more or less public, written conversation, either in real time (as on an IRC channel) or not (as a in a Usenet newsgroup).

connection: There are different types, or levels, of connection to the Internet, ranging from a direct network connection, through SLIP or PPP dial-up access, to character-based shell-account dial-up access, and simple e-mail gateways to the Net.

Connection dosed by foreign host: A message during a telnet or other remote login session that tells you that the host you've logged in to has closed the connection.

Connection Control Language (CCL): An Apple Talk scripting language for controlling modem functions.

connectionless communication: A form of communication between applications in which data can be requested and supplied during intermittent connections.

connection-oriented communication: A form of communication between applications in which all data is exchanged during a single connection.

connect time: The amount of time you spend connected to your service provider. Many providers charge a fee based on your connect time, Others are flat-rate providers,

Consortium for School Networking (CoSN): A nonprofit organization that studies the uses of networking in K-12 schooling. For more information, send e-mail to cosn@bitnic.bitnet.

conspiracy: The Internet is home to many conspiracy theorists and provides an excellent means for the sharing of theories, rumors, and evidence. Don't try to keep all the conspiracies straight or you'll lose your mind. Some of them deal with the creation and "control" of the Internet itself.

contention: The situation when two devices both try to use the same channel. Every network must have some protocol in place to deal with issues of contention.

control bus: The channel within a computer along which control signals (signals that control a device or routine) are carried.

control character: A special character, usually nonprinting, that starts or stops a computer function.

Control key: The key marked *Ctrl* on most computer keyboards (the closest Macintosh analogy is the Command key). In combination with other keys, the Control key can send control characters to the computer. It is sometimes symbolized by, so Control-C might be written ^IC or Ctrl-C.

Conversational Monitor System (CMS): The command-line interface of IBM's VM operating system.

cookie: A fortune cookie program that spits out a different fortune every time you run it. Some systems run cookie as part of their startup or login procedure.

Coordinating Committee for Intercontinental Research Networks (CCIRN): A committee that coordinates research networks in North America and Europe.

copyleft: The General Public License carried by Free Software Foundation software (such as GNU). It grants reuse ,and reproduction rights to anyone and everyone.

copyright: People debate how standing copyright law applies to articles posted to Usenet or to texts in general made available on the Internet. This is thus far not settled law, Some people attach copyright notices to their Usenet posts.

core (n): 1. RAM, on UNIX and some IBM machines; 2. The name of a file that appears in your UNIX directory after a core dump. This file contains everything that was in memory at the time of the dump.

core dump (In): 1. A copy of the contents of memory, dumped into a file when an unrecoverable error occurs; 2. A brain dump.

Corporation for Research and Educational Networking (CREN): An organization formed by the merger of BITNET and CSNET. CREN can be reached via gopher at info.educom.edu.

corrupted (adj): Said of a file, block of data, or other communication, damaged transmission.

cp: The UNIX *copy file* command.

cpio: A UNIX command that makes whole directories into a single file, for easy transportation.

CP/M: A PC operating system that preceded DOS. If someone mentions, CP/M, they're bragging about how long they've been working with microcomputers.

.cpt: The extension of a file compressed with Compact Pro, a Macintosh program.

CPU: *Central processing unit,* the heart of a computer, the part that does the "thinking"

cracker: One who breaks into computer systems. What many people in the real world call a hacker.

cracking: The act of breaking into a computer system.

crack root (v): To break into the root account of a UNIX machine and, most likely, use the root privileges to break into other accounts.

crash (n): An unrecoverable failure of a computer system, requiring rebooting as a minimum response.
(v) To suffer from a crash.

crippleware: Shareware that lacks a useful or even crucial functionality, in order to entice you Into registering as an owner to obtain the uncrippled version of the program.

crlf: A combination of two characters (carriage return and line feed) that on some computer systems constitutes a newline.

crosspost (n): A Usenet article posted simultaneously to more than one newsgroup. Most newsreaders will show you crossposted articles only the first time you encounter them.

cross-post (v): To post a Usenet article to several newsgroups at once. This takes up less disk space than posting it separately and repeatedly.

crosstalk: Interference between two wires in a cable.

CrossTalk: A communications and terminal emulation program for DOS and Windows.

cryptography: The study of codes and ciphers and other security issues.

C shell: A common flavor of UNIX shells.

.cshrc: A startup file for the UNIX C shell.

CSLIP: *Compressed Serial Line Internet* Protocol, a faster version of SLIP in which Internet address information is compressed

CSO: *Computing Services Office,* a system for searching campus telephone and address listings, reachable by gopher.

CSO name server: A searchable white pages listing of real names and associated e-mail addresses, usually reached via gopher.

The Cuckoo's Egg: A book by Clifford Stoll describing how he tracked East German crackers breaking into a system at Lawrence Berkeley Labs at the University of California at Berkeley.

CUSeeMe *(see-you-see-me)*: A new Internet protocol for synchronous video and sound communication.

cyber: A prefix overused to indicate a connection to computers, networks, technology, or futurism.

cyberdelics: 1. Mind-altering effects brought about by computer technology (as opposed to hallucinogenic drugs); 2. Eye-bending screen savers.

cybernaut: A traveler in cyberspace, someone who uses their Internet connection to explore the furthest realms of cyberspace.

cyberpunk: 1. A largely hype-driven category of popular culture at the crossroads of computer technology, science fiction, and youth culture, 2. A genre of science fiction that appeared in the mid-to-late'80s and combined a bleak, noirish view of the future with a fetishization of technology and human-computer interaction.

cyberspace: A term, popularized by author William Gibson, for the shared imaginary reality of computer networks, Some people use cyberspace as a synonym for the Internet. Others hold out for the more complete physical-seeming consensual reality of Gibson's novels.

cycle power (v): To turn a computer off and then on again.

cyclic redundancy check (CRC): An error-detection technique used during file transfers and other forms of data transmission.

D

daemon (*day-min*): In UNIX and other operating systems, a program that runs all, the time, in the background, waiting for things to do (possibly from Maxwell's Demon). When you post an article to a *.test newsgroup, daemons all over the world send you e-mail confirmations when they receive your post.

daisy chain: A network architecture, also called *bus topology* in which all nodes are connected to a single cable.

Daisy Wheel Printer: A type of impact printer that uses a print wheel with characters embedded on a series of spokes or stems radiating out froth the central core.. The term "daisy wheel" is used since the wheel resembles the flowering head of a daisy, where the characters are embedded on the ends of the petals. During printer operation the daisy wheel is rotated until the appropriate character appears under the strike hammer and the relevant character is imprinted, via a ribbon, on to the paper.

Although daisy wheel printers produce very well defined characters they are often inconvenient to use since each daisy wheel has only one font. If more than one font is required for a document then it is a tiresome task to have to stop the printer, change wheels, and continue with the print job. The characters embedded on the wheel are not necessarily arranged in alphabetical order. Frequently used combinations are used so as to minimise the amount of wheel rotation.

dark fiber: Unused cable in the fiber-optic network.

DARPA: *Defense Advanced Research Projects* the official name of ARPA during the 1980s and early 1990s.

Data: Any computer usable information. This may be numerical, for example the depth of snow at a skiresort over the past fifty years is numerical data; it may be textual, for example a list of customers; or it may be graphical, for example the input from a graphic scanner. Data may be entered into the computer via the keyboard, secondary storage, for example, a disk or tape, via another computer or via a peripheral device such as a scanner, or a remote sensing device, for example, a weather station. Data is then stored in computer memory or in secondary storage. Unprocessed data is often called "raw data"

Database: A collection of data, usually related in some manner. For example a list of customer names, addresses and telephone numbers constitutes a database. Another example is a payroll listing of employee names, employee numbers, bank details, tax file numbers, pay rates etc. The telephone directory is a classic example of a database, however the name "database" is generally not used until the data has been entered into and stored by the computer. Database software applications are commonly found on mainframe computers and are popular, useful,' items for personal computer users.

Database Management System: A collection of software applications that allow the computer user to setup, maintain and manipulate a database. Management tasks may include controlling access to the database, or sections of it, extracting data selectively from different parts of the database, financial and statistical analysis. Usually abbreviated to DBMS.

Database Query Language: A command and/or programming language, forming an integral part of a database package. A query language allows the user to extract and manipulate data from the database based on user defined criteria, Data, Bus. A set of wires or printed circuit tracks that is used for transferring data within the computer and its peripherals.

data bits: In asynchronous data transmission, the bits between a start bit (and sometimes a parity bit) and a stop bit, the only bits actually carrying data, There are usually seven or eight data bits, depending on the size of a character, or byte.

Data bits is therefore one of the settings you have to specify on your modem to make a connection. Usually 7 or 8, it depends on the, modem you're calling.

data block: A unit of data sent from one device to another.

data bus: The channel within a computer along which communication signals are carried.

data channel: Any channel over which data is sent in the form of a signal.

Data Communications: A communications system used primarily, but not necessarily exclusively, for the transmission of data. Data communications has become an increasingly important revenue source to common carriers over the past 20 years. Since the mid-1970s most common carriers in the USA have made more money out of data communication than voice communication. Increasingly, air-waves and cables are congested by machines talking to other machines. The process of transmitting data from one computer to another, or from any device to another device.

Data Communications Equipment: Any equipment involved in a communications link.

Data Compression: This refers to the compressing of data prior to transmission in order to save transmission time, and therefore money. There are several methods of compression, one is to eliminate any unnecessary spaces and to condense repeated characters to a code, for example, instead of transmitting GGGGGGGGG, use G@9. The other is to transfer the message into the most efficient coding system

Data Dictionary: These are used in Systems Analysis, program and database design. A data dictionary, also called MetaData lists all the attributes of the data that is to constitute the data fields of a database.

The following is an example of data dictionary entries,

Name of data item.

Usage of the data item. Ensures that the data item is definitely required in the database, clears out redundant data. Number of characters. Number of decimal places. For numeric characters, it may be necessary to specify the number of decimal places, for example, two for financial records, none for PostCode.

A data dictionary provides c and relates organisational activities to program design. Some countries have formal standards for data dictionaries.

Data Element: A single entity within a dataset or database. For example, a person's tax file number would be a data element of a payroll database. Also referred to as a data item.

data encryption key (DEK): An element of key encryption that is used to encrypt and decrypt data.

data encryption standard (DES): A security protocol defined by the U.S. government.

Data Entry: The process of entering data into a computer. Traditionally this has been a manual process, performed by computer operators but much of this work is now automated. For example, stock control in many large shops is now achieved by direct data entry from cash register transactions. Similarly, bank account records are updated by transactions conducted by members of the public through automatic teller machines (ATMs).

data/fax modem: A modem that can transmit raw data or a fax image.

Datagram: The basic unit of data transmission across a network, containing a header and the data itself. The header describes the data, its destination, and its relationship to other datagrams.

Datagram: Delivery Protocol (DDP) An AppleTalk protocol that handles the routing of datagrams over an AppleTalk network.

Data Integrity: This refers to the reliability of any particular data. For example, data on the world's climate from 500 years ago would be very sketchy, and unsuitable for indepth analysis. In another example, the data collected during a vehicle count on Sydney Harbour Bridge may be of doubtful integrity if it is known that one of the recorders had an intermittent fault.

data link: 1 The device that enables data transmission; 2. An active connection for data transmission.

data link layer: The second layer of the OSI Model that deals with transmission of data frames from node to node.

Data Processing: The manipulation of data to produce usable information for example, the processing of time sheet information to Produce a list of payroll bank transfers.

Data Source: Any organisation, person, place or device that generates a dataset or database. For example, the data source for information (data) on world food prices may he the United Nations, the data source on Australian household incomes may be a professional pollster or the Australian Bureau of Statistics.

data stream: A series of data blocks sent from one device to another.

Data Terminal Equipment: The terminating hardware involved in the transmission process. Usually located in an organisation's premises.

Data Transfer Rate: The rate, in kilobytes or megabytes per second, at which data can be read/written from/to CDROM, disk, tape etc.

Data Verification: In many applications, particularly databases, it is essential to verify that the data being entered in to the database is of the right type, length etc. For example, a payroll database would record, amongst other things, an employee's address and postcode. A professionally designed database would cheek that the entry for postcode is totally numeric and exactly four digits long. An entry for postcode of "abcd" would be rejected, as would "31889". Checks such as this are known as data verification. A more thorough verification would also ensure that the postcode is within the accepted range of numbers.

Another aspect of data verification is to check for duplication of entries. Using a payroll database as an example, this database would record an employee number and tax file number for each employee. Obviously there could never be more than one person with the same employee number, or the same tax file number, Each new entry to the database would need to be checked in this manner against existing database entries. However, most data items in a database would riot need to be checked for duplication. For example, surname, first names, address, postcode etc can all be quite legitimately duplicated.

DCE: data communications equipment or Distributed Computing Environment.

Ad: The extension of a file compressed with DiskDoubler on the Macintosh.

DDCMP: Digital Data Communications Message Protocol.

DDN: Defense Data Network.

DDN NIC: Defense Data Network Network Information Center.

DDP: Datagrarn Delivery Protocol.

DEC *(deck)*: *Digital Equipment Corporation,* manufacturer of VAX (and before that PDP-11) boxes and the VMS operating system.

Deadly Embrace: A clash of hardware/software that results in a system lockup. Often the only solution to this situation lies in the Power On/Off switch or rebooting.

Debugging: Jargon for fault finding, usually in software but also in hardware. A phrase first used by computer developers in the US Navy in 1945. At this time a US Navy prototype computer ground to a halt and after a long period of investigation the fault was found to be a moth that had died amongst the wiring panels of the computer. Getting the computer up-and-running again was a merely a matter of debugging.

DEchead *(deck-head)*: 1. An employee of Digital Equipment Corporation; 2. A Deadhead (Grateful Dead fan) employee of DEC.

Decimal Numbering: A numbering system which uses a cycle of ten digits as the basis for the counting procedure. The only digits are 0,1, 2,3,4,5,6,7,8,9.

Decision Support System: A database system whose purpose is largely geared towards decision making. A Decision Support System is not necessarily an online, working database. It may draw data from the day-to-day activities of the organisation, but it is generally not involved in actual transaction processing.

Declaration: A technique used in some programming languages where the programmer must "declare", that is notify, the software/compiler/ translator of the variables that will be used in the program and their type.

DECnet *(deck-net)*: Network protocols designed for VAX and PDP-11 computers, used by Digital Equipment Corporation operating systems instead of TCP/IP.

DECnet/DNA: DEC's implementation of DNA (Digital Network Architecture).

DECnet tunnel: A protocol for packaging AppleTalk datagrams within DECnet packets.

decrypt: To remove the encryption from a file or e-mail message and make it readable.

decryption key: In key encryption, a key used to decipher an encrypted message and make it readable.

dedicated (adj): Assigned to a single task or able to perform only a single task.

dedicated line: A telephone line dedicated to telecommunications.

deep hack: The extreme state of concentration, bordering on a trance, that hackers enter after long hours of hacking.

Default: A group of settings applied to a computer in the absence of' specific instructions from the user or software application. For example, the default setting for reading and writing data in a spreadsheet package may he a specific hard disk directory, the default setting for text blocks in a word processing package may be 90mm, the default data transmission settings for communications between two computers may be 9600 baud.

default route: An entry in a routing table indicating where to route packets intended for destinations not otherwise listed in the table.

Defense Data Network (DDN): The network of networks used by the U.S. military, connecting with the, Internet in some places and not in others.

Defense Data Network Network Information Center (DDN NIC): The Network Information Center for the DDN, a source of information as well as an administrative authority over the DDN.

Defense Information Systems Agency (DISA): The U.S. government agency that, oversees the Defense Data Network.

DEK: data encryption key.

delete (v): To erase a character, file, or directory.

Delete key: A key used in most environments to erase the character that the cursor or insertion point is on or just before. On some systems, Delete erases the character just typed or to the left of the cursor.

delimiter: A character or symbol that indicates a break between two pieces of information, items in a table, or fields in a database.

delurk *(dee-lurk,* v): To post to a list or newsgroup for the first time. (n) A first post to a newsgroup or list after the writer has lurked for a while.

demon: A routine in a program that waits until it is needed (possibly from Maxwell's Demon):

Depew, Dick: The inventor of ARMM, a roboposting utility designed to retroactively cancel off-topic Usenet posts. Depew's 'bot had a serious flaw and followed up its own posts, eventually bringing down part of the internet in sorcerers apprentice mode.

deprecated (adj): Being phased out in favour of a new standard,

DES: data encryption standard.

despew (v): From [Dick] Depew, to robopost reams of junk to the Net.

developer: A software publisher.

Device: A software, utility program used to enhance or change the default settings of a computer, particularly with reference to how memory is managed.

Device Driver: A software utility program used to enhance or change the default settings of a computer, particularly with reference to how memory is managed. Also a utility program that describes the protocol for accessing a particular part of computer hardware.

/dev/null: On UNIX boxes, the null device. Data piped to /dev/null disappears. People posting controversial articles to Usenet sometimes add the notice "flames to /dev/null."

Dhrystone: This is an industry standard that measures the number of times a particular task, or group of tasks, can be executed per second. Dhrystones are used as a standardised measure of processing speed, for example, the Intel 80386 microprocessor running at 16MHz has been rated at 6000-7000 Dhrystones.

Dialog Box: A menu that poses a number of questions or alternatives to the user, the user responds to all or some of the questions and then returns to the main menu or the previous/next task.

dial up (v) To use a modem to call up another computer or network and log in to it.

dial-up (adj) Said of an Internet access that requires the user to connect via a modem.

dial-up account An Internet account on a host machine that you must dial up with your modem to use

DIALOG Information Retrieval Database A commercial online database service with hundreds of databases and millions of records. To connect to DIALOG, telnet to dialog.com.

dictionary flame A flame that focuses on someone's use of a particular word or their vocabulary, a weak sort of flame that indicates that the flamer has nothing substantial to say against the flamee.

digest (n) A collection of mailing list posts, sent out as one message.

digestified (adj) Turned into a digest. Not all mailing lists are available in a digestified form.

digital (adj) Representing values as discrete bits. CD is a digital medium because the second or other information is digitized ,converted into bits) and then stored. A CD player converts the digital information encoded on the CD into an analog signal sent to the amplifier.

Digital Data Communications Message Protocol (DDCMP) A DECnet data link protocol that can handle a both synchronous and asynchronous links.

Digital Equipment Corporation (DEC) Manufacturer of VAX (and before that PDP-11) boxes and the VMS operating system.

Digital Network Architecture (DNA) A set of protocols for network architecture.

DIP *Dual in-line package,* the housing for an integrated circuit.

DIP switch A switch used to select the operating mode of a device.

directed information Information intended for a particular recipient, such as private e-mail.

directory An organizing structure for files. In most operating systems, directories can themselves be organized hierarchically into a "tree" of parent and children directories.

Directory Access Protocol (DAP) An X.500 protocol governing communication between a Directory User Agent and a Directory System Agent.

directory listing A summary list of available files, possibly including file sizes, attributes, date and time of creation or last changes, and the owner, where appropriate.

directory service A database of sites and usernames that enables users to locate other users, hosts, and services.

Directory System Agent (DSA) X.500 software that serves directory information to Directory User Agents.

Directory User Agent (DUA) X.500 software that queries a Directory System Agent for directory information.

DISA Defense Information Systems Agency.

disable To temporarily disconnect or make nonfunctional (without necessarily shutting off).

disclaimer The line in some sig blocks asserting that the opinions of the writer are not necessarily those of the organization providing her internet access.

Disclaimer

>thus my 10 years of research culminate
>in these findings.
1 agree!
- jojo
--
jojo@yoyodyne.com
joey joe-joe "Junior" Shabadoo

The opinions in this message are those of joey joe-joe Jr.'s and not those of Yoyodyne, Inc., unless explicitly stated.

Discordianism The principles of the Discordian Society, as set clown in the *Principia* Discordia and other sacred (or profane) texts.

Discordian Society Followers of the goddess Eris (or Discordia), a mostly farcical organization spawned from Robert Anton Wilson's *Illuminati*! trilogy.

discussion group Any online group of likeminded people who may communicate via a mailing list, in a newsgroup, on an IRC channel, etc.

disk A medium for storing computer data, either built into the computer, (a hard disk) or removable (a floppy disk).

disk drive The mechanism that spins, reads from, and writes to the disk itself.

disk server A network program that enables a computer to use a disk drive on another computer (or a partition of such a disk drive) as if it were a local disk drive.

Distinct TCP/IP Tools A set of Internet tools for Windows sold by Distinct Corporation.

distributed computing An approach to computing that allows applications to run the same way across different types of networks,

Distributed Computing Environment (DCE) A set of standards for servers, interfaces, and protocols promoted by the Open Software Foundation to enable distributed computing.

distributed database A repository of information stored on various hosts and accessible to searches as if stored in a single location.

distributed server Peer-to-peer network architecture, in which server functions are shared among the peer computers in the network and disk drives, printers, and other devices are available to all.

distribution The geographic range that a Usenet post is distributed to. By default, most newsreaders will give posts World distribution.

distribution list A simple form of mailing list in which an alias is assigned to a list of e-mail addresses. Mail directed to the alias is sent to every address on the list.

disusered (adj) Denied access to the Net, having an account cancelled.

DIX *Digital, Intel and Xerox,* together the developers of the Ethernet protocol.

documentation Paper or online manuals that describe the functions of a computer system, often in incomprehensible terms.

dogpile (v) To quickly follow up a **Usenet post** with a large volume of critical replies.

domain The main subdivision of Internet addresses, the last part of an Internet address after the final dot. In the United States, the standard domains are as follows:

Domain	*Meaning*
.com	Commercial
.edu	Educational
.gov	Government
.mil	Military
.org	Non-profit organisation
.net	Network

Outside the United States, the top-level domain is usually the country domain, such as *.ca* for Canada, *.de* for Germany (Deutschland), *.uk* for the United Kingdom, and so on.

domain name:: A complete description of an Internet site including a host name, subdomain, and domain, all separated by dots.

domain name address An Internet address expressed in terms of host, subdomain, and domain, as opposed to the numerical IP address.

domain name resolution The process of converting domain names to numerical IP addresses, by consulting domain name servers.

domain name server An application that maintains a table of domain names and corresponding IP addresses in order to resolve the domain names of messages.

Domain Name System (DNS) A collection of distributed databases (domain name servers) that maintain the correlations between domain name addresses and numerical IP addresses, for example, the domain name address ruby.ora.com gets resolved into the numeric Internet address 134.65.87.3, and vice versa. DNS allows human beings to use the Internet with remembering long lists of numbers.

d00dz B1FFspeak for *dudes,* a term of address.

DOS *Disk Operating System,* the operating system developed for IBM PCs.

dos2unix A UNIX program that converts DOS text files to UNIX format (by stripping the carriage return character from the end of each line).

dot The separator character for domain names, newsgroup names, and other UNIX-oriented files. Dots should only be used to separate hierarchical levels in newsgroup names, not to split compound names. So, for example, alt.fan.dave.barry would be improper, but alt.fan.dave-barry is fine.

dot address A 32-bit numerical IP address of the form *number-dot-number-dot-number-dot-number (such* as 192.100.81.101). Each of the four numbers can range from 0 to 255.

dot file A UNIX file whose name begins with a dot, such as profile, .netrc, .cshrc, and so on. Dot files will not show up in a normal directory listing.

double dot.., an abbreviation for the parent directory of the current directory in both UNIX and DOS.

doubled sig A sig block that appears twice at the end the of an e-mail message or Usenet post, a sign that the writer is a newbie or that the software is hiccupping.

down (adj) Said of a network or device that is not functioning.

download To transfer a file over a modem from a remote computer to your desktop computer. (Technically, to transfer a file from a larger computer to a smaller computer.)

downstream Where your newsfeed goes after it has reached your host and your host a DUA has sent it along to other sites.

driver Software that controls peripheral devices, such as monitors, printers, or keyboards.

drop-ins Random characters that appear on the screen due to a faulty connection and/or line noise.

drop-outs Characters that are missing from the screen or not passed on by the keyboard.

DS4 *Digital Signal Level 4 is 274.176* Mbps, a standard level of digital transmission service.

DS1 *Digital Signal Level 1 is 1.544* Mbps, a standard level of digital transmission service.

DS3 *Digital Signal Level 3 is 44.7,36* Mbps, a standard level of digital transmission service.

DS2 *Digital Signal Level 2 is 6.312* Mbps, a standard level of digital transmission service.

DSO *Digital Signal Level 0 is 64* Kbps, a standard level of digital transmission service.

dual in-line package The housing for an integrated circuit.

dumb terminal A keyboard-and-monitor device that sends keystrokes to a computer and displays output on the screen. If you dial up to a UNIX shell, then your PC is being used as a dumb terminal.

dummy variable A meaningless variable used in an example to demonstrate correct syntax, such as foo, bar, or baz.

dump (v) To send tire contents of a file (or other data) to a device or another file, in order to print, display, or store the data.

dup killer *(doop killer)* FidoNet software that tries to detect and eliminate duplicate copies 0', the same message that may have arrived via different routes.

duplex Transmission of signals in two directions at once,

dup loop *(doop loop)* A series of nearly identical messages that have eluded the dup killer.

dynamic adaptive routing A method of directing network traffic based on the current state of the network.

dynamic node addressing A method of addressing used on AppleTalk networks in which nodes are assigned network addresses as needed, but do not have stable consistent network addresses, as in an IP network.

dynamic SLIP A type of SLIP access to the Internet, in which the user is supplied with a new IP address, drawn from a pool of possibilities, every time she connects. This enables the service provider to assign fewer IP addresses to its SLIP customers, with the trade-off being that the users cannot function as a host without a consistent address.

E

EBCDIC: An abbreviation for Extended Binary Coded Decimal Interchange Code. This is an eight bit character coding system and is one of the most popular binary coding systems.

echo (n): 1. A discussion group on FidoNet; 2. The, method by which the characters you type ire displayed on your screen, also know as local echo; 3. The method by which characters sent from a remote system are displayed on your screen, also known *as remote echo.*

EcoNet *(ee-coe-net)*: A BBS dedicated to environmental issues. Its Internet domain name is igc.org.

ed (rhymes with *bed)*: A UNIX, line-at-a-time text editor.

EDGAR: *Electronic Data Gathering Archiving and Retrieval,* a database of corporate disclosure, transaction, and financial status data maintained by the United States Security Exchange Commission.

EDIFACT: Abbreviation for Electronic Data Interchange For Administration, Commerce and Transport.

Editing: The process of reviewing, and if necessary, changing the content and/or format of a document, spreadsheet etc.

editor: 1. A text editor, a program used to edit simple text files; 2. Any program used to edit any type of file, such as a .WAV (Windows sound file) editor.

EDLIS: *Exchange of Dylan Lyrics—Internet Service,* an underground organization whose respond to requests posted in rec.music.dylan and elsewhere on the Net.

EDT: A text editor available on VMS machines and at Delphi Information Service.

.edu: The Internet domain dedicated to educational institutions.

Educational Resources Information Center (BRIC): A service for schools providing online bibliography and journal abstracts, via gopher at ericir.syr.edu and via e-mail at askeric@ricir.syr.edu.

EDUCOM *(ed-you-com)*: An *organization* dedicated to facilitating the use of computers in educational institutions. It is a supporter of the National Research and Education Network (NREN). Gopher: educom.com, e-mail: inquiry@ bitnic.educom.com.

EFFs Guide to the Internet: Formerly Big *Dummy's Guide to the Electronic Frontier* Foundation's excellent free Internet guide, available via FTP, gopher, and the Web.

EGP: External Gateway Protocol.

EIA/TIA-568: A document coauthored by the American National Standards Institute, the Electronics Industry Association, and the Telecommunications Industry Association that specifies a wiring standard for buildings suitable for both LANs and telecommunications systems.

8-bit clean (adj): Said of a modem connection with 8 data bits and no corruption of the signal from line noise.

802.x: A set of communications standards (802.1 through 802.5) for physical and electrical connections in LANs, defined by the Institute of Electrical and Electronic Engineers.

80-character line length: The standard line length for an IBM or UNIX terminal, a recommended maximum line length for e-mail and Usenet posts (some prefer 75 characters to allow for quotation, since most e-mail and newsreader programs quote text by preceding it with a > or other character).

EISA: Abbreviation for Extended Industry Standard Architecture. This is a bus architecture standard for personal computers proposed by a number of computer manufacturers and software developers. EISA provides for a clock speed of 8MHz and a 32-bit data bus.

e-journal: An *electronic journal,* an academic journal that circulates via an e-mail mailing list. One advantage-journals have over Print journals is that they are searchable.

Electronic Data Interchange: A national standard which specifies the protocol and format for the interchange of commercial documents. Abbreviation EDI.

Electronically Erasable Programmable Read Only Memory: A type of read only memory (ROM) that can be programmed (or reprogrammed) by electronic means. Electronically Erasable Programmable Read Only Memory is used in many electronic devices, not just computers.

Electronic Frontier Foundation: A lobbying and advocacy organization, founded by Mitch Kapor and John Barlow, working for the preservation of freedom on the cyberspace frontier.

Electronic Funds Transfer: Financial transaction processing via data communications links, abbreviation EFT.

Electronic Funds Transfer-Point of Sale: Financial transaction processing via data communications links. Examples include supermarket check-outs, service stations etc. The retailer keys in the relevant transaction details and the customer then keys in a Personal Indentification Number (PIN) to validate the transaction.

electronic journal: An academic journal that circulates via an e-mail mailing list. One advantage e-journals have over print journals is that they are searchable.

Electronic Mail: Any information that is transmitted via a computer system or communications network. Abbreviation e-Mail or E-Mail.

Electronic Office: A generic term for a hi-tech office that uses many electronic business machines such as computers, modems, fax, photocopiers, cordless telephones etc.

Electronics Industries Association (EIA): A standards organization for the electronics industry, the coauthor of EIA/TIA-568.

Electronic White Pages: A service provided by Telecom Australia which enables computer users to access the white pages telephone directory via a data communications network.

elm (rhymes with *helm)*: A full-screen UNIX e-mail program, easier to use than the basic, line-at-a-time mail but still more difficult than pine, which is much closer to modern word processors.

.elmrc: A setup file for elm.

emacs *(ee-macs)*: Also written EMACS, a UNIX text editor that doubles as an operating environment, mail program, and newsreader.

e-mail (n): Short for *electronic mail,* one of the most popular features of networks, online services, and the Internet in general, but you already knew that, didn't you? The term *e-mail is* used both for the overall process and for the messages carried electronically from computer to computer.

(v) To send e-mail.

e-mail address: 1. An Internet mail address of the form *username@host.domain;* 2. The username portion of a mail account on a network.

e me: Send me e-mail, please reply by e-mail.

emoticon: A smiley or other sideways punctuation face such as these: :-) :-(:-p %^) ;-) B-) :D. Emoticons can convey some insight into the writer's emotional state.

Emulation: To copy the characteristics of a particular hardware device. For example, the ABCD Laser Printer has three emulations, the VFG 200, the YUK 90 and the ARG 50, meaning that the ABCD can be treated as being "identical" in most aspects to the other printers in terms of printer drivers.

encapsulate: To embed a higher-level protocol within a lower-level protocol to create a single frame for transportation over a network

Encapsulated PostScript (EPS): A device-independent file format for PostScript files. EPS files are portable and can be printed with any PostScript printer.

encoding: The process of converting data to a coded format, generally to make it more easily transportable.

encrypt: To scramble the contents of a file or e-mail message so that only those with the key can unscramble and read them.

Encryption: A coding technique used to provide security for data being transmitted over a communications channel. The data is encrypted into an agreed format by the sender and restored to its original format at the receiving end.

encryption key: A unique, secret data block used to encrypt e-mail.

end-to-end (adj) Direct, said of a connection between two computers.

end-user (n): From a programmer's perspective, the ultimate customer, the regular person using the program, operating system, or computer.

Enter key: A large key on the right side of most keyboards used to submit commands or insert hard returns into text.

enterprise computing: Corporate network computing, bridging a variety of platforms, operating systems, and networking protocols.

Enterzone: A hyperzine on the World Wide Web at http://enterzone.berkeley,

environment: A front end for an operating system, a set of tools and a consistent look and feel that allow the user to interact with the computer, Windows is an environment that runs on top of die MSDOS operating system.

End-Of-File: A phrase used in many programming languages to indicate that processes are complete. A character used to denote that the end of a file has been reached. *The* end-of-file marker is often a Control-Z (^Z), a particular combination of binary digits which is recognised by the program control. Abbreviation EOF.

End-User: In Systems Analysis, this is the final user of the computer system. For example, a Systems Analyst may discuss computer software with a software developer and talk of the "enduser's requirements".

ENIAC: Abbreviation for Electronic Numerical Integrator and Calculator. One of the first computers of the First Generation, developed in the USA during the early 1940s. ENIAC used vacuum tubes and had a MTBF of about two hours.

ENTER Key: The key used to signal that keyboard input is ready for processing. Typically the ENTER key is pressed after each command. In some documentation the ENTER key is designated RETURN. Pressing the ENTER key empties the keyboard buffer.

.eps: The file extension for an Encapsulated PostScript file.

Ergonomics: The study of the Workplace and furniture design in relation to work processes. The key aim of ergonomics is to improve health, safety, and efficiency in the workplace. Recent studies in ergonomics have also investigated the impact of colour in the workplace, not only the colour of office furniture, walls etc, but the colours used on computer monitors. It has been found that a monochrome monitor using green is the least tiring to the eyes whereas amber produces the least number of operator mistakes.

Eris: The Goddess of Discord.worshipped by members of the Discordian Society.

error: An unexpected action or result, or incorrectly transmitted data, Any process that causes results which a computer cannot properly interpret.

error control: Any method for verifying the correctness of transmitted data.

Error Message: A message generated by a software application or hardware device in response to a hardware, software or user error. Error messages are notoriously brief and usually require cross-reference to the system or software manuals.

Error Rate: This is the number of errors that occur during data transmission. There is a need to monitor error rates as high rates , are obviously unacceptable.

escape character: 1. ASCII 26; 2. Any character which, when preceded by an escape (usually ASCII 26, the character that is transmitted when the Escape key is pressed), sends a command to a device, such as a terminal or printer. They are often represented on the screen as capital letters preceded by carets, such as ^E, ^X, etc.

Escape Key: This is a key found on many computer keyboards which is used to start an "escape" sequence. This may be backtracking out of a menu or activating a menu etc.

escape out (v): 1. To substitute a special symbol for a character that would otherwise be misinterpreted; 2. To run a temporary shell from within an application in order to send commands to the operating system.

Escape Sequence: A series of command codes sent to a peripheral device to instruct the printer to perform a particular task, such as change the font for the next character, to indent the text, change the line spacing etc. Different printer command languages have their own codes, as do different printers. Escape codes are embedded into the data being sent from the computer and are invariably user-transparent.

e-text: Written works made available electronically.

Ethernet: A Local Area Network (LAN) implementation protocol developed by Xerox Corporation, Digital Equipment Corporation and Intel. Ethernet is one of the most popular LAN implementations and several industry standards are based on it.

EtherTalk: AppleTalk protocols for Ethernet LANs, encapsulating DDP datagrams into Ethernet frames.

EtherTalk Link Access Protocol (ELAP): AppleTalk's Ethernet data link protocol.

ETLA *(ee-tee-ell-ay)*: *Extended three-letter acronym (i.e.,* a four-letter acronym). The acronym is a facetious comment on the proliferation of bewildering TLAs in the technical world. Too many TLAs and ETLAs thrown around make MEGO.

.etx: File extension for a setext file.

Eudora: An e-mail program for Windows or the Macintosh that can use the Post Office Protocol and function as an offline mail reader. Available via anonymous FTP from ftp.qualcomm.com.

European Academic and Research Network (EARN): A network of universities and research facilities in Europe that has e-mail and file-transfer connections to BITNET.

even parity: A method of verifying the correctness of transmitted data by summing each byte, adding a parity bit of 1 if necessary to ask the sum even before sending the data, and then repeating the summation on the receiving end.

exclamation point (!): 1. A bang—it precedes each site in a bang path; 2. In some UNIX programs, an exclamation mark enables the user to shell out; 3. Overuse of exclamation marks to punctuate Usenet posts is one of the hallmarks of a newbie or a BIFF.

.exe: A DOS file extension used to indicate an executable file (such as a program or self-extracting archive file).

execute: To perforın a command or run a program, something operating systems do.

Executable File: This is computer software that contains instructions for the CPU and computer peripherals. Executable files can be "run", that is they produce tangible events via the CPU instruction set. Conversely, data files are passive and are only useful in conjunction with an executable file. Executable files are generally referred to simply as "software" or "programs". Under many operating system, executable files have the file extension "exe". In each case, the software can be loaded by typing the name of the executable file, the file extension "exe" need not necessarily be typed.

exit (v): To quit a program or leave a shell.

Expanded Memory On an IBM and IBM compatible PC, this is memory that is accessible via a 16KB "window" within the first 1MB of RAM. Expanded memory is therefore accessed in 16KB "pages" and requires sophisticated memory management. The industry standard for this is the LIM EMS (Lotus-Intel-Microsoft Expanded Memory Specification). Expanded memory is primarily used on XT, and XT compatible computers since the eight bit microprocessor used in these machines cannot address any area of memory above 1MB.

Expansion Slot: These are slots (electrical connectors) on a motherboard reserved for the addition of more RAM, extra peripherals etc. Expansion slots are normally specified x by the number available and their size, for example, two 8 bit expansion slots and one 16-bit expansion slot.

Expert System: A specialised computer system, usually dealing with a narrow range of expertise, for example, land management, scientific analysis. Expert Systems are designed to act as a "consultant" or "troubleshooter" for the management of an organisation.

expire: Applied to Usenet articles, to be removed after an expiration date to keep the newsfeed from growing too large.

export (v): 1. To save a file in a different format (that of another program); 2. To send a product to a foreign country (whether physically or over the Internet).

Extended Binary Coded Decimal Interchange Code (EBCDIC): A proprietary IBM character set that is not entirely compatible with ASCII.

Extended Memory: On an IBM and IBM compatible PC, this is memory above the first 1MB boundary, that is, above "conventional" memory. The first IMB of conventional memory contains RAM, video RAM etc.

Extension: This usually refers to the second part of a file name. Operating systems allow a certain number of characters for the file name and an additional group of characters as a file extension. The file name is usually separated from the extension by a full stop. In many operating systems the file extension can be up to three characters.

External Command: In MS-DOS this is a command that is not available via the generic command processor (COMMAND.COM) and requires the loading of an executable file.

External Disk Drive: A disk drive whose hardware is physically separate to the computer hardware. Electrically it will perform the same function as an internal drive.

External Gateway Protocol (EGP): A routing protocol by which connected net works signal their availability to each other.

External Reference: A technique which allows one data file to extract or load data from another data file. Each rile contains a reference to the other data file, which the relevant program then accesses as necessary. This software link between two *data files* means that as one file is updated the other is also updated.

e-zine: An electronically distributed fanzine or magazine. Many are sent as e-mail. Others are made available via gopher or the Web.

face time: Time spent meeting with a person as contrasted with spent communicating via e-mail, etc.

Facsimile: A data communications device that can transmit images via ordinary telephone circuits. At the transmitting end a document is fed into the facsimile machine (also known as a fax machine or simply fax) which then scans and digitises the document. The digital bitstream so generated is transmitted to the distant end where the image is reassembled on the receiving facsimile machine.

fair use: The legal doctrine that allows limited quotation of other people's work if the use of their work does not undercut its market value.

fall off: Said of a portion of data that exceeds the size of a memory register and is lost.

fanzine: An underground, do-it-yourself magazine, often dedicated to a band, celebrity, or cult figure.

FAQ (fack,n): 1. *frequently asked question;* 2. A file containing frequently asked questions and their answers, sometimes called a FAQL (*frequently asked question list).* To find FAQs, look in the answers newsgroups or the FTP archive at rtfm.mit.edu. Many mailing lists and Usenet newsgroups maintain FAQs so that participants won't have to spend lots of time answering the same set of questions.

FAQL (*fackle,* n): *Frequently asked question list,* a file containing frequently asked questions and their answers, usually compiled and maintained by a newsgroup, mailing list, or Internet site.

FARNET (Federation of American Research Networks): A nonprofit organization that works to promote the use of computer networks for research and education.

FAST: Abbreviation for Federation Against Software Theft. An American software industry association with obvious objectives.

fast packet: A standard for highspeed, high-traffic, cellswitching networks.

fax: 1. A *facsimile* of a document, digitized and transmitted over phone lines. While faxes are usually sent and received with a stand-alone fax machine, faxes may also be sent to and from computers using fax software and a fax modem; 2. A machine that can send and receive faxes.

fax modem: A modem that can fulfill some of the functions of a fax machine.

FCC: Abbreviation for Federal Communications Commission, an American statutory body, concerned with many aspects of communications. For example, the FCC issues Class A and Class B certificates, relating to suppression of radio interference (RE). Class A certificates cover usage in commercial premises, whilst the more stringent Class B certificate covers residential usage. Most countries have an equivalent system of certification.

FDC: Abbreviation for Floppy Disk Controller.

FDD: 1) Floppy Disk Drive. 2) Fixed Disk Drive. Another name for Hard Disk Drive.

Federal Information Exchange (FIX): A gateway linking U.S. government net works with the Internet.

Federal Information Processing Standards (FIPS): A United States Department of Defense document specifying U.S. government networking plans.

Federal Networking Council (FNC): An organization that coordinates the net working standards of U.S. government agencies.

FEDIX: An online information service linking educational institutions and the U.S. government. It offers the Minority On-Line Information Service (MOLIS).

Fetch: A step in a machine cycle where the next instruction or batch of required data is retrieved from RAM or secondary memory.

Fiber Distributed Data Interface (FDDI): A backbone, system for large networks, employing two rings of fiber-optic cabling, with a signaling rate of 80 Mbps.

Fibre Optics: A data communications method that uses glass fibres to channel light through a cable. Given the high frequency of light this provides a very powerful transmission media, with many thousands of connections per fibre being possible.

fiber-optic cable: Class cabling designed to carry light pulses, often used for backbones; more dependable, lighter, and smaller than copper cable carrying electronic signals, but much more expensive and more difficult to repair.

FidoNet: A network of BBSs with Internet e-mail access.

Field: This is a data entry area in a database, with each field being specified by a label, a size and a data type.

First in -First out (FIFO): A design philosophy employed in queueing, gating and spooling systems. This philosophy ensures that waiting times are roughly equally for all users.

Fight-o-net: A pejorative name for FidoNet, alluding to the frequent arguments on FidoNet echoes and mailing lists.

File: A collection of data items, text or numerical information created by computer software during the execution of a program. Files are normally stored on tape or disk. A word processing file may contain, for example, a quotation for a job, a chapter of a book, an annual report or a memo. A database file may contain a listing of names, addresses, postcodes, telephone numbers and employee numbers. A spreadsheet file may contain financial data for the present financial year.

File Allocation Table: A data file, on a floppy disk or hard disk, detailing the location of each file that has been written on to the disk. This enables the operating system to locate and read or update each file whenever necessary. The File Allocation Table (abbreviation FAT) is stored in duplicate because of the possibility of bad sectors making the FAT unreadable and the disk therefore useless.

File Attach: A FidoNet procedure for attaching a file to an e-mail message to send it to another BBS.

file locking: Preventing all but the first user from changes to a file that is opened by more than one user on a network.

File Name: The name given to a data file, system file or executable file. In many cases the file name must be given by the computer user before the computer can write the file to disk or tape. When a software application makes a request for access to a particular file, the operating system converts the file name to a storage address ready for retrieval. Most operating systems restrict the file name length to a maximum number of characters (for example, under MS-DOS this is eight characters). It is useful to make a file name indicative of the file contents. For example a word processing file called XYZ-AP8.doc might be a letter sent to X= P/L on April 8th. FIN89-90.WKI might be a company's financial records spreadsheet for the financial year 1989-90.

File Protection Ring: A small plastic ring on a reel-to-reel tape that is used to "write-protect" the tape.

File request: A FidoNet procedure for transferring a file from one BBS to another.

File Server: A microprocessor controlled device that controls the flow of data to and from terminals in a Local Area Network. A File Server "serves" software and data to each terminal.

file transfer: The copying of a file over a network connection from a remote site to the localhost.

Fill-in Screen: A data entry screen that provides a number of boxes and lines as data entry points. Each data entry point is presented in a logical order and has an appropriate label to indicate which data item should go where. This type of screen is often used for airline reservations and similar systems and is also known as a Data Entry Screen.

film at 11: A common tag line in Usenet follow-up posts mocking the timeliness of the original article. Often follows "Imminent death of the Net predicted!"

Filter: A software command that either extracts data items from a database in a particular order and/or extracts only certain data items from the database. The first case is sometimes referred to as indexing, the second case as querying.

Finder: A part of the operating system on an Apple computer, which provides file and directory management facilities.

finger: To seek the identity of a user or the status of a network. The UNIX command that performs the finger function.

finn: To pull rank on someone else in IRC by showing that you've been around a lot longer than the other person—a relative newbie compared to you.

firewall: A security measure on the Internet, protecting information, preventing access, or ensuring that users cannot do any harm to underlying systems. Some networks are connected to the Internet via a firewall machine.

Firmware: This term is used to describe the software embedded into ROM (read-only-memory). This software is usually written into ROM during manufacture and cannot subsequently be changed by programmers or users. Firmware provides basic control routines for the CPU and computer hardware.

First Generation Computer: These were computers developed between about 1940-1960, First Generation Computers used vacuum tube technology and consumed awesome amounts of power and floor space. See also Fourth Generation Computer, Generation, Second Generation Computer, Third Generation Computer.

FirstSearch Catalog: A catalog maintained by the Online Computer Library Center that gives member libraries access to many databases of books and magazines in print.

Fixed Disk: A type of hard disk.

Fixed Length Record: A data record that has a fixed amount of space reserved for it regardless of whether that space will be used or not. For example, in a database it may be necessary to reserve up to 30 characters for a person's surname, but in practice most surnames would fall far short of this size. In large databases (such as a payroll database for a large organisation) fixed length records can mean an enormous amount of wasted data storage capability.

Fixed Space Font: A design of font that allocates the same linear space to each printed character. By comparison a Proportionally Spaced Font allocates variable linear space to different characters. For example, using proportional spacing, the letter 'w' would be given more space than the letter "i". Use of proportional spacing gives a much more professional appearance to text. Most word processors can specify proportional spacing (proportionally spaced fonts) but not all printers can produce 'the necessary output.

Flag: A register that stores the status of a device (microprocessor, hardware etc).

flame: An insulting e-mail or Usenet post. Flames are often illconsidered kneejerk expressions of anger, but they can also be cruelly detailed and intended for the amusement of the general audience at the expense of the flamee.

flamebait: A post to a mailing list or newsgroup designed to elicit flames.

Flamebait: can be recognized by the fact that it goes beyond the premises of the list or newsgroup. Nobody objects to provocative or even argumentative posts, but posts to the alt.fank.frank-zappa newsgroup saying "Zappa was a no-talent potty-mouthed dweeb" betray a lack of legitimate interest in the subject hand.

flamefest: A flame war, particularly one involving many participants.

flame on: A comment in a post meaning either "Here is where I start flaming" or "I'm prepared to be flamed for the following comment."

flamer: 1. One who flames; 2. One who flames habitually or incessantly.

flames to /dev/null: A tag line in posts to mailing lists and newsgroups meaning "I'll ignore any flames", from the UNIX name for the null device, a sort of trash can.

flame war: Often written *flamewar,* a prolonged series of flames and counterflames, drowning out the on-topic posts in a newsgroup or mailing list. Traditionally, flame wars end when Nazis are mentioned.

flavor (n): A variety, as in "BSD is a flavor of UNIX"

Flip-Flop: A part of the internal circuitry of a register. It recognises and responds to binary input, the circuitry of the register "flips" and "flops" between two states (0 and 1). In combinations it is used as a logic gate, as well as a shift register.

Floating Point Numbers: These are numbers that can be represented by a variable amount of decimal places. Decimal representation can be achieved in binary numbering by allocating certain positions as "decimals". For example, in a 16-bit word, 12 bits can be allocated to be the actual number and the remaining 4 bits to represent the decimal places

The normal method of storing numbers is referred to a "fixed point" numbers, that is the decimal point is not moved throughout any computer operation, either for data storage or for processing. This creates problems when dealing with large numbers and "floating point" notation is used. For example, the number 13678123410 can be represented by using floating point notation. In this system each large number is converted to a decimal and a, corresponding "power of ten" multiplier. In the example given, this could be 0. 1367812341 x 10 ^ 11 or 1367.7812341 x 10 ^ 7. In this manner the CPU is able to manipulate otherwise unwieldy numbers with accuracy.

In some programming languages (for example, C) program variables can be declared as being "floating point". Variables should only be declared as floating point if absolutely necessary as these numbers will have a large amount of RAM allocated to them.

flood (v): To spam an IRC channel, that is, to type or paste in huge amounts of text, effectively drowning out the conversation.

Floppy Disk: A magnetic storage media, using flat, circular platters. Floppy disks are primarily used on PCs. Physical size and storage capabilities vary. Some examples are,

Size capacity

5.25"160KB, 360KB, 1.2MB

3.5" 160KB, 360KB, 400KB, 720KB, 800KB, 1M, 1.44MB; 2.8MB

Floppy disks first came on the market in the early-1970s. The 5.25" (135mm) disk appeared to be the industry standard for many years but is now being challenged by the more robust, more compact, larger storage, 3.5" (90mm) disks. The even smaller 2" disk has yet to make its impact.

Floppy Disk Drive: An electro-mechanical device that performs read/write operations on a floppy disk. The disk drive has a read/write head which accesses and, if necessary, updates data files on disk. The disk drive rotates the internal magnetic media of the disk at about 360 revolutions per minute, ensuring that all areas of the disk appear under the read/write head at frequent intervals.

Floptical Disk: A type of floppy disk that combines optical and magnetic techniques. These disks have a very high density of data storage tracks and hence a high storage capacity. As this is a comparatively new technology, floptical disks have yet to make their impact.

Flow Chart: A graphical representation of the major steps in a computer program or the manufacturing/commercial processes involved in producing goods or services. Most flow charts are based upon a standard method of indicating the different types of processes that may be involved. The following is an example of a flow chart using ANSI symbols,

flow control: The method by which two devices, generally modems, signal to each other when to start and stop sending data.

fnord: A nonsense word embedded in posts or sig blocks, alluding to Robert Anton Wilson's Illuminati! trilogy.

FOAF: A *friend of a friend,* the most comon source or attribution for urban legends, implying that the teller doesn't personelly know the participants, but knows someone who does.

folder: 1. A directory, especially on a Macintosh; 2. An e-mail file containing related messages.

follow-up: To respond to a post with a replying post.

follow-up: A post that replies to and possibly quotes an earlier post.

follow-up line: A line in the header of some Usenet posts directing follow-ups to a particular newsgroup or newsgroups. Newbies who fail to heed the follow-up line can be tricked into posting replies to inappropriate newsgroups.

foo: A dummy variable used by programmers as a stand-in for a real variable, often paired with bar.

foobar: A dummy variable used by programmers as a stand-in for a real variable.

footprint: The portion of a surface that the computer or other device occupies.

foreground: In a multitasking computer environment, a process that takes place in full view or with higher prioriy than other running processes is said to take place in the foreground.

FORTRAN: An early computer programming language (the name comes from FOR*mula* TRAN*slator*).

Fortrash: A pejorative term for FORTRAN.

fortune cookie: A program that spits out a different fortune every time you run it. Some systems run cookie as part of their startup or login procedure.

forum: A discussion group on CompuServe and other online services and BBSs where interests may find valuable information exchange ideas and share files.

forward: To send received e-mail to another address, either manually or automatically.

forward slash: Used to divide directories in a path.

FQA: *Frequentlly questioned acronym.*

frame: A block of data encapsulated with a header and trailer for transmission over a network.

frame relay: A standard for transmission of frames over a packet-switching network, a variant of the X.25 standard.

fred: 1. An easy-to-use X.500 interface; 2. A dummy variable used by programmers to stand for a real variable.

FrEdMail *(fred-mail)*: A network of BBSs for students and teachers.

free-net: A free public network providing Internet access to members of a community.

Free Software Foundation (FSF): An organization dedicated to the production and distribution of the free software the creators of GNU, reachable via FTP at prep.ai.mit.edu.

free-WAIS: A free version of a WAIS server produced and distributed, by CNIDR (Clearinghouse for Networked Information Discovery and Retrieval).

freeware: Software distributed for free (or bragging rights) via the Net. The culture, of the Internet encourages freeware.

frequency: A measurement of the number ot cycles per second of an electronic signal, roughly a measurement of the speed of a process or device.

fringeware: Software of dubious stability, value, or appeal, made available as freeware.

frink: The sound that lemurs make, according to the alt.fan lemurs newsgroup.

front end: The part of a computer process that the end-user interacts with. In client/server applications, the client acts as a front end for the server.

FSLIST: The Forgotten Site List. A list of Internet service providers available via anonymous FTP from freedom.nmsu.edu in the /pub/docs/fslist directory.

ftp: The UNIX FTP program.

FTP: Internet *file transfer protocol,* the standard TCP/IP protocol for transferring files over the Internet, across any platforms.

FTPmail: A way to use FTP by e-mail if you don't have an FTP application. One address for an FTPmail server is ftpmail@ pa.dec.com.

FTP server: An FTP file server, a computer serving files from an FTP archive.

FTP site: A host on the Internet containing archives and set up for FTP.

f2f: *Face-to-face,* meeting in person.

FUBAR: *Fucked up beyond all recogni*tion, an old U.S. Army term used frequently on the Net.

full duplex: Two-way communication in which the computers at either end of the transmission both send and receive at the same time.

full name: The real name associated with an e-mail address; can be an alias.

full-screen editor: A text editor that allows the user to move around the screen, editing the entire file.

fully qualified domain name (FQDN): The complete domain name that identifies a specific computer (or host network, at the very least) on the Internet, including a host name, a subdomain name, and a domain name.

furrfu (fur-foo): rot13 for *sheesh!*

fwiw (written only): *For what it's worth.*

FYI: An Internet document that provides information about the Internet itself, but which does not define standards. Available via anonymous FTP from rtfm.mit.edu.

G

G: This is a symbol for the word "Giga" (one thousand million) and in computer usage this is the quantity 1073741824 (2^30) not 1000000000 as in normal business and scientific usage.

Gantt Chart: An activity monitoring method commonly used in business. It is usually in the form of a bar chart, and shows actual progress against planned progress of an activity. Named after Henry Gantt (1861-1919) a management theorist and a writer of the scientific management school.

Gas Plasma Display: This is a type of monitor display which is used in some portable computers. Gas plasma provides better definition than a Liquid Crystal Display, but at the price of higher power consumption. It uses inert gases, such as neon.

gate (n): Also called a gateway a computer providing a connection between two works, two e-mail handling systems, or a Usenet newsgroup and a mailing list illustration below). A gate reformats the data so that it will be acceptable to the system it is passing into. (v) To establish a gate.

gated (adj): Connected to another network or discussion group via a gateway.

gated newsgroup: A newsgroup whose posts are sent to a mailing list and which receives (or includes) posts from the mailing list.

Gateway: Any link between two data communications networks.

<gd&<r>: Grinning, ducking, and running (what you post you've tweaked someone). Also <gr&d>.

geek: Someone who knows a lot about computers, networks, or the Internet and thinks they're interesting (not necessarily an insult).

geek code: A set of coded ratings in a sig block. describing the poster in humorous, geeky terms.

geek out (v): 1. To get lost in the minutiae of a computer process; 2. To talk computers or networking in a social setting.

Gender Bender: A small electrical connector that inverts the gender of an electrical connector (male > female, female--> male).

General Public License (GPL): Also called copyleft, the license carried by Free Software Foundation software (such as GNU), granting reuse and reproduction rights to anyone and everyone.

General Public Virus (GPV): A pejorative name for the General Public License carried by Free Software Foundation software, so called because some developers believe it opens them up to legal liability if they include GPL code in their products.

Generation (computers): Evolutionary steps in technological progress are often referred to as being "of the next generation". The actual boundary between one generation and another is hard to define, but the concept of successive generations remains.

In computers it is acknowledged that First Generation was from 1940-1960, using vacuum tube technology; Second Generation from approximately 1955-1965, using transistor technology, but only as discrete components; Third Generation from approximately 1965-1980, using low density integrated circuits and microprocessors; Fourth Generation from approximately 1980, using Very Large Scale Integration (VLSI).

Generation (languages): In computer programming the present crop of formal, structured, syntax dependent languages are Third Generation (also known as 3GL). Examples include BASIC, PASCAL and C. The newer, less .formal languages, for example, DataFlex, are known as Fourth Generation languages.

Geographic Information System: A computer system, both hardware and software, which is used to analyse geographic information, for example, the distribution of natural resources, land usage patterns, demographic trends etc. A Geographic Information System (abbreviation GIS) is not necessarily an on-line system. It usually draws data from external primary and secondary sources. Its tasks may include cartography, time-series analysis, statistics and databases.

get (v) To copy a file from a remote source to your host computer, particularly via FIT. (n) The FTP command to get a file.

Get a life: A common flame, suggesting that the flame is too involved in the Internet or her/his computer.

Get a real: A common geeky type of flame (such as "Get a real computer," "Get a real operating system," "Get a real service provider," and so on) directed at someone's inferior hardware, software, or network connection.

Ghod: An alternative spelling for God preferred by some hackers and other netizens /also spelled *ghod).*

Ghu: A deity some hackers and other netizens offer their praises and curses to, as in "Great Ghu! Where'd you get an idea like that?"

GIF (Graphics Interchange Format): 1. An extremely popular compressed graphics (image) file format originated by *CompuServe* but readable in most platforms; 2. A file in the GIF format.

GIF! GIF! GIF!: A ritual follow-up to a post mentioning an image (such as a photograph), requesting that someone scan the image, save it as a GIF, uuencode it, and post it to the newsgroup.

Gigabyte: A measure of secondary memory capacity. One gigabyte (abbreviation GB) is 1024 Megabytes. Secondary memory on a mainframe computer is typically measured in GB.

GIGO: Abbreviation for Garbage in Garbage out. A reminder that the finished product is only as good as the raw materials, hardware, software, data and personnel involved in a project.

Glitch: Computer jargon for a program failure or human mistake.

global: Affecting an entire document or system (for example, a global search and replace is a search and replace operation performed on an entire document than a small selection or a single item)

Global variable: A variable whose value is controlled by any part of the program (subroutine, module, or main program). A global variable is accessible to the main program and other modules, any of which may be able to alter its value.

Glossary: A listing of definitions, usually found at the back of the more professional computing books.

gnu: A hierarchy in the Usenet mold devoted to the Free software foundation and its free products, such as GNU and emacs.

GNU (noo): A freely distributed set of applications and utilities intended as replacement for UNIX GNU is distributed by the Free Software Foundation.

GNUMACS: A contracted form of GNU emacs.

Godwin's Rule: Usenet Rule #4, which states that a thread in which Nazis or Hitler have been invoked has reached irrelevancy and will end soon. For some (but not all) of the other Rules see the net.legends FAQ at gopher://dixie.aiss.uinc.edu: 6969/00/ urban.legends/net.legends/Net.Legends.FAQ.

Good Thing: Something generally or widely accepted to be good. Tolerance is a Good thing. so is reading the FAQ before asking questions.

gopher: A client/server application that allows you to browse huge amounts of information by performing FTP transfers, remote logins, archie searches, and on, presenting everything to the end-user in the form of menus. This saves the user from having to know (or type in) the address of the Internet resources being tapped.

Gopher Book for Windows: A gopher client for Windows, available via anonymous FTP from sunsite.unc.edu.

gopher client: The gopher program that an end-user runs to get information from a gopher server. The gopher client retrieves the menus and documents and displays them for the user.

gopher.micro.umn.edu: The site of the University of Minnesota Gopher, the original gopher server.

Gopher for Nextstep: A gopher client for the Nextstep operating system, available via anonymous FTP from sonata.cc. purdue.edu.

gopher server: An application that provides documents and menus to gopher client, a starting point for a gopher search.

gopher site: A computer with a gopher server running on it.

gopherspace: A conceptual space encompassing all of the menus and documents that can be reached via the interconnected system of gopher serves on the Internet.

gorets (n): A generic noun that can have any meaning, especially as elaborated in the alt.gorets, especially as elaborated in the alt.gorets newsgroup.

go root (v): To log in as root, a UNIX superuser or system administrator account, in order to exercise the extended privileges of that account.

GOTO: A program statement used in several high-level programming languages, for example, BASIC, PASCAL, C. GOTO statements transfer program control to another line of code and may be conditional or unconditional.

Although a very powerful and precise programming tool, many programmers advise against excessive use of GOTO statements. Reasons given are that a program with many GOTOs is like a bowl of spaghetti, it is difficult to find which program segment belongs where and the program logic is hard to follow. This makes the program hard to debug. Several academics have shown that GOTO statements are not necessary and that sufficient program control can be achieved through DO WHILE and REPEAT UNTIL loops. The general consensus is that GOTO statements are acceptable in moderation. For professional programmers they often provide the only solution to program control in the depths of a large program.

.gov: An Internet domain corresponding to U.S government, including federal , state, and logical governments.

Government OSI Profile (GOSIP): A set of OSI standards that the U.S government follows in the procurement of computers in order to preserve compatibility among various government computer networks.

grape juice!: Something you yell at a computer when it isn't working, akin to banging it on the side.

Graph: Any pictorial representation of business or statistical information, often called charts, rather than graphs. Many PC software applications provide graphics capabilities, for example, SYSTAT, Excel, Lotus 123, Quattro, SPSS etc.

graphical user interface (GUI): A full-screen graphical Interface (meaning not limited to just letters and numbers) that allows users to run programs, execute commands, and generally interact with the computer by using a pointing device such as mouse to manipulate graphical screen elements, as opposed to typing commands at a prompt.

Dial-up Internet users generally need SLIP or PPP access to be able to interact direclty with Internet facilities within their GUI.

<gr&d> (written only): Grinning running and ducking (what you post after you've tweaked someone). Also <gd&r>.

Graphics Program: Software that can be used to generate general purpose drawings or specific industry drawings, for example, engineering, cartography, business etc.

Great Renaming: A day in 1985 on which nonlocal Usenet newsgroup names were changed from the form net.* to the hierarchy still in use today.

Great Worm: The 1988 worm that got out of control and crashed systems all over the internet. throwing a scare into many.

Greeking: The use of symbols to show text or graphics that cannot be shown in sufficient detail to be legible. For example a very small font may be shown on the monitor as xxxxx

green-card lawyer: A pejorative term for people who *spam* the Net with unwanted advertisements and then go on TV to defend their actions (In 1993, a pair of lawyers posted an advertisement obtain green cards [to work in the United States] separately and individually to over six thousand *newsgroups*, provoking a huge backlash of fury and indignation.)

grep (rhymes with prep, v): To globally search a document, set of files, or *newsfeed* for a particular word or expression. (n) The UNIX grep command.

grok (v): To understand deeply or intimately, from Robert A. Heinlein's Stranger in a Strange Land.

group (n): Generally, a news group, a Usenet or similar style discussion group

groupware: Software that gives multiple users access to the same information over a network, allowing collaboration on documents, scheduling of meetings, tracking of mission-critical projects, and so on.

grovel: 1. To beg for something in a Usenet newsgroup,. 2. For a programmer, to hunt through code looking for a problem.

guest: A special login account reserved for visitors checking out a *BBS*, online service, or service provider.

GUI: Abbreviation for Graphical User Interface. This is an adjunct to a computer operating system which provides an enhanced environment for the computer user. Since a GUI uses graphics based (pixel based) images, rather than text based images, it provides for on-screen integration of several different software applications.

guiltware: Shareware that reminds you to register (and pay for) the product.

gunzip (n): The UNIX *uncompression* program for *gzip*ped files.

guru: A helpful expert, someone to whom regular users turn to solve problems with their computer or network.

GW-BASIC.: A proprietary version of BASIC, developed by computer guru Bill Gates. According to Gates, GW stands for Gee Whiz!

.gz: A file extension for files that have been compressed with *gzip*.

gzip (n): A UNIX file compression program.

h: The help command in some UNIX applications.

-h-: The letter *h is* often stuck inside other words to make them appear odd, as in Ghod.

^H: The backspace character. Use of the Backspace key in terminal emulations chat don't support it sometimes leaves the original text on-screen, followed by one ^H character for every time Backspace is pressed, as in "Let me be the first to call you a ^H^H^H^H friend."

hack: To write code, to work on a computer, to cleverly diagnose and fix a problem, to dig beneath the surface of a computer process, reinventing things when hack around To figure a software program out for yourself, by trial and error, rather by reading the manual.

hacker: A computer adept, someone who enjoys working with computer, and testing the limits of systems, an enthusiastic or fast (or both) programmer.

hacker ethic: The philosophy, common among hackers, that information, technology, and clever tricks should be shared and disseminated rather than hoarded.

half bridge: A device that connects a network to a communications link via a modem without passing routing information, which must be supplied by the network software

half duplex: Two-way communication in which the computers at each end of the transmission take turns sending.

half router: A device that connects a network to a communications link via a modem, passing routing information along with data.

handle: A nickname or one-word name, such as a nick on IRC or a user-name. Network connections provided by employers often assign a strung-together version of a person's full name as their user-name, instead of a handle.

Handshake: Protocol for a data communications or data transfer circuit, for example, agreement on Baud Rate, Parity etc. Engineers may talk of "handshaking problems".

Hands-on: This refers to situations where a person actually uses computer hardware/software. Often called "hands-on experience". A computer operator may write in a job application "Five years hands-on experience, IBM 370. In an educational/training situation the syllabus may say "One hour lecture, followed by three hours hands-on"

hang: Said of a computer, to, stop working, to freeze, to become unresponsive, to wait for something that will never happen.

Hard Card: In a PC, this is secondary memory in the form of a plug-in card which includes a hard disk. Typically a hard card has 20-40MB capacity and is a useful way of getting a quick extension to a computer's memory.

Hard Copy: A generic term used to describe any form of computer output that produces a permanent record, for example, on paper, transparency, microfiche etc.

Hard Disk: A magnetic storage media, using flat, circular platters which are rotated at very high speed, typically 3600 revolutions per minute. The high speed of rotation ensures that all areas of the disk appear under the read/write heads at very frequent intervals. Physical size and storage capabilities vary. For PCs, sizes vary from 20MB to about 200MB. On mainframe computers, sizes vary from 500MB to several GB. Hard disks have been in use since the mid-1950s, when IBM introduced their "Ramac" hard disk.

Hard Disk Controller: Electronic circuitry that provides an interface to, and supeivises, a hard disk drive. Abbreviation HDC. There are several different controller philosophies in use, for example, ESDI, MFM, SCSI, ST506.

Hard Disk Drive: An electro-mechanical device that performs read/write operations to a hard disk. The disk drive has at least one read/write head which accesses and, if necessary, updates data files on disk. The disk drive rotates the platter(s) of the disk at about 3600 revolutions per minute, ensuring that all areas of the disk appear under the read/write head at very frequent intervals. Abbreviation HDD.

Hard Space: In word processing this is a space that is important for the meaning of the text. For example it may be considered bad style to allow word wrap to split the name "Ms Bingham!" over two lines. The insertion of a "hard" space between the two words will ensure that white space appears between the two words but that the words are treated as one.

Hardware: A generic term used for all of the electronic and electromechanical devices associated with a computer. This includes the computer cabinet itself, disk and tape drives, monitors, mice etc.

hardware address: A specific physical address assigned to a device.

hardware flow control: A form of flow control that is governed by devices themselves, instead of by communications software.

Hard Wiring: Fixed wiring that is a part of any computer or communications system. Once installed, hard wiring is rarely changed during the lifetime of the system.

Harris' Lament: "All the good ones are taken!"

hash: A symbol (usually #) echoed at regular intervals to show that a process is still underway. The ftp command that causes the hash symbols to be displayed.

hat: A common name for the caret character, ^ (ASCII 94), used to indicate exponents and to underscore text on the previous line in e-mail and Usenet posts.

Hayes-compatible: Said of a modem that understands the Hayes AT instruction set. Most modems today are Hayes- compatible.

HD: Abbreviation for High Density.

Head Cresh: A term used to describe the collision of a read/write head with a disk platter. Ibis is mostly a problem on hard disks as the separation of read/write head and platter is often less that 20 microns. A head crash can occur if the disk is subject to violent shock whilst in motion or if a foreign particle gets wedged under the head.

header: The rows of information at the top of an e-mail message that include who the message is from, who it's to, when it was sent, and what it's about. Information preceding the data in a packet, specifying the addresses of the source and the destination as well as error-checking information.

Heap: Part of random access memory (RAM) set aside for usage during program execution.

Hello world: The output of most C programmers' first program, from Kernighan & Ritchie's canonical C text, The C programming Language.

help: A command that will bring up help information in some programs and in some operating systems. When you are stuck, it never hurts to type *help,* or h, or ?, and press Enter to see what happens.

Help Menu: An on-screen display of user-friendly information, designed to help users of software applications to answer queries about the software without resorting to instruction manuals. Help Menus are usually called up by pressing a single key or by making a selection from another menu. Many are context sensitive, this means, for example, that if the user wants help during the setting up of a style sheet, then the Help Menu would immediately provide information on this aspect of the package.

Hercules Card: A high resolution video (monitor) controller card. Commonly used for high resolution monochrome displays.

hetboy: A heterosexual male, used most often in alt.sex groups.

heterogeneous network: A network that includes various types of computers, operating systems, network cards, and so on, which therefore must be capable of different network protocols.

hetgirl: A heterosexual female, used most often in alt.sex groups.

Hex: Abbreviation for Hexadecimal. Pertaining to a numerical system base 16. Hexadecimal digits are represented by the numerals 0 through 9 and the letters A through F. Because 16 is a multiple of 2, it is easy tom convert binary numbers into hexadecimal numbers, and some programs display data in hexadecimal form.

Hexadecimal Numbering: A numbering system that has 16 possible digits, 0-9 and A-F. Hexadecimal numbering is a convenient shorthand notation for binary numbering and is widely used in writing assembly language code and for addressing different parts of computer memory. The following table shows the relationship between hexa-decimal, binary and decimal.

HEX	DECIMAL	BINARY
0	0	0000
1	1	0001
2	2	0010

3	3	0011
4	4	0100
5	5	0101
6	6	0110
7	7	0111
8	8	1000
9	9	1001
A	10	1010
B	11	1011
c	12	1100
D	13	1101
E	14	1110
F	15	1111

When counting in HEX, each digit is increased by 1 from 0 to F. Once the digit position reaches F it is reset to 0 and the next digit position is incremented. Ibis is illustrated in the following HEX counting sequences,

38, 39, 3A, 3B, 3C, 3D, 3E, 3F, 40, 41, 42

6F8, 6F9, 6FA, 6FB, 6FC, 6FD, 6FE, 6FF, 700

Arithmetic operations can be carried out using hexadecimals (and any other numbering system) so long as the rules of the particular system are adhered to.

hiccup: Said of a network or applicamistakenly skip some data or send it more than once.

Hidden File: A file that is not normally displayed by a file listing, for example, the MS-DOS and VAX DIR command. Under MS-DOS the files IO.SYS and DOS.SYS are hidden files.

Hierarchical Database: A database in which the relationship of different data elements to one another is similar to the relationship of leaves on a tree to twigs, branches, large branches, the tree trunk itself and leaves, twigs etc on other branches.

hierarchical file system: A system of arranging files in directories and subdirectories to maintain hierarchical relationships between the files and make them easier to find and retrieve.

hierarchical routing: A system of routing in which different parts of a large network are arranged in a hierarchical tree and each level takes care of routing information to subordinate levels. The Internet maintains three different routing levels: backbone networks, mid-level networks, and stub networks.

hierarchy: In file storage, the arrangement of directories into a tree of parents and children. In networks, the arrangement of levels for routing purposes. In Usenet, the organization of newsgroups into general areas, topics, and subtopics, or the major groupings themselves.

High Density: On a "high density" floppy disk, the amount (areal density) of magnetic coating is much greater than that of a single or double density coating. Ibis obviously increases the memory capacity of the disk. The number of usable sides on a disk will also affect capacity. A single sided 5.25" disk may have 160KB capacity, a double sided double density (abbreviation DSDD) may have 36OKB and double sided high density (abbreviation DSHD) disk 1.2MB, or 1.6MB.

High-Level Data Link Control (HDLC): An ISO protocol for the data link layer of X.25 and OSI networks. It specifies that data is sent in frames that may vary in length.

High Level Language: A programming language that uses grammatical and mathematical notation reasonably similar to everyday language. Examples include BASIC, FORTRAN and PASCAL.

Highlighting: This is when a selection of on-screen text is differentiated from other text by means of keyboard commands or a mouse. The selected text is distinguished in some way, for example by a change in colour or the text may go to an enhanced display or inverse (reverse) video.

High Performance Parallel Interface (HPPI): An ANSI standard for connecting supercomputers to other devices, such as routers and other computers.

High Resolution: A measure of the precision of computer output, hard copy and soft copy. In the case of hard copy printed characters, high resolution implies an output of at least 240dpi. In the case of soft copy (monitor display) about 1000 x 850 pixels. High resolution monitors are kind to the eyes and less fatiguing to work in front of than low resolution monitors.

Hi-Tech: Abbreviation for high-technology. Used to describe hardware of any kind that uses the latest technology

HIPO Chart: Abbreviation for Hierarchical Input-Process-Output Chart. A type of flow chart that uses standardised flowchart symbols to show the data flow through an organisation or program. HIPO charts generally use a three box structure to show the three entities Input, Process and Output.

hit: A successful match in a database search; A connection made to a Web server.

Hit Rate: This relates to cache memory management, is the rate (percentage of times) that the cache memory the data needed by the CPU. Most cache controllers aim a 90% hit rate.

Hoff, Ted: An exceptional engineer who, as leader of a re., search team at Intel, conceptualised and developed the Intel 4004 microprocessor, the first of its kind. In the early 1970s, Intel were trying to design a processor and circuit board that needed to accommodate at least 2000 transistors. Hoffs approach was to rely more on software than hardware, enabling the Intel design to incorporate the entire processor on a single integrated circuit, introducing the word "microprocessor" to the language.

Hollerith Code: This code, developed by Herman Hollerith, is used to enter data on a punched card. Hollerith designed the code specifically for use in tabulating the data from the 1890 census in America. The code was revised in 1994 into its present 80 column format. In 1896 Hollerith formed the Tabulating Company, a successful enterprise that was later sold and, after a few mergers, became International Business Machines (IBM).

holy war: An neverending argument between intractable sides, such as over gun control, abortion, or IBM vs. Mac. There are usually special talk newsgroups set up for the people who can't resist arguing with their opposites, and it's considered bad form to bring up a holy war topic in an inappropriate forum.

$HOME: In UNIX, a variable that serves as an abbreviation home directory.

home directory: The directory allotted to your specific account, where you start off when you log into your UNIX account, and where you store your files.

home page: On the Web, a starting page with links to other related pages. Many people have personal home pages with biographical information and a hotlist of favorite Web destinations.

homogeneous network: A network that includes only one part of computer, operating system, network card, and so on, and there fore a single network protocol.

hop: Each short, individual trip that packets make many times over, from router to router, on their way to their destinations.

hop count: The number of hops it will take for a packet to make it from a source to a destination.

Horizontal Motion Index (HMI): The minimum distance that a print head can be advanced in a horizontal direction. This is a measure of the resolution of the printer.

host: A computer on a network that allows many users access at once. If you connect to the Internet by dialing up a provider via a modem, then the computer you log into is your local host.

host address: A numerical IP address of the form *number-dot-number-dot-number-dot-number.*

Host Computer: A computer, usually a mainframe, which controls (that is, supervises) other computers in a network or complex computer system.

host name: Also *hostname,* the leftmost portion of a fully qualified domain name, uniquely identifying a specific computer on a network in a subdomain in a domain.

hotlist: A list of frequent destinations, or sites, arranged on a menu, such as a list of Web pages.

Housekeeping Tasks: These are background tasks performed by a software application and/or operating system. Examples include reading and writing data to temporary storage locations (Cache, Heap, Stack) establishing files, clearing areas of RAM etc.

HP-SUX: A derogatory term for HP-UX.

HP-UX: Hewlett-Packard's version of UNIX.

.hqx: A file extension that indicates the file has been compressed with the Macintosh BinHex compression.

HTML: *Hypertext markup language,* the hypertext language used in

Web pages. It consists of regular text and tags that tell the browser what to do when a link is activated.

HTTP *Hypertext transport protocol*, the Internet protocol that defines how a Web server respond to requests for files, made via anchors and URLs.

hub In networks arranged with star topology, the central connecting device, a device ,that allows a network to add workstations by extending the transmission signal.

HWD An acronym for the physical dimensions of hardware (HWD = height/width/depth). For example an external 3.5" floppy disk drive may be referred to as 6/17/31 HWD (6cm high, 17cm wide, 31cm deep). The units, in this case centimetres, are generally not stated. Assume inches for USA manufacturers, centimetres elsewhere.

hung Said of a computer, unresponsive, frozen, and possibly stuck in an infinite loop.

Hypercard A computer based card filing system and database.

hypermedia An extension of the concept of hypertext to include pictures, sounds, movies, and so on, along with text and links to other documents.

hypermedia link A link from one document to another, from an anchor to a named location, or from an anchor to another form of media entirely, such as a picture, sound, or movie.

hypertext Text that contains links to other text documents, allowing the reader to skip around and read the documents in various orders.

hypertext link A link from one text document to another or from a text anchor to a named location.

hyperzine An electronic hypermedia magazine or zine.

hyphen On computer keyboards, the—character, used also to indicate a dash.

Hyphenation The process of hyphenating text so that it will more easily fit into the prescribed text block size. Many word processors and desktop publishing packages offer automatic hyphenation. These use specialised dictionaries to determine whether a word should be hyphenated or not.

I

IBM: International Business Machines, a large, US based, multinational corporation. IBM has been the instigator of many de-facto industry standards and is generally seen as an industry leader. Also known as "Big Blue" from their distinctive blue logo.

ice: Slang for security software, popularized William Gibson's *Neuromancer* trilogy.

Icon: An on-screen symbol that is used, to represent a menu choice or a task being processed. For example a caricature of a printer may be used to indicate the menu choice "Print a File". During updating or loading of a file an hour-glass (egg-timer) may be used to indicate that the computer user should wait.

IEEE: Abbreviation for Institute of Electrical and Electronics Engineers. The Institute is a professional association (USA) and has been the instigator of many industry standards.

IF: A programming statement used in many high level languages which is used to make a comparison between different parameters of the program. The following lines of program code show the usage of the IF statement,

```
IF A > B THEN GOSUB 1900
IF A < F/12 THEN GOSUB 2200
```

The IF statement can be expanded into an IF THEN, ELSE statement. In this case the program can take one of two different paths depending on the outcome of the initial comparison. For example,

```
    Begin;
    IF A < B THEN;
    Begin;
            A = A + (X/Y);
```

```
            B = SQRT(L*M);
            C = LEN(IPDATA);
      End;
Else
      Begin;
            A = 0;
            B = 0.5
      End;
      End;
```

ignore: On IRC or in any other type of chat, to screen out the contributions of a participant who is annoying you.

IMAP *Internet Message Access Protocol,* a protocol for the storage and retrieval of e-mail, not yet a widespread standard.

Imminent Death of the Net Predicted: A parody of the perennial warnings that traffic on the Net has gotten to be too much.

inbox: Also *in box* and *in-box* a file in which a mail program stores incoming e-mail messages.

include: To copy some or all of the message to which you are responding. Most e-mail programs and newsreaders will add a character such as > before each line of included text.

#include <disclaimer.h>: A C joke that appears in sig blocks, meaning that a standard disclaimer should be understood to have been included there.

include war A flame war in which so many previous posts have been included that it's impossible to follow the argument amidst all the >s

Incremental Backup. A backup process that only updates those flies that have changed since the last backup operation. This is a useful, time saving feature.

Indent. In word processing this refers to reducing the size of a text block, or parts of a text block, to set that section apart from the rest of the text. This technique is used to draw attention to a particular item, for example, a quotation, or to improve presentation of the material in a general sense.

index. A file in a directory at a site that describes the contents of the directory; An archie database; A default Web page that a Web server provides when no file is specified.

Industrial Espionage. The stealing/copying of unpublished or proprietary information from an organisation or individual, with the objective of gaining benefit from that information. New processes, product designs and marketing plans are common targets. Industrial espionage is increasingly hard to thwart given the small size and portability of many secondary storage devices. Such devices allow an employee to remove a vast amount of data from an organisation's premises undetected.

INET: An annual conference put on by the Internet Society; An abbreviation for Internet.

Infinite loop A computer process that repeats forever due to a programming error, causing the computer to hang. The instructions on the back of many a shampoo bottle—lather, rinse, repeat—would cause an infinite loop in a computer.

info: A common username for a mailbot providing information about a network, service provider, or information service.

Info-Mac archives A huge collection of Macintosh software at the sumexaim. stanford.edu FTP site, in the /info-mac directory. It's also mirrored at wuarchive. wustl.edu in the /mirrors/info-mac directory.

Information: This is a generic term applied to any knowledge of a particular fact, event or situation.

information agent: A program that searches databases for information without requiring that the user know where the information is stored.

Information Management: The gathering, storage, or.ganisation and use of information. Information is the basis of most organisational activities and plays a vital part in managing an organisation.

Information Overload This occurs when a person receives more, information than he or she can effectively absorb or deal with. It often leads to confusion and sometimes inertia on the part of the recipient

information pooper-highway Some people think that the Internet won't reach its ultimate potential until computers are taken into the bathroom as easily as newspapers.

Information Science: The study of the collection, management and organisation of information and information systems.

information wants to be free: A slogan popular on the Internet, suggesting that it is impossible,, ultimately, to hoard information, as it finds its way into general availability much as water proverbially seeks its own level.

info-server: An e-mail address that triggers a mail server, responding to messages that contain key words by sending stored information.

In-house: Activities that are completed by an organisation using its own resources. Some examples of usage of the phrase are, "we can use in-house expertise for that programming" or "we can do that disk conversion in-house".

initgame: An IRC variation on the guessing game called Botticelli, in which one participant changes their nick to the initials of a famous or fictional person and the other participants ask yes-or-no questions trying to guess the secret, identity. Winner gets to start the next game.

Initialise: To set the initial values of program variables, some will be set to zero, others to designated values. The following is an example of an initialising statement from a C program header,

```
/* initialising variables */
    float   PI = 3.142;
            RA = 1.667;
    int J = 5;
            K= 0;
```

initialization string: A string of seemingly nonsense, characters sent to a modem to get it ready to make a connection.

Ink Jet Printer: A non-impact printer that shoots minute bubbles of ink on to the print surface to form the image. This is a very quiet printer that lends itself to colour output since it is easy to have more than one source of ink.

Input: The process of entering data into a computer. Traditionally this has been a manual process, performed by computer operators, but much of this work is now automated. For example, stock control in many large shops is now achieved by direct data entry from cash register transactions. Similarly, bank account records are updated by transactions conducted by members of the public through automatic teller machines (ATMs).

Input Device: Any hardware, such as a keyboard, scanner, digitiser, barcode reader, light-pen, mouse, ATM, remote sensing equipment etc, that generates computer compatible input.

Inquiry Screen: A screen design philosophy used where the user may not necessarily be computer literate and/or where rapid information retrieval is required. Inquiry Screens are commonly used in large libraries for accessing books by title/subject/author etc. They use a simple command structure and a user-friendly interface.

insert mode: In text editors such as vi, a special mode the user has to switch into insert text.

Installation: The process of setting up hardware and/or software for use by a particular organisation or on a particular computer system. Software is increasingly setup by running a special install program.

Institute of Electrical and Electronic Engineering (IEEE) A professional organization among other things, has defined a number of networking standards, such as the 802.x protocols.

Instruction: A command that is recognised by the CPU (processor). Commands are usually generated by a single step in a computer program, often several instructions may be generated per line of code. Each processor has its own instruction set and these may not necessarily be compatible with other processors.

Instruction Word: A combination of an opcode (an instruction) and an operand, which specifies the data (memory locations) that will take part in the process called for. In machine language this combination produces a typical instruction word such as that shown below,

0100 0101101001110010

Here the first four digits are the opcode and the remainder is the operand. If only four digits are used for the opcode then only 16 different opcodes are possible.

For convenience the instruction word is stored in hex format (the above instruction word would then become 4 5A72). The complete instruction word may, for example, tell the microprocesor to fetch the word stored in address 5A72, add it to the number already stored in the accumulator and store the result in the accumulator.

Integer: A number that does not have any decimal points, also known as a whole number. Integers are typically used to represent a telephone number, a postcode, the number of people in an organisation etc. The following numbers are integers 47, 3188, 2001. Program variables can be declared in the program header as being integers.

Integrated Circuit: An electronic assembly that contains many hundreds, if not thousands/hundreds of thousands, of individual electronic components (transistors, diodes, etc). Integrated circuit technology has had a major impact on the evolution of computers, enabling them to become both smaller and faster. An integrated circuit (abbreviation IC) is manufactured using photochemical techniques on a silicon substrate, a highly automated process that has ensured that the price of most electronic devices has fallen dramatically over the past twenty years. Silicon is used because of its favourable chemistry (a Group 4 element on the boundary between metals and nonmetals, silicon is a semiconductor). ICs are also known as silicon chips.

Integrated Services Digital Net Work: A service provided by a common carrier which combines voice, data and video communications. Abbreviation ISDN.

Intel: An American developer/manufacturer of highly successful IC designs. One of the pioneers of today's microprocessors. See separate entries under "0-9" for details of some Intel designs.

intelligent agent: A type of computer program that can handle a user's mail, database searches, file transfers, and so on over the Internet with out the user having to oversee the process directly or even remain connected to the Net.

interactive: Said of programs or environments, able to respond and give feedback to a user and to take instruction from user commands.

Interactive Menu: A menu philosophy that poses questions on a one-at-a-time basis. As each question is answered the next one is placed on the screen. Often used in Business Information Processing.

Interactive Processing The processing of data as and when it becomes available, not in a batch at the end of a data entry session. See also Batch Processing, Interactive Menu, Real Time Processing.

Interagency Interim National Research and Education Network (IINREN) A set of network and operating, system protocols under development for the National Research and Education Network.

Interblock Gap: The space between a group (block) of records on a computer tape.

Interface: An item of hardware interposed between two other devices.

Interior Gateway Protocol (IGP): A protocol that defines how routing information is distributed among routers in a network.

Interleave: This is one of the protocols used when data is written to disk. It may seem logical to write data on contiguous sectors but in many cases this is not the best method. Because of microprocessor and/or read/write delays it may be beneficial to write the data on sector 1, and then wait for sector 4. The gap between sectors is taken up by processing time and/or data read times during which time sector 2 has been and gone from under the read/write head. Just coming over the horizon is sector 4 and it will be quicker (more efficient) to write to this sector than wait the latency period for sector 2 to come round again.

In practice many computers aim for a 1:1 Interleave, indicating that contiguous sectors are in fact used. However the fact that a 1.1 Interleave is used may not necessarily indicate efficiency. The Interleave capability of a computer is setup during low-level formatting.

Intermediate System (IS): An OSI system that moves packets across a network.

Intermediate System to Intermediate System Protocol (ISIS): An OSI Interior Gateway Protocol that can route both OSI and IP packets.

intermittent: Said of a connection, riot constant, occurring irregularly.

Internal Command: In MS-DOS this is a command that is available via the generic command processor and does not require the loading of any executable file.

internal modem: A modem chip mounted on a board installed inside a computer.

International Organization for Standardization (ISO) An international standards organization attempting to foster international cooperation in science, engineering, and technology. Creator of the OSI Model.

International Telegraph and Telephone Consultative Committee (Comite Consultatif International de Telegraphique et Telephonique CCITT): An international standards organization comprising telecommunications companies, part of the United Nations' International Telecommunications Union, creator of the X.25, X.400, and X.500 standards.

Internet: An international network of well over ten thousand networks linked using the TCP/IP protocols. Also used more loosely to mean either the worldwide information net or the conglomeration of all computers and networks that can be reached via an Internet e-mail address.

Internet Adapter, The (TIA): A UNIX program that enables a dial-up shell account to emulate a SLIP connection, allowing the user to run Internet software native to his or her desktop environment without the full costs of real SLIP.

Internet addressing: In IP, transmission of data and headers is done as shown in Figure. Octet I is transmitted first, then octet 2, and so on. An IP address has two parts network number and host number. The IP layer recognizes the IP address only. IP address classes are Class A, Class B, Class C, Class D, and Class E. The main distinction among Class A, Class B, and Class C is in the division between network number and host number, also referred to as the *rest field.* In Class D, the first four bits are 1110, and the remaining 28 bits are known as the *multicast address.* When IP packets have to be sent to a group of stations, this is known as multicasting. *Broadcasting* is an extension of multicasting, in which all the stations in a subnet receive the IP packet. In Class E, the first four bits are 1111. Class E addresses are reserved for future uses.

The main advantage of these classes is flexibility for arranging the networks. For example, a large number of workstations may need to be connected to form a network. In such a case, the Class A addressing scheme is convenient. If a relatively small number of workstations are to be connected to form a LAN, Class C may be appropriate.

The 32 bits of IP address are divided into four eight-bit fields. The IP addresses in *Dotted Decimal Notation* are formed by decimal numbers obtained from each of the eight-bit fields, and they are separated by periods. As an example, 183.127.2.35, a class B address, is shown in Figure. The network numbers are assigned by the Network Information Center (NIC). At the time this manuscript was written, work on IP version 6 was ongoing. In IP version 6, an IP address will be 16 octets (128 bits). This will solve the present problem of a shortage of IP addresses.

A process in the application layer chooses the transport it requires. It decides whether it wants to use a connection-oriented service such as TCP or a connectionless service such as UDR The next layer (TCP/UDP) wraps its own header to the data it received from the process in the application layer. The action of wrapping a header on the data received from an upper layer is known as *encapsulation.* The internet layer, in turn, adds its own header and sends the data to the local NI. The local NI maps the IP address to the local network address. If a packet is to be transmitted from one host in a network to a host in another network, then the local gateway address must be found and the packet must be transmitted to the right gateway. The gateway maps the IP address to the local network address and routes the packet to the destination host or another gateway in the path of the destination host. A packet may be delivered to a destination host by more than one path. To avoid such a situation, the gateways have algorithms to calculate the right path.

Internet Architecture Board (IAB) A group that oversees the maintenance of TCP/IP protocols and promulgates other Internet standards.

Internet Assigned Numbers Authority (IANA) A group that assigns the standard numbers used for ports, sockets, and so on. Assigned numbers can be found in the Internet document called STD2.

Internet Control Message Protocol, (ICMP): An Internet protocol that defines error messages and governs how test packets and the ping command function.

Internet-Draft (I-D): Draft documents written by the Internet Engineering Task Force dealing with potential problems and networking developments. They are archived at the ftp.internic.net anonymous FTP site.

Internet Engineering Steering Group (IESG): A group that manages the Internet Engineering Task Force and reviews Internet standards.

Internet Engineering Task Force (IETF): A voluntary group made up of researchers that studies technical problems and proposes solutions to the Internet Architecture Board.

Internet Experiment Note (IEN): A now-obsolete series of reports on the development of the Internet, parallel to the RFCs.

Internet Hunt: A monthly contest consisting of ten questions whose answers must be dug up on the Internet. The contest is reachable by gopher via gopher. cic.net in the hunt directory.

Internet Monthly Report (IMR) A monthly publication about the Internet, produced for the Internet Research Task Force.

Internet Protocol (IP): The protocol that handles routing of datagrams from one Internet host to another. It works along with the Transmission Control Protocol to ensure that data is trasmitted accurately across the Internet. The IP is a connectionless best-effort packet delivery service. In this protocol, there is no end-to-end guaranteed delivery, acknowledgment, flow control, retransmission, or error recovery. This protocol tries its best to deliver packets to the destination. The frames are discarded as a last resort. If connection-oriented support is required, then it must be provided by the upper layers. The IP layer deals with fouroctet IP addresses.

The IP datagram is as shown in Figure, consisting of the IP header and the data portion. The first field in the IP header is the *version* of IP, which version is provided to furnish details of the IP software. Like any technology, changes do occur to account for advances. The present version is 4. The version field alerts the system to these changes and facilitates compatibility. The IP header length is in multiples of 32 bits. The *length* field extends from the version field to the beginning of the data portion. Total length is inclusive of the IP header and data, and is measured in octets. Because the length field is 16 bits, it can accommodate up to 65,535 octets. However, there is also a restriction that hosts must be able to accept IP datagrams larger than 576 octets.

Though IP imposes an upper limit of 65,535, protocols used in the lower levels impose their own restrictions. For example, Ethernet has its minimum of 64 octets and maximum of 1518 octet frame length limitations. So the length of datagrams sent in networks will be guided by limitations other than the ones imposed by the IP layer. The *type of service* (TOS) field is one octet long. The first three bits indicate *precedence,* for which different levels are defined. High-precedence traffic is regarded as more important than low-precedence traffic.

Bits 6 and 7 of the TOS field are reserved for future use, and they are set to zero. However, RFC 1349 redefines the TOS field. Here the TOS field is taken as four bits; the last bit is labeled Must Be Zero (MBZ), and this bit is unused. TOS values mentioned in Table are the values which will be tried. If the network cannot provide the TOS requested, then values used will be those of the network.

When a datagram is larger than the size that can be handled by a network, then a gateway converts the datagram into smaller-size fragments which are multiples of eight. As an example, the IP datagram shown in Figure can be converted to smaller datagrams as shown. This action of forming smaller datagrams out of a large one is known as *fragmentation,* also sometimes known as segmentation. However, these fragments are reassembled only in the destination host and not in the intermediate gateways.

The *identification* field is 16 bits in length. It has three bits of the *flag* field and 13 bits of *fragment offset.* In the flag field, the fist bit (bit 0) is set to 0. Bit I has two options. If it is set to 0, then it indicates that the datagram may be fragmented. If it is set to 1, then the datagram cannot be fragmented. Bit 2 of flag again has two options. When fragmentation is done, this bit in the last fragment is set to 0. However, in other fragments, this bit is 1, indicating that there are more fragments of the datagram. The other IP field, *fragment offset,* furnishes the offset of the datagram, which is in units of eight octets. The first fragment has a fragment offset of 0. The next IP header field, known as the *time to live* (TTL) field, is eight bits long and has time in seconds. TTL specifies how long a datagram remains in a system. Because a gateway is able to process a packet in less than a second, the TTL count is reduced by one. In such a case, the TTL counter becomes a maximum allowable count of hops for a packet to reach the destination host. When the TTL becomes zero, then a datagram destroys itself. This process is also known as *self-destruction* and prevents a datagram from making unnecessary cycles in the network.

The *protocol* field has the protocol number of the upper layer. For example, ICMP has a protocol number of 1, and the protocol number for TCP is 6. Assigned numbers of higher-layer protocols are furnished in Reference. The *header checksum* field provides the checksum of the IP header field only, and does not include the checksum of the data portion. It is obtained by adding the ones complement of different fields and then taking the ones complement of the sum. The source and destination IP addresses are the addresses of the sender and receiver. The destination IP address does not refer to the addresses of intermediate gateways.

The *options* field must be implemented in all hosts and gateways, but it is optional in datagrams. There are two types of options field, Case 1 and Case 2, as shown in Figure. In Case 1, the *option type* field is one octet long. Case 2 has a one-octet option type, one octet of *option length,* and the option data. The option length octet includes the length of the option data and two octets that include one octet of option type and one octet of option length fields. The option field has one bit of flag, two bits of option class, and five bits of option number.

One bit of flag indicates whether the option field is copied into fragments on fragmentation. If it is zero, then the option field is not copied and if it is set to one, then the option field is copied into all the fragments. The option field is quite useful for adding a variety of features, but options cannot be used unless they are accepted by the general Internet community. The *padding* field is used to ensure that the IP header aligns on a 32-bit boundary.

Internet control message protocol(ICMP) ICMP is used for communicating error or control messages from one host to another host or from routers (gateways) to the host. ICMP is required in every IP layer. The ICMP message occupies the data portion of the IP. It has a header of its own and data. For an ICMP message, the protocol field in the IP header is set to 1. For ICMP, TOS is always set to 0000. The source address refers to the host address or router address which generated the ICMP message. The destination address is the address of the host or router to which the ICMP message must be sent.

The ICMP field always has an ICMP type field, which distinguishes different ICMP messages. There is also a code field, which gives more details about messages, and the checksum field, which furnishes the checksum for the ICMP message portion only.

The IP header and first 64 bits of the original datagram refer to the header and the data of the layer above ICMP. The layer above can be either TCP or UDP. The first 64 bits of data are used for matching processes which may use the ICMP message. The ICMP message is quite useful for discovering hosts and routers. The Packet InterNet Groper (PING) is used for checking the connectivity of a host with a remote host and getting the details of a host. It is also quite useful for network management. PING is an echo request and echo reply, and is useful for gathering data on hosts and routers. The ICMP message for an echo request and echo reply is shown in Figure. When an echo request is to be sent, the ICMP type is 8. The destination address is the address of the router or host IP which must send an echo of the message back to the sender.

Identifier and sequence numbers are used for identifying and matching a message and its replies. If code is 0, then both identifier and sequence number may be 0. As we have seen earlier, echo request and echo reply can be used to gather data and statistics on the network and hosts and routers.

Transmission control protocol (TCP): TCP is a connection-oriented, reliable, packet-switching protocol used for communication between processes in host computers. These host computers are distinct and are part of a communication network. The data transfer is full-duplex, which means that the sender sends data in one direction and can simultaneously receive data from the opposite direction. One of the strengths of the TCP protocol is its flexibility. It does not specifically mandate any protocol for the layer above it or the layer below. Usually, in Internet, the lower-layer protocol is IP. TCP is a stream-oriented protocol, and the combination of TCP layer data and headers is known as a *segment.*

An important concept in TCP is that of a connection. TCP provides for a set of addresses or *ports* within each host. Many processes can be associated with a port. The IP address and port number identify a *socket.* A pair of sockets identify a *connection.* Before communication can take place, a connection must be established between processes. This connection is referred to as a *virtual circuit,* which is analogous to a telephone connection being formed before the start of a conversation.

In a network, segments of data may be damaged or corrupted, lost, duplicated, or delivered out of order. To account for this, there is provision for acknowledgment and retransmission. When data is sent by a sender, the sequence number of the first octet of data in the segment is also sent. At the same time, the sender starts a timer. The receiving end sends an acknowledgment number. This acknowledgment refers to the sequence number of the next expected data octet to be sent by the sender. However, if the acknowledgment is not received before the timer runs out, then the sender retransmits the segment. There is also provision for a checksum of the data to identify whether the data has been corrupted. We have seen earlier that IP does not provide a checksum of the data; it provides for a checksum of the IP header only. So TCP takes account of this fact to provide a reliable communication mechanism.

Flow control is achieved by means of a variable window that can be sent along with an acknowledgment by a receiver. If the receiver does not have much buffer space left, then it sends a smaller window. Conversely, where the receiver is willing to accept and process data at a faster rate, it adjusts the window to a larger number than the existing one. The destination IP address identifies the destination host, and the source IP address identifies the source host address. In this figure, SA1 is the source host IP address, and DA1 is the destination host IP address. The applications Al, A2, and A3 are the source ports. It is assumed that they want to communicate with destination ports B1, B2, and B3, respectively. The process in Host 1, where applications are combined, is analogous to multiplexing, and the process in Host 2, where they are directed to the respective ports, is similar to demultiplexing seen in the data transmissions across a transmission medium.

A TCP segment has a TCP header part and a data part. The TCP header has the following fields:

Source port number: A 16-bit field, containing a source port number.

Destination port number: Also a 16-bit field, with a destination port number where a data segment must be sent.

Sequence number: The sequence number of a data octet of a segment that is being sent from a sender. In the case of synchronization or when the SYN bit is set, it is the *initial sequence number* (ISN). The first octet of data starts from ISN + 1. Here note that the ISN need not always start with 0, or the first octet sequence number need not always start with 1. The sequence number is a 32-bit field.

Acknowledgment number: A 32-bit field, always sent once a connection has been established. This is the number of the first data octet which a receiver expects to receive next. For example, if a receiver has received data up to 100 octets, the receiver puts the acknowledgment number as 101. The receiver next expects a segment in which the data octet starts with 101.

Data offset: A four-bit field. A TCP header is a multiple of 32 bits. This field contains the length of the TCP header measured in terms of 32 bits. In a segment, data offset indicates where the data starts.

Reserved: Intended for future use and set to 0. It is six bits in length. It is a good idea to provide for a reserved field in any protocol. When technology changes or new technologies are incorporated, these reserved bits can be used. The first six fields in the following list are all one-bit fields.

URG: Urgent pointer significant field. TCP has provided for sending out-of-band urgent data. When this bit is set, the receiver is expected to process this segment first, interrupting all other activities. When the URG bit is set, the urgent pointer field has relevance.

ACK. Acknowledgment significant field. When this field is set, an acknowledgment number is sent.

PSH: Push function field. When this field is set, the sender is expected to send whatever data is available in the buffer instead of waiting for the send buffer to be filled up.

RST. Used for resetting a connection. When this bit is set, depending on the states of sender and receiver, actions are taken. For example, reset is sent when a segment for another connection is received.

SYN: For synchronizing sequence numbers. This is used in the beginning to establish a connection by means of a three-way handshake.

FIN: Used for closing a connection.

Window: A 16-bit field. Because the data in IP segments are in terms of octets, window states the number of octets which a receiver is willing to receive, starting from one.

Checksum: A 16-bit field. The checksum is calculated and includes a TCP pseudo header and TCP segment. The TCP pseudo header has source and destination addresses, eight bits set to 0, the protocol, and TCP length. The pseudo header is used for computing the checksum and is not transmitted while transmitting data. That is the reason for naming it a pseudo header. Here, TCP length is the sum of the TCP header and TCP data. This TCP length does not, however, include 12 octets of the TCP pseudo header. For checksum, header and text octets must be even. To make these even, sometimes the last octet is padded with 0. To form the checksum, the ones complement of the TCP header is taken, then the ones complement of the result is taken.

Urgent pointer: Provides positive offset from the sequence number in a segment. This points to data offset following urgent data. As mentioned earlier, this field is taken into consideration only if the URG bit is set. This is a 16-bit field.

Options: A variable-length field, with length in multiples of eight bits. Here, too, there are two options: *Case 1*: Has one octet of option; *Case 2*: Has one octet of option, one octet of option length, and variable-length options data. Here, as in the IP, length includes two octets due to the option and option length.

User datagram protocol (UDP) SNMP, Internet Name Server, and Trivial File Transfer use the UDP protocol. This is a connectionless datagram service. UDP, in turn, depends upon the connectionless IP layer. As a result, there is no guarantee that data will be delivered; there may be duplicate frames sent, or data may be received in an order different from the order in which they were sent. Also, there is no acknowledgment that data has been delivered. However, if an application wishes to provide services that are available in a connection oriented service, it is the responsibility of the application to incorporate them in upper-layer software. In UDP, an application that wants to transmit data to another application uses a scheme similar to TCP The data of the application are initially enveloped with a UDP header. Then, at the IP layer, the IP header is appended. In the NI layer, the network header is appended to the IP frame. This frame is transmitted over the Internet to the other end. On the receiving end, the NI layer removes the network layer header, and the IP layer strips off the IP header. The UDP layer, in turn, removes the UDP header and routes data to the appropriate application. If there is a mismatch or the proper frame is not received, the ICMP message can be sent to the original application with causes for the error.

The UDP datagram is as shown in Figure. It has 16 bits each of source port and destination numbers. The length field contains the number of octets of the UDP frame and includes the length of the UDP frame headers. The next field in the UDP header is the checksum field, which is an optional field. If it is not used, then this field has zeros; however, if the checksum field is used, it contains the ones complement of the checksum derived from a pseudo header.

The UDP pseudo header is similar to the TCP pseudo header. The UDP pseudo header has four octets each of source IP address and destination IP address, zero padding, protocol, and UDP length. One octet of zero padding is done to make the UDP frame a multiple of two. One octet protocol field is 17 for IP, and the two-byte UDP length field is the length of the UDP datagram in octets. However ' the UDP length field does not include the length of the pseudo header. Thus, an application that wants to send data needs to know the IP addresses of source and destination beforehand in the UDP layer itself.

The use of checksum is mostly guided by the application. Note here that IP uses only the header checksum; it does not use the checksum over the IP data portion. Hence, if some validation of whether the UDP frame is the correct one is required, then the checksum in UDP is required. In some cases, we may not want to have the overhead of computing the checksum., since the loss of some UDP frames may not matter much. One such case is that of monitoring the performance of a resource, where the loss of a UDP datagram may not mean much. Also, in some cases, a network may be very reliable, without the risk of losing frames. In other cases, the application may be critical and the loss of a frame may lead to problems. In such cases, it is better to use checksum. Also, when a network is unreliable, it is appropriate to use the cheeksum to make sure that the data delivered is correct.

Address resolution protocol (ARP) We have seen that Internet knows only the IP address. Let us investigate how an IP packet is sent to the other end. An IP packet has a destination IP address. Then the local host looks at the ARP table and checks where the destination is. An ARP table is a sort of lookup table which has a mapping between an IP address and its corresponding physical address. Then the NI layer inserts the actual physical address of the destination host. The Ethernet or tokenring frame has this destination physical address. On the destination side, this Ethernet frame is stripped of its physical address and routed to the right IP layer. When this happens, the destination is in the same network. However, it is possible that the destination could be another network, in which case, instead of the physical address of the destination host, the physical address of the IP router is appended in the Ethernet frame. In the IP router, a check is again made with a routing table to see where the destination IP address is. If there are many hops or steps required before a destination can be reached, then the physical addresses of the IP routers are successively inserted. In the last IP router, the destination host physical address is retrieved from the destination IP address to route the IP packet to the correct destination.

The next issue is how to build an ARP table. This is done by broadcasting an ARP request packet, which has a source IP address, source physical address, and destination IP address. When this packet is broadcast, each host examines the IP address and looks whether it matches its own IP address. If it matches, the host puts its IP address and physical address in the source. The earlier source IP and physical addresses are transferred to the destination IP address and the destination physical address, and the response is sent back.

In the original host that sent the ARP request packet, the ARP table now has the mapping of the destination IP address and physical address. It is possible that no host has a matching IP address when an ARP request packet is sent. In such a case, the IP address is not, known.

The manner in which the IP packet handles cases in which mapping between the IP address and physical address is not known is, implementation dependent. In some cases, when the mapping is not there, the IP packet is queued and an ARP request packet is sent. When the destination physical address becomes known, the ARP request packet is received. The IP packet is dequeued and sent to the destination. If the address is not known, the IP layer discards the packets. In some cases, these IP packets may not be queued. If the IP packets are not delivered, the upper layers are alerted by *timeouts.*

Reverse address resolution protocol (RARP) RARP is the reverse process of ARP, in which mapping is from a physical address to the IP address. A station may have its physical address; it sends a RARP to a server giving its IP address, and the server maps the IP address and sends back the physical address.

Internet Research Steering Group (IRSG): A group that manages the Internet Research Task Force.

Internet Research Task Force (IRTF): A voluntary group that projects long-term issues and problems for the Internet and proposes solutions and new directions, reporting to the Internet Architecture Board.

Internet Service List An exhaustive list of Internet services, maintained by Scott Yanoff and available via anonymous FTP.

Internet Society (ISOC): A nonprofit organization that promotes the use of the Internet in academic and research communities and supports networking research, publishing the *Internet Society News* and putting on the INET conference every year.

Internet Talk Radio (ITR): A set of audio programs, similar to radio broadcasts, distributed over the Internet via the MBONE.

Internet tools: A set of utility programs that can use various Internet facilities and that have interoperability.

Internet Underground Music Archive (IUMA): A database of bands, including sound clips, video clips, information, and many other music-related links.

Internetwork Packet Exchange (IPX): Novell's Netware network layer protocol that specifies addressing, routing, and switching packets between a server and workstations and across interconnected LANs. Encapsulated TX packets can be carried by Ethernet packets and token ring frames.

InterNIC: Short for the Internet Net work Information Center, a service of the National Science Foundation. It provides information about the Internet and registers domain names.

interoperability: The ability of devices by different manufacturers or as part of different computer systems to communication and share information over a network.

Interpreter: Software that reads each line of program code and converts it on a line by line basis into machine code.

Interrecord Gap: The space between records on a tape. Abbreviation IRG.

Interrupt: An instruction to the CPU. This instruction suspends the current task in favour of a new task. The previous task is resumed when the CPU becomes free again.

InterSLIP Macintosh SLIP software, developed by InterCon Systems Corporation.

Intuitive Command: A command whose name is indicative of the outcome of the command. For example, Controls is an intuitive command to save a file since the result of the command begins with the letter S, Control-X is an intuitive command to exit from an application since X rhymes with exit Control-P is an intuitive command to print a file. Conversely, Control-F10 to list the contents of a directory is not intuitive, neither is Alt-F7 to underline text. Software Applications that use intuitive commands have a faster learning curve and higher productivity than other applications.

IP address: Internet Protocol address that uniquely identifies each computer on the Internet, made up of four numbers separated by three dots.

ISO: Abbreviation for International Standards Organisation, an agency of the United Nations. The ISO is actively involved in negotiating worldwide standards in many aspects of industry, technology and commerce. Several facets of the computer industry are covered by ISO standards, for example ISO 7185-1983(E) defines a standardised version of the programming language PASCAL.

ISO Development Environment (ISODE): Software that enables networks using OSI standards to communicate with TCP/IP networks.

ISO OSI: Abbreviation for International Standards Organisation Open System Inter-connection. The ISO OSI model has been developed since the late 1970s and is intended to provide protocols for different manufacturers and administrations to interconnect their data transmission systems.

The OSI uses a seven layer model to indicate the various control process necessary for successful data transmission. These layers are,

Application Layer—the initial contact between user and the transmission of data, a friendly environment for nontechnical people. It provides screen formatting in conjunction with presentation layer, error and information messages. It allows users to generate some of the housekeeping items for the transmission of data such as message destination, length of message etc.

Presentation Layer—provides code and format translation if necessary, also compression and encryption of data. It is also involved in presentation of data transmission to the sender and receiver.

Session Layer—provides data transmission management for the current session (involved in some error checking functions). It also controls prioritising of messages and queueing, if necessary, of data packets.

Transport Layer—provides error checking (also covered in data layer and session layer) and resolution of errors (repeat message if necessary). It also controls the flow of information between network layer and session layer (avoiding congestion, unnecessary delays etc).

The Transport Layer establishes an outside connection for messages using information derived in-house and is involved in multiplexing of data from different sources where necessary.

Network Layer—includes various management functions, such as charging for services, as well as controlling the end-to-end routing of the data blocks (this may vary on switched networks). It also provides an interface between the external aspects of data transmission (the transmission medium) and internal aspects, starting with the transport layer. Determines protocols to be observed for one-way/two-way messages etc.

Data Layer—provides various monitoring and housekeeping tasks such as error checking, defining data blocks, resolving contentions, identification and sequencing of data blocks, monitoring of transmission quality.

Physical Layer—the actual connection between sender and receiver. It describes such things as how many wires are to be used for the connection, the size and shape of connectors, the transmission medium and the means of data representation.

J

Janet The major United Kingdom backbone network.

jargon file: A list of hacker jargon and slang—compiled and maintained collectively since the 1960s—with excellent definitions, great humour, and lots of interesting anecdotes, available via the Web at http:// www.ccil.org/jargon/jargon.htmI and as a paper book from MIT Press under the name *The New Hacker's Dictionary, Second Edition* (buy the book!).

Job control language: A batch oriented control language used on mainframe and mini-computers. It identifies data files to be used for processing, storage locations to be used and the sequence of each job

joe: A UNIX text editor.

Joint Photographics Experts Group: An ISO committee that proposed the JPEG image compression standard.

JPEG: A compressed file format for images that is more efficient than CIF (but newer and therefore not so widespread).

.jpg: A file extension that indicates compression.

Jughead: An index of high-level gopher menus. (After the creation of archie, other internet tool developers have not been able to resist naming their applications after other Archie Comics characters. Besides Jughead, there is also Veronica. What's next, Big Moose?)

Jumper: A temporary wire linking two or more hardware connections. Jumpers are usually flexible wires, often with simple connectors at each end, and are often used for fault-finding or for introducing optional facilities, for example, different lock speeds, to computers. The word jumper, like many others in computer jargon, is borrowed from the communications industry.

jupiter (v): To kill an IRC 'bot or kick a user and then keep the 'bot or user from reconnecting by adopting its nick. (Jupiter is the handle of the first user to use this tactic.)

Justification: A process used in desktop publishing, typesetting and word processing which ensures that the text block is even on each side, that is, the left and right margins are a straight line. Justification is achieved by manipulating character widths, the space between characters, the space between words and by kerning.

K

K: This is a symbol for the word "Kilo" (one thousand) and in computer usage is the quantity 1024 (2^10), not 1000 as in normal business and scientific usage. For example, 5 kilobytes is 5 x 1024 bytes, not 5000 bytes.

k12: An alternative newsgroup hierarchy in the Usenet mold, dedicated to elementary and secondary school (kindergarten through 12th grade) education.

KA9Q: An adaptation of TCP/IP protocols for radio systems.

Kb: An abbreviation for kilobit.

KB: An abbreviation for kilobyte.

kbps: An abbreviation for kilobits pc second, a measurement of transmission speed.

Kbyte: An abbreviation for kilobyte.

Kermit: A transmission protocol for transferring files between computers. This includes error checking routines and retransmit capabilities after errors are detected. See also Protocol.

Kernel: A part of a memory resident program. A kernel is the core (hence the name kernel) of such a program and remains in memory (RAM) whilst other parts of the program may be removed from memory and only recalled from disk in response to specific commands. A memory resident program may have an executable file size of 90KB, but this may shrink to a kernel of 12KB. Kernel techniques are used to keep the usage of RAM to a minimum, thereby allowing other programs to have access to as much free RAM as possible.

Kerning: A technique used in desktop publishing, typesetting and word processing which attempts to improve the appearance of text. In kerning, the space occupied by a character may be shared with an adjoining character.

kevork (v): To abort a process or reboot a computer (from Dr. jack Kevorkian, a.k.a. Dr. Death, a Michigan physician who routinely assists terminally ill patients in committing suicide).

key: 1. In encryption, a phrase or string that allows you to decrypt encrypted text. In public-key encryption, there are two kinds of keys, public keys and private keys; 2. A key word.

Keyboard: A typewriter-like console used for communicating with the computer and for entering text and data. The keyboard in most common use is the QWERTY Board. There are many proprietary variations of the QWERTY Board but the basic layout of the alpha-numerics remains the same. The QWERTY board is not the most efficient in ergonomic terms but remains the most commonly used keyboard design. The QWERTY layout originates from the earliest typewriters where the main concern was the mechanics of the machine and the minimisation of typewriter printhead clashes. Several alternative designs have been proposed, using a more efficient, productive layout, but there are few takers. Everyone's keyboard skills are geared to QWERTYs.

Keyboard Initialisation A procedure that is run during the booting of many computers. Keyboard Initialisation is started by ROM BIOS (Read Only Memory, Basic Input Output System) to check that the keyboard is plugged in and that the correct scan codes are used. Successful keyboard initialisation is usually signalled by the Num Lock LED coming on.

Keyboard Skills: The ability to use a computer keyboard effectively and efficiently. Keyboard skills are considered essential for computer professionals and increasingly a life skill for everyone as they are often required in daily life.

Keyboard Template: A plastic proforma that fits over the keys of a computer keyboard, providing quick and easy reference to particular software application key functions. Keyboard templates are increasingly supplied as part of a Software package.

key encryption A form of encryption that relies upon keys for the encrypting, and decrypting of messages or files.

Key Punch Operator: A person who operates a key punch machine. This was one of the early methods of entering data into a computer. The key punch machine converted the typed entries into code on a series of paper cards, which were then read by an electromechanical card reader. Key punch machines are infrequently used today as they have been replaced by faster, more reliable means of entering data, although the term key punch operator remains.

keyword: 1. In a database search, a word to search for in target documents—hits must include the key word; 2. In online services, a word used to jump directly to a topic area.

kgbvax: One of the machines on the bang path of the famous April Fool's kremvax post.

Kibo: The username of James F. Parry, acclaimed by some as the first deity of the Internet. Kibo reportedly notes every mention of his name on Usenet and follows up worthy posts. He is also the founder of HappyNet. Students of kibology can read more on the subject in the alt.religion.kibology newsgroup.

kibology: The religion of Kibo. Its main doctrine is You're Allowed. Only Spot, Kibo's dog, is Not Allowed. For more adept instruction in the ways of kibology, try to follow the alt.religion.kibology newsgroup or wait for the kibologists to start crossposting their metaposts into your favourite newsgroup. Beware of trolls.

Kibo number: Also *Kibo #*, a number that represents how close you are to Kibo in terms of e-mail. Kibo's Kibo number is 0. Anyone who has gotten mail from Kibo has the Kibo number 1. Mail from someone with a lower Kibo number than yours lowers your Kibo number to that person's Kibo number plus 1.

kiboze: (v) To grep the newsfeed to find every single post that mentions the key word you're grepping for.

kick (v): To eject a participant from an IRC conversation and prevent the user from rejoining.

kill (v): 1. To delete a post (mark it as having been read),. 2. To delete posts traumatically, using a kill file; 3. To stop a process; 4. To erase a file.

kill file: a file containing search instructions for automatically killing or autoselecting Usenet posts. Sometimes called a bozo filter, a kill file can be used to screen out annoying posters and avoid uninteresting threads.

Kilobit: One thousand (2^ 10) bits. This term is often used to describe the memory capacity of RAM chips, for example, "this is a 256 kilobit chip".

kilobits per second: A measurement of the speed of a medium, meaning the number of kilobits that can pass through the medium in one second.

Kilobyte: A unit which equals 1024 (2^ 10) bytes. A byte is eights bits (binary digits) of information and is roughly synonymous with one character of data storage. On most computers a byte is the smallest amount of memory that can be reached via the address bus.

Kludge A temporary solution to a programming hitch. Many become permanent solutions, leaving inappropriate and inadequate coding for the next person to sort out.

kluge *(klooj,* n): The original and more phonetically correct spelling of *kludge,* a clumsily assembled program or feature of a program that functions well enough but is not elegant, similar to the noncomputer expression *jury-rigged.*

Knowbot Information Services (KIS) An experimental information service on the Net, intended to function as a robotic librarian that can search databases and, among other things, help find e-mail addresses. To access the Knowbot, telnet to nri.reston.va.us.

kremvax: An imaginary Usenet site, the source of a famous April Fool's hoax posting in 1984, supposedly the first Soviet communication over the Internet, a direct message from Premier Konstantin Chernenko. The post was met with both welcoming and scornful responses.

L

LAN (n): *Local area network,* a computer network, usually confined to a single office that allows for the sharing of files and other resources among several users and makes interoperability among various systems possible.

LAN adapter: A card installed into a PC to attach it to a LAN.

Land Information System: A computer system (hardware and software) which is used to analyse land management information, for example, the distribution of natural resources, land usage patterns, property ownership, rateable values etc. A Land Information System (abbreviation LIS) is not necessarily an online system. It draws data from external, primary and secondary, sources and its tasks may include cartography, statistics and databases.

LAN Workplace: Novell's TCP/IP client software for Macintosh and DOS computers.

Landing Zone: An area on a hard disk platter reserved for 64 parking" the read/write head. Early designs of hard disk required a manual "parking" command but this is now included as the last action in the dying moments of power availability. The landing zone is a non-data storage area, and is often the highest numbered track/cylinder on the disk.

Landmark A proprietary hardware/software evaluation system developed in America.

Landscape: This refers to the hard copy images. Landscape indicates that the job was printed across the long side of the page rather than the vertical orientation which is far more common.

LapTop Computer: A PC specifically designed to be easily portable (light and compact) and to be easily usable on a person's lap. LapTop computers started out as very basic machines but many now have very powerful' processing capabilities.

Laser Printer: A high resolution printer, typically 300 dpi, which uses electrostatic techniques and laser beams to produce images. The printer uses laser beams to create an electrostatic charge on selected parts of the image surface which is then transferred to the print surface. Dry powder ink, usually referred to as "toner", is attracted to the charged area and forms the appropriate image. Laser printers are frequently used with PCs, to provide high quality output. Print speeds are in the range 5-10 pages per minute for text, much slower for graphics. Many mainframe computers use a laser printer as an output device for hard copy. Output of these machines is often measured in metres of paper per minute or boxes of paper per hour.

Latency: The amount of time required, on average, for the required data to appear under the read\write head of a disk drive. If the required data has just passed under the read\write head at the time of data request then the latency period will be close to the maximum possible. A full revolution of the disk platter is necessary before the data again appears under the read\write head. On a hard disk spinning at 3600 revolutions per minute this will be approximately 16 milliseconds.

lcd: The UNIX ftp command to change the local directory (as opposed to the working directory at the ftp host site).

Leading: The spacing between lines of text measured in points. The leading or a given point size would always be greater than the point size of the font. Leading and font point sizes are often quoted together to give an impression, to the trained mind, of how the finished product would look on paper. The text in this book is set in 11/12 Times Roman, indicating an 11 point typeface with 12 points of leading.

leaf: 1. In network architecture, a computer that receives a signal from a more central computer but does not pass a signal along to a more remote computer, 2. *In (audio* cassette) tape trees, a participant who receives a copy of the tape being distributed but does not make copies of the tape for anyone else.

leaf site: A Usenet computer that receives a newsfeed from another site but does not distribute news to any other computers.

League for Programming Freedom: A group that opposes software patents and copyrights; information available via anonymous FTP at prep.ai.mit. edu in the pub/lpf directory or by e-mail at league@prep.ai.mit. edu.

Learning Curve A graph showing the relationship between continued practice at a given task and the resulting gains in proficiency, speed and accuracy. Sometimes called an experience curve. Software users may talk of "an easy learning curve" or "a long learning curve".

leased line: A telephone line leased from the telephone company to provide a permanent connection from a LAN to an Internet service provider or to a WAN.

letterbomb: An e-mail message containing either escape characters that can lock up certain types or terminals, or harmful commands to be interpreted by the user's shell.

Lexis/Nexis: A proprietary system of searchable databases of legal briefs (Lexis) and newspaper and magazine articles (Nexis)

lharc: A file compression program for DOS.

.lhz: A file extension that indicates lharc compression.

Library: A collection of pre-written, pre-tested program modules that can be called upon to form part of a new program. Libraries are usually stored on disk and are made available during compile-time and run-time as required.

library catalogs: Most university and library catalogs are available via telnet. Hytelnet index of library catalogs.

Library of Congress: The main repository of information of the U. S. government, available by telnet at locis.loc.gov or on the

Light Emitting Diode: An electronic device that emits light when a voltage is applied to it. They are often used as a "Power On" indicator on computers and computer hardware.

Light Pen: A hand held device, connected to a computer, that can read bar-codes. They are commonly used in supermarkets and other retail stores. Light pens can also be used as a pointing device in conjunction with a computer monitor. The pen is pointed at an object, for example, a menu choice, on the monitor screen in order to make a selection.

LIM-EMS: Abbreviation for Lotus Intel Microsoft Expanded Memory Specification.

Line: A generic term for a transmission medium. It may actually be a line, as in a cable, but increasingly it is likely to be a microwave or optical fibre link.

line cater A bug in older versions of Usenet newsreader software for UNIX that caused certain lines at the beginning of posts to vanish. To appease the line cater, posters would include lines of spurious text to be sacrificed instead of the actual con^ tents of the message.

line feed A character that moves the cursor down one line (ASCII 10) usually starting a new line in combination with a carriage return character.

Line Graph: A type of graph that links, or attempts to link, all of the data points of a dataset. A Line Graph may be used to demonstrate trends in a dataset over a period of time.

line length: The number of characters that fit on a line—fixed on some systems, settable on others. The standard, line length on the Internet is 80 characters: e-mail or Usenet posts produced with software using longer line lengths will wrap irregularly and appear awkward to users with 80-character lines.

line noise: Static or interference on a wire that corrupts the signal. On a character-based modern connection, for example, line noise might result in random gibberish and escape characters polated with the intended text.

line-oriented (adj): Said of applications and interfaces that display text one line at a time, rather than making an entire screenful of text available at once.

link (n): 1. In UNIX, a reference to a directory or file contained elsewhere that appears in directory listings just as if the remote directory or file were in the current, directory; 2. On Web pages, a hypertext connection, a button or high-lighted bit of text that, when selected, jumps the reader to another page.

Linear Programming A mathematical procedure used to determine the best combination of limited resources and activities necessary to fulfil a specific objective. Although termed "Linear Programming" this technique predates "programming" in its modem sense.

Line Printer: A fast moving printer, used on mainframe and minicomputers only. Line printers are also known as "Line-at-a-time-Printers" as they assemble the characters on a line by line basis, not on a character basis as do most other printers. Output of line printers is often measured in metres of paper per minute or boxes of paper per hour! Types of line printer include a Band Printer, a Chain Printer and a Drum Printer. See separate entries for each of these.

Link Access Protocol (LAP): A data link layer protocol for AppleTalk that specifies the interface to network hardware.

Linker: A software application that links object files, library routines, procedures and variables into a, form ready for execution as a program. Some compilers are also linkers, they take source code and produce an executable file, by passing a separate linking process.

Linotronic: A proprietary brand of typesetting equipment, developed and manufactured by Linotype Corporation. Lino-tronic typesetters provide very high resolution (1200-2500dpi) and are commonly used at commercial printing premises.

Linux *(line-ux)*: An implementation of UNIX for IBM PC-compatibles. It has been developed as a collaborative effort by widespread Internet users and is distributed for free.

Liquid Crystal Display: This is a type of monitor which uses an alternative to cathode ray technology and is particularly useful where power supplies are limited. A Liquid Crystal Display (abbreviation LCD) uses aromatic hydrocarbons, for example, quinones, which polarize when a voltage is applied to them. This enables the quinones to either pass or block light. Background lighting falling on a LCD screen is normally reflected, however where the quinones allow light to pass through, the image of the appropriate character is formed. LCD technology depends on background lighting, in the absence of this the LCD display is useless. Many manufacturers have overcome this by providing "background" lighting.

LISP: A high level language designed in the late 1950s at Massachusetts Institute of Technology (USA). LISP is used for Artificial Intelligence and other complex applications.

list (v): 1. To view the names of files in a directory; 2. *To* display the contents of a file.

listserv: A type of automated mailing list software that runs on IBM mainframes and originated on the BITNET network.

little-endian (adj): A storage format in which the most significant byte has the highest address, as opposed to big-endian.

liveware: People (as opposed to hardware or software)

local (adj): Said of a computer to which a user is connected directly or of a device (such as a printer) or process under the user's direct control, as contrasted with remote hosts, devices, and processes.

Local Area Network: A computer network whose participants are located close together often within the same building. Local Area Networks have the advantage that they can utilise very high data transmission speeds and the terminals, which are often personal computers, can share expensive resources such as laser printers and software.

Local Area Transport (LAT): Digital (DEC) architecture for connecting terminal servers on Ethernet networks to host computers.

local echo: 1. A copy of the data being sent (usually typed) over a communications device (such as a modem) displayed in a terminal window so that the sender can monitor the process; 2. *A* terminal mode in some communications programs, specifying half duplex transmission, in which the communications program displays the user's input on the screen, instead of relaying an echo from the host.

localhost (n): Also local host, the host computer a user is currently logged in to. The *address of* any user's current localhost is always 127.0.0.1.

local node: The computer on a network to which a user is connected directly.

LocalTalk: Shielded, twisted-pair wiring and connectors for using the Macintosh's built-in AppleTalk network hardware.

Local Variable: A variable whose value is controlled by a program module, such as a subroutine. The variable may or may not be accessible to the main program and/or other modules, however only the module containing the "local variable" can alter its value. This is a useful programming technique as it allows compartmentalisation, and therefore safe-guarding, of different program variables.

locative domain name: A two-letter geographical domain name, such as us for the United States, *uk* for the United Kingdom, *de* for Germany, and so on.

LOCIS: The *Library of Congress Information Service*, available by telnet at locis.loc.gov or on the Web at http://www,loc,gov/.

lock up (v): To freeze, as when certain sequences of characters, freeze a keyboard, preventing the user from typing.

Log Book: Nautical jargon borrowed by the computer profession. A log book is often used to keep a record of computer staff on duty and the processing tasks performed. It may also be used to keep a record of hardware maintenance schedules and breakdowns.

logical: Said of a computer address or device, identified by a numerical reference, which may or may not correspond to a physical address or device.

Logic Error: A program fault that does not necessarily prevent the program running but produces an output error. Programs with logic errors invariably run through from first to last statement but produce the wrong answer or output.

logical conjunction: A word that joins two or more key words by specifying a logical relationship between them.

Logical Drive: Part of a physical storage medium (for example, a hard disk) that has been separated by the operating system into distinct storage locations. The hard disk may have a storage capacity of 42MB, but for operational reasons (users preference or operating system restrictions) it may be necessary to divide the 42MB into two logical drives". Under MS-DOS the two locations may be designated as the C and D drives (A and B are usually reserved for floppy disk drives). In this case the C and D drives share a common physical storage medium.

Logic Gate: A flip-flop, or collection of flip-flops, that will 1 and respond to varying input conditions. Widely used in a CPU and in registers.

Logical Link Control (LLC): The Institute of Electrical and Electronic Engineering 802 standard that specifies a uniform user interface.

logical tree Any logical arrangement of devices, files, data, and so on in which all relationships stem from a root; child branches are subordinate to parent branches, and an element without any children is called a leaf.

Logical Unit: Software that communicates with an IBM SNA network.

log in (v): To connect to a network or computer, identify oneself as a user, supply a password, and start a session.

login (n): 1. A username, the *handle a* user logs in with, corresponding to an account; 2. An instance of logging in.

login script: A prerecorded sequence of login steps that can play back automatically to connect a user to a computer or network. Login scripts can breach security if they automate the process of supplying a password, thereby allowing anyone who runs the script to log in.

Log-on: The process of gaining access to computer facilities. This may include entering a password.

log out (v): To end a session and disconnect from a computer or network.

Longitudinal Redundancy Check: An error checking technique, used in data communications, in which the parity check character is applied to each column of bits within a data block.

loopback (n): A test in which a signal is sent from a source to an intermediate point and 'hen back to the original source to evaluate the accuracy of the transmission.

loopback address: The Internet address (127.0, 0.1) that always points back to the localhost.

low-bandwidth: 1. Said of a connection that can only manage a slow connect speed or of a resource on the Internet that a user with a slow connection will still find useful. 2. Colloquially, con dining little useful information.

Low Level Format: The basic installation of a hard disk, usually only performed once in the lifetime of a hard disk. A low level format is also known as a pre-format and can be performed by many disk management utilities.

Low Level Language A programming language that is fairly close to the machine code used by the processor. Low level languages are often hardware specific and are not necessarily portable between computers.

LSI: Abbreviation for Large Scale Integration, the manufacture of integrated circuits where many thousands of electronic circuits are placed on one silicon chip.

lurk: To read a mailing list or newsgroup without posting to it. Every new user should lurk for a while before posting to get a feel for what the group is all about and how others in the group behave.

lurker: One who lurks. On any mailing list or in any newsgroup, there are usually many times more lurkers than regular contributors.

M: This is a symbol for the word "Mega" (one million) and in computer usage is the quantity 1048576 (2^ 20), not 1000000 as in normal business and scientific usage. For example, 5 megabytes is 5 x 1048576 bytes, not 5000000 bytes.

M: Abbreviation for megabyte.

^M: One way that the carriage return character (ASCII 13) can appear. Some computers use a carriage return to indicate a newline, some use a linefeed, and some use both. If an ASCII file is transferred from a computer that uses carriage returns to one that doesn't, and a binary file transfer rather than an ASCII file transfer is used, ^M appear at the end of each line.

MaasInfo Package: A set of documents written by Robert E. Maas explaining how to use various Internet resources, available via anonymous FTP from aarnet.edu.au in the pub/doc subdirectory.

MAC address: The address that identifies a particular piece of hardware out of several connected to shared media.

MacBinary: A Macintosh file transfer protocol that specifies how files should be transmitted over modems.

Machine Code: A series of on/off signals (binary 0 and 1), the only method of communicating with a processor. The loading of data and instructions into the CPU can only be accomplished by using machine code. Regardless of what type of language (low level or high level) a computer programmer uses, the program must eventually be converted into machine code (binary format). In machine code the program will consist of a series of os and 1s.

Machine Cycle The fundamental operating cycle of the CPU, during which the CPU fetches, interprets and executes an instruction word.

Macintosh A personal computer, based on a Motorola microprocessor, employing a GUI. It was introduced by Apple Corporation in 1984.

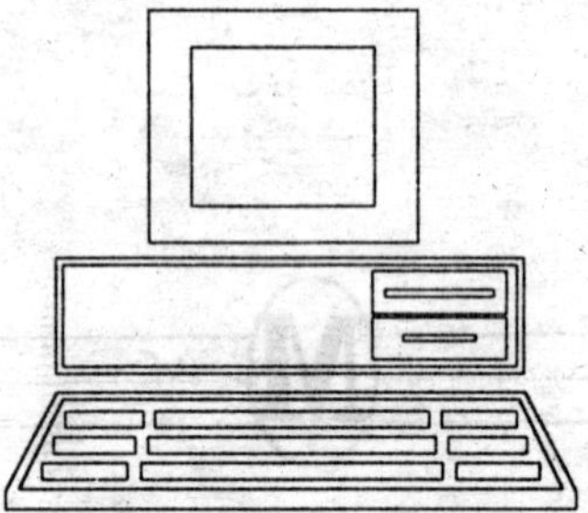

Macintosh archive The largest source of Macintosh shareware and files is the Macintosh archive at Stanford University. Connect via anonymous FTP to sumex-aim.stanford.edu and look in the info-mac directory. This site is also mirrored at the wuarchive.wustl.edu FTP site in the/mirrors/info-mac directory.

Macintoy: A derogatory term for a Macintosh, implying that it is a toy computer, not suitable for hardcore computing.

Macintrash: A derogatory term for a Macintosh.

MacPPP: PPP (Point-to-Protocol) software for the Macintosh, developed by Merit Computer Network and available as freeware via anonymous FTP from ftp.merit. edu in the internet.tool /ppp/mac directory.

Macro: A series of instructions that may be recalled by pressing a single key or entering a simple code. Macros are a mini programming language and are typically used on spreadsheets and word processors.

MacSLIP: SLIP (Serial Line Internet Protocol) software for the. Macintosh, developed by Hyde Park Software.

MacTCP TCP/IP protocol software for the Macintosh, built into version 7,5 of the Macintosh operating system. For more information, send e-mail to apda@ applelink.apple. com.

MacWeb: A Web browser for the Macintosh, created by EINET and available via anonymous FTP from ftp.einet. net in the /einet/mac/ macweb directory.

Mac weenie: A pejorative or affectionate term for a Macintosh aficionado.

magick: Magic in the sense of the occult, natural or supernatural mysteries, study of the kaballah, and so on, spelled with a *k* to distinguish from stage magic.

Magnetic Core: One of the first forms of computer memory, magnetic core uses windings of copper wire to store magnetic pulses (representing 0 or 1). Magnetic cores are rarely used today as they are bulky and expensive to manufacture. They have been superseded by solid state memory devices.

Magnetic Disk: A disk that is coated with iron oxide, thereby enabling the introduction (writing), retention (memory) and reading of magnetically recorded information. The absence or presence of magnetism is interpreted during read operations as a binary 0 or 1. Magnetic disks are sensitive to environmental conditions (humidity and temperature) as well as external magnetic fields and need to be stored carefully.

Magnetic Ink Character Recognition: A technology used by many financial institutions. The numbers on a cheque are printed in magnetic ink (ink with a high iron oxide content). For cancellation, the cheques are fed into a Magnetic Ink Character Recognition (abbreviation MICR) reader where the MICR hardware/software identifies the customer who wrote out a particular cheque. All the operator has to do is key in the value of the cheque and the transaction is processed.

mail (n): 1. On the Internet, synonymous with e-mail, that is, *electronic mail,* messages carried electronically from computer to computer; 2. The name of a simple UNIX mail program.

(v) 10 send an e-mail message.

mail address: 1 An Internet e-mail address of the form *username@host.domain;* 1 The *username* portion of a mail account on a network.

mailbomb: (n) A huge number of messages or an enormous chunk of data, such as a core dump, sent to an e-mail address as a prank or attack on the recipient, in hopes that the bomb will overload or even crash the user's mailer program.

(v) To send or encourage others to send a huge number of messages or an enormous chunk of data.

mailbot: A *mail server,* a program that automatically responds to mail by sending information or performing functions specified in the incoming mail.

mailbox: A file, directory, or area of hard disk space used to store e-mail messages,

mail bridge A device that connects networks and filters mail between them, passing only messages that meet certain criteria.

mail-enabled application: A program that, in addition to its normal capabilities, can also handle the sending and receiving of mail.

Mail Exchange Record: A record type in the Domain Name System that identifies the mail-serving host for a given domain.

mail exploder: A program that forwards an e-mail message to all the addresses on a mailing list.

mail gateway: A computer that passes e-mail from one network to another, from a network to the Internet, or vice versa, reformatting the headers as necessary.

mailing list: A discussion group, commonly referred to on the Internet simply as a list, consisting of people with a common interest, all of whom receive all the mail sent, or posted, to the list. Mailing lists are often more specialized than Usenet newsgroups. Lists can be moderated or unmoderated.

Mail Merge: A facility provided on most word processors, where, for example, a predesigned form (a proforma) is merged with a database of customer addresses. The proforma may be a standardised letter, for example, a letter of reminder about outstanding accounts, or a memo, for example, a notice of meeting.

mail-news gateway: A computer that collects posts from a mailing list and forwards them to a corresponding newsgroup, and vice versa.

mail path: A list of sites an e-mail message must pass through on the way from the sender to the receiver. Although it is rarely necessary any longer to specify the route your mail will take, mail headers still often include the entire mail *in* back to the sender.

mail program: Also mail *reader,* the program a user reads, replies to, forwards, and saves mail with. Common UNIX mail programs include mail, elm, and pine. Eudora is a popular mail program for PCs and Macs.

.mailrc: A setup file for UNIX mail programs (other than elm).

mail reflector: A mail address that automatically forwards any mail it receives to a list of other addresses.

mail server: A mailbot, a program that automatically distributes files or information in response to e-mail requests.

Main Distribution Frame A communications cabling distribution rack, usually located in basement areas of multistory buildings. It is the meeting point of external and internal communications cables.

Mainframe: A generic name for a large computer installation. A mainframe computer used to be distinguished from other computers, such as PCs, by superior processing speed, but this is not so today. Distinguishing features of mainframe computers are vast amounts of memory, typically several hard disks in the gigabyte range, one or more tape drives, cassettes, several line printers, a separate computer operators' room, a false floor (for underfloor cabling) and tight security.

majordomo: A type of automated mailing list software, similar to listserv.

MAKE.MONEY.FAST: A chain letter still making its rounds on the Net after many years. It's a classic Ponzi/pyramid scheme.

As someone replied last time 1 saw this garbage reposted, "Don't make your first Federal crime one that includes your name and address at the top!"

man: The UNIX command that displays the man pages, online documentation for UNIX programs and commands.

MAN: A Metropolitan Area Network, a highspeed (100 Mbps) public network, capable of voice and data transmission over long distances, connecting LANs across a city or campus.

Management Information Base (MIB) A database, on a host, router, or bridge that

Management Information System: A database system that is used to support the management of an organisation, project or resource. For example, a Management Information System (abbreviation MIS) may be used to assist in the management of an airline, a large building project or a National Park. A MIS is not necessarily an online, working database. It may draw data from the day-to-day activities of the organisation, project or resource but it is generally not involved in actual transaction processing.

Manchester encoding: A method of data-transmission tnat enables network interface cards to transmit digital signals using direct current, encoding data, and timing signals in the same data stream, as opposed to non-return to zero (NRZ) encoding, which employs two voltage levels—negative and positive—to represent 0 and 1.

mang: 1. An undefined expletive, uttered or written in response to statements or actions so outrageous or bewildering as to overload a civilized person's ability to respond; 2. The sound the boo tree makes, straining to express the ineffable.

man pages The *manual pages*—online documentation for UNIX commands and programs.

marble Teleconnect SLIP (Serial Line Internet Protocol) software for the Nextstep operating system, developed by Marble Associates.

mark as unread: To save a newsgroup article as if it were still unread.

Martian (adj): Said of a packet that arrives with an incorrect or impossible source address.

MASM: Abbreviation for Macro Assembler, a low level programming language that incorporates the use of macros as a programming tool.

Mass ACK: A message sent to a mailing list requesting a response, in order to test the currency of the addresses on the list.

Mass Storage: A form of secondary storage that uses automated methods of retrieving and loading individual storage devices, for example, cartridges and cassettes. A mass storage system may incorporate an open fronted rack of several hundred cartridges, any of which can be retrieved and loaded automatically.

massage (v) To edit, extract, information from, or format a file, as in 'I'll have to massage this data some to figure out what it means.

match (n): In a search, a record or document that meets the specified criteria.

Matrix News: A newsletter of the Matrix Information and Directory Services, on the subject of networks, avaible via WAIS at matrix_news.src.

Maximum Transmission Unit (MTU): The greatest datagram length allowed on a particular network.

Maxwell's Demon: Nineteenth-century Scottish philosopher James

Clerk Maxwell postulated that temperature could be regulated in a room by posting a demon at the entrance who would only allow air

Maxwell's Demon: molecules moving at a certain speed or higher to enter. This theory is the probable source for the computer terms daemon and demon

Mb: Abbreviation for megabit.

MB: Abbreviation for megabyte.

MBONE: The *multicast backbone,* an experimental, highspeed virtual network that can send packets simultaneously to a large number of Internet sites, suitable for audio and visual transmission. In 1994, a Rolling Stones concert was multicast to workstations around the world via the MBONE

Mbps: Abbreviation for megabits per second.

MCA: Abbreviation for Micro Channel Architecture. A proprietary (IBM) computer architecture for personal computers.

Mean Time Between Failure: A measure of the elapsed time between equipment failures, usually quoted in the number of operational hours. For example, the Mean Time Between Failure (abbreviation MTBF) of a hard disk may be 20000 hours.

Media Access Control (MAC) The lower component of the data link layer, which defines how computers on a LAN share access to a transmission medium, used in CSMA/CD (Carrier Sense Multiple Access with Collision Detection) and token ring LANs.

media filter: A device that converts the signal from a token ring adapter board for a particular type of wiring.

Median: The middle value of a dataset. In the following dataset the median value is 4. As there are nineteen items in this dataset the median is the middle value. In the case of an even number of data items, the median is the mean of the two middle items.

medium Any substance that conveys a signal from a sender to a receiver, such as copper or other wire, coaxial cable, optical fiber, and so on.

Megabit One million (2^ 20) bits. This term is often used to describe the memory capacity of RAM chips, for example, "this is a, one megabit chip". Eight one megabit chips would be required to store one megabyte of data, since one byte = 8 bits (on most computers a ninth "parity" bit is added to the data so one megabyte of data would actually require nine one megabit chips). Abbreviation Mb.

megabits per second A measurement of transmission speed (such as modern speed or network speed).

Megabyte This term is used as a measure of the memory capacity of hard disks and tapes. A byte is eights bits (binary digits) of information and is roughly synonymous with one character of data storage (that is, each character stored in memory will take up one byte of storage). A megabyte (abbreviation MB) is 1048576 (2^ 20) bytes.

Megahertz One megahertz (abbreviation MHz) is one million Hertz (or one million cycles). A signal (sine wave) that completes one cycle once per second is said to have a frequency of one Hertz (also one cycle per second). The unit Hertz is a metric unit (named after H R Hertz, 18571894, a German scientist) that replaces cycles per second. MHz is the unit used to measure processor clock speed. For example an Intel 8088 microprocessor based computer may run at 9.5MHz, whereas an 80386 computer may run at 20MHz and often much faster.

MEGO (written only) My *eyes glaze over.*

meltdown: What happens when a network is so overloaded that it crashes.

Membrane Keyboard: A keyboard that uses very low profile keys, sealed from the external environment. This type of keyboard is used for computer applications where dust, moisture, hygiene or vandalism may be a problem. Examples of usage include Automatic Teller Machines (ATMs) and industrial control processes.

meme (rhymes with *seem,* n): A self-replicating and self perpetuating idea, concept, saying, pun, or way of thinking. For example, how many times have you heard "The Eskimo language has a thousand words for snow" or words to that effect? It doesn't matter that it's not actually true; it is such an infectious or useful metaphor that it sticks in the mind and circulates from person to person perpetually.

The word *meme* was coined as an analogy to *gene* (in the sense of the "selfish" gene that propagates itself, using people as a medium) as well as *phoneme* and *morpheme* (in the sense of a "unit" of thought). The study of memes is called *memetics.* When i powerful set of memes (such as a religious philosophy) is unleashed on the Internet, it is called a *meme plague.*

Memory: A generic term used to describe any data storage area of a computer. Memory may be broadly divided into two types, primary memory, which in most cases requires a power source to retain data; and secondary memory which does not require a power source once the write operation is complete. Primary memory is always located very close to the CPU, often on the same circuit board, whereas secondary memory may be several hundred metres away. Some examples of memory are RAM (primary memory) floppy disks, hard disks, tapes and CDROM (secondary memory).

Memory Chip: A generic name for any form of integrated circuit memory, for example, DIPP, DRAM, FRAM, RAM, SIMM, SRAM.

Memory Management Unit: A part of the CPU or an adjunct to it, which provides specific memory management services. For example, it may provide cache memory management.

Menu: An on-screen display where the computer user can make selections of different programs, software tasks or options. Selections can be made either by highlighting the desired item via the cursor control keys, by using a pointing device, such as a mouse, or by typing the first, or other designated letter of the menu selection.

A selection may be made by highlighting the desired item or by typing the underlined character in combination with another key, for example ALTS. Each menu selection may lead to other menus (sub-menus) and many software applications, for example, Lotus 1-2-3, have many different levels of menus.

Menu Driven A computer system or software application tnat is dependent on commands given by menu selections. In practice most applications use a mixture of direct commands and menu selections.

message: 1. An e-mail letter; 2. A comment sent to a specific person on IRC and not to the entire channel; 3. A packet.

message cancel: A feature of some mail programs that allows the user to catch a message and "unsend" it

message of the day: A message from a network's system administrator that is displayed whenever a user logs in.

message handling service (MHS): A popular e-mail protocol for storage management, and exchange, especially in corporate offices, licensed by Novell.

message handling system: The CCITT X.400 protocol for store-and-forward messaging.

message switching: Also called *packet switching,* a store-and-forward method for routing messages in which each message is passed from a source through intermediate nodes to a destination address.

message switchin: A store-and-forward method for routing messages in which each message is passed from a source through intermediate nodes to a destination address.

mess-dos: A pejorative term for MS-DOS, impugning its elegance.

metanetwork: A network made up of other networks.

MFLOPS: Abbreviation for Millions of Floating Point Operations per second. MFLOPS are used as a measure of processing speed. The present generation of micro-processors are recording processing speeds of 0.1-0.7 MFLOPS.

metasyntactic variable A dummy variable, a stand-in variable used in an example to clarify a point of syntax.

MFM: A type of hard disk drive technology which uses Modified Frequency Modulation (MFM) for read/write operations. This is a more efficient method than the older Frequency Modulation techniques and provides higher data transfer rates.

mget: The command in the UNIX ftp program for multiple get, to get a number of files at once.

Microcom Networking Protocol (MNP) An error-checking feature built into many modems. MNP organizes data into frames, then transmits the frames, sometimes compressing the data as well.

Microcomputer: Analogous to personal computer, the term microcomputer is generally only used in educational situations, giving the categories of computers, micro, mini and mainframe. The dividing line between the three categories is by no means clear. Boundaries have blurred over the past few years as personal computers have become so powerful.

MicroDroid: An employee of Microsoft, especially one who defends the company in Usenet newsgroups.

Microfiche: A film negative, approximately 15cm x 11cm, that is used to record/archive data, for example, stock control records, national library records, meteorological data etc. It requires a special "microfiche reader" in order to be accessed. Microfiche can be produced directly from computer output and is an example of 'hard copy'.

Microfilm: A film negative that is used to archive textual information, for example, newspapers.

Microphone: A communications program for the Macintosh.

Microprocessor: The main brain of most modern computers, providing the fundamental command and instruction environment for the computer. The microprocessor contains a processor, registers, a Control Unit (controls the execution of a program and provides housekeeping functions), a clock and an Arithmetic Logic Unit (performs mathematical operations, comparisons). A microprocessor is contained on a single chip, hence the name "microprocessor"

Microsecond: A unit of time representing one millionth of a second. The symbol for a microsecond is us.

MicroSerf: An employee of Microsoft.

Microsloth Windows A derogatory term for Microsoft Windows.

Microsoft: An American software developer, founded by Bill Gates and Paul Allen in 1975. Microsoft developed the word's most popular operating system (MS-DOS) and many other very successful software applications.

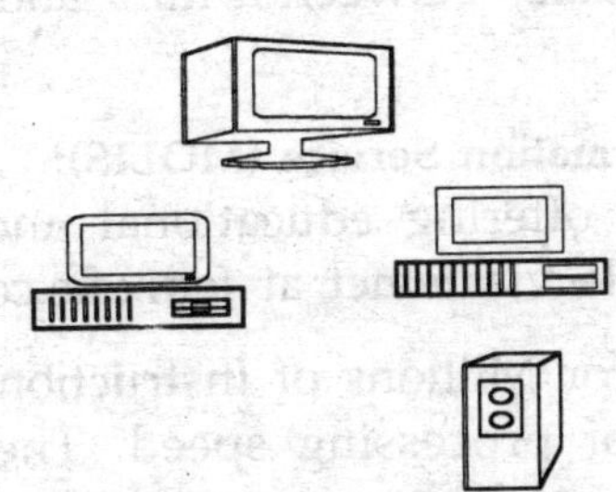

Microsoft Network An upcoming online service from Microsoft, access to which will come built-in with Windows 95.

Microwave An ultra high frequency section of the electromagnetic spectrum (of which visible light is just a small part). Microwave is used in many communications applications, such as satellites. One microwave channel can accommodate a vast amount of data/voice/ television circuits. Microwave is also used for ground based communications, many communications links that were previously serviced by underground cables now use a series of microwave stations.

Microsoft Windows A multitasking operating environment that runs on top of MS-DOS and provides IBM PCs and compatibles with a GUI (graphical user interface) not unlike that of the Macintosh, including icons, dialogue boxes, menus, and a mouse pointer.

The upcoming version of Windows, called windows 95, is rumored to include TCP/IP support as well as direct access to Microsoft Network, which itself will include full access to the Internet.

mid-level network A regional network, a vague Internet level category between backbone and rib levels.

.mil: An Internet domain corresponding to U.S. military organizations.

Millisecond: A unit of time representing one thousandth of a second. Hard disk access times are typically measured in milliseconds (abbreviation ms).

MIME: *Multipurpose Internet Mail Extensions,* a protocol that allows e-mail to contain simple text plus colour pictures, video, sound, and binary data. Both the sender and the receiver need MIME-aware mail programs to use it.

Minicomputer: A small mainframe computer, typically used in businesses with less than 100 employees and in small academic institutions. The boundary between a mini and an actual mainframe is blurred.

Minority On-Line Information Service (MOLIS): A service maintained by the U.S. government offering educational and other information, as part of Fedix, available via telnet at fedix.fie.com (log in as *fedix).*

MIPS: Abbreviation for Millions of Instructions per Second. MIPS are used as a measure of processing speed. The present generation of microprocessors are recording processing speeds of 28 MIPS.

mirror (v): To store an exact copy of files at another archive site (in order to minimize the load at the original site or provide an archive site geographically closer to some users).

mirror site An archive site (generally FTP) containing an exact copy of the files at another site.

misc: A Usenet hierarchy devoted to whatever doesn't fit in the other hierarchies.

mkdir: The UNIX command to make a directory.

mnemonic (*ne-mon-ic,* n): A word that helps one remember a command or shortcut. For example, in WordStar (an archaic word processing language), the *cut text* command is Ctrl-Y; the mnemonic to help remember this is *yank* (because you're yanking the text out of the document).

By association, the term has also taken on the meaning of the shortcut or command itself; thus, in the WordStar example, *Ctrl-Y* can also be called the mnemonic for *cut*.

mode: One of several possible states a program can be in. The most common example of this is the requirement some older text editors such as vi have that the user must first enter insert mode before typing anything.

modeless editor: A text editor that does not require the user to execute a special command to enter insert mode in order to begin typing. Most new text editors are modeless. On UNIX systems, pico is a modeless editor and vi is not.

Modem: A telecommunications device used to convert digital signals, typically the output from a computer, into a form (analog signals) suitable for transmission over a communications channel (often part of the telephone network). Two modems are required for each channel as the analog signals must be converted back to digital at the receiving end. The name modem comes from the processes involved, modulation demodulation.

modem bank: A set of shelved modems connected to a host or BBS to allow many callers to log in.

moderate (v): To review articles submitted to a list or newsgroup and post only those which meet certain criteria (minimally, they must be on topic).

moderated (adj): Said of lists and newsgroups whose posts must pass muster with a moderator before appearing.

moderator: The volunteer who decides which submissions to a moderated list or newsgroup will be posted.

Modula-2.: A high level language devised by Nicholas Wirth. This is an up-dated version of PASCAL which was also devised by Wirth.

Module: 1) Part of a hardware device, usually a plug-in item.

Module: 2) Part of a computer program. Many programmers build up a library of modules which they can call on at any time to form part of many different programs. For example, a programmer may have written a module which uses Newton's Approximation to solve an equation a module that prints out her company logo; a module that monitors the number of hard disk read/write operations. Some or all of these modules can be utilised as and when required by using the appropriate lines of code or compiler directive.

Monitor: A computer peripheral that provides the user with an instant status and update of computer activities. Monitors use similar, but for many reasons different, technology to a television screen. On some "home computers" a monitor is not supplied and the user must plug the computer into a TV set. There are many different monitor technologies in use.

Some of these are:

CGA (Color Graphics Adapter). Low resolution screen, with colour capabilities.

EGA (Enhanced Graphics Adapter). Middle resolution screen with colour capabilities. Introduced by IBM in 1984.

HGC. Hercules Graphics Card. Monochrome output (single colour, often green or amber) with high resolution. Introduced by Hercules Computer Technology in 1982.

MDA. Monochrome Display Adapter. High resolution monochrome screen with a limited number of display lines.

Monochrome. Single colour with high resolution.

Multisync. Capable of a variety of screen and adaptation to different control cards. It also has colour capability.

RGB. Colour monitor that is often used with a CGA card. The initials RGB stand for Red-Green-Blue, a reference to the colours it can display.

VGA (Video Graphics Array). High resolution screen with colour capabilities. VGA uses analog logic whereas most other devices use digital logic. Introduced by IBM in 1987.

Super VGA Uses more pixels (56% more) than VGA Introduced by a group of American companies in 1988.

Some of these names refer to the monitor, some to monitor types and control cards. For example, a dealer may offer a monitor with a CGA/EGA card.

monospace font: A font in which all the characters are the same width (as opposed to a proportional-width font, in which the letters *w* and i, for instance vary greatly in width).

For e-mail and newsgroup posts, the 80-character line length standard presupposes a monospace font.

MorF (written only) Short for *Male or Female* asking about another user's sex.

Morning Star PPP: PPP (Point-to-point Protocol) software for Nextstep, developed by Morning Star Technologies.

Mosaic: The first graphical Web browser, developed by National Center for Super computing Applications, which greatly popularized the Web in the last few years, and by extension the Internet, as it made the multimedia capabilities of the Net accessible via mouse clicks.

Mosaic exists in freeware and shareware versions for the Macintosh, Windows, and X Window systems and is available via anonymous FTP at ftp.ncsa.uiuc.edu.

moskvax One of the sites in the path c: the famous April Fool's kremvax post in 1984.

MOTAS (written only) A member *of the appropriate sex.* A way of referring to a potential partner without specifying that person's sex.

motd (written only): *Message of the day.*

Motherboard: The main printed circuit board of a computer. The motherboard usually houses the microprocessor, ROM, RAM and many other devices. These items are said to be "on-board". Additional circuitry may be mounted on "daughterboards" which plug into the motherboard.

Motion Picture Experts Group: An ISO committee that proposed the JPEG audiovideo compression standard.

MOTOS (written only): *Member of the opposite sex.*

MOTSS (written only): *Member of the same sex.*

motto! A follow-up post on a newsgroup, proposing the previous post as a motto for the group or for Usenet as a whole, perhaps facetiously.

Mouse: An electromechanical device used as a pointer to select items from an on-screen menu. Mice were originally designed with the idea of reducing the number of key strokes required for a particular task. The most common mouse uses an internal, magnetically coated ball to detect movement of the mouse across a flat surface, usually a desk top. Movement of the mouse is monitored via an input port and this is translated into movement of an icon, usually an arrow, on the screen. Menu selections can be made by pressing one or more buttons on the mouse body when the arrow is located on the required item. Many software applications provide for use of a mouse, but equally as many do not. Mice are increasingly becoming hi-tech and more sophisticated control mechanism can be expected to appear in the future.

mouse potato: A human being who spends inordinate, chunks of his or her waking life glued to a computer screen, mouse in hand.

Mozilla: A slang name for the Netscape Web browser.

MPEG: A compressed file format for movies (audiovideo files).

.mpg: A file extension that indicates MPEG compression.

mput: The command in the UNIX ftp program for *multiple put,* to send a number of files at once.

Multiplexor: A communications device which combines the signals (data) from many different, usually unrelated, sources for transmission purposes. At the receiving end another multiplexor separates the individual signals. Multiplexors provide a convenient means of maximising the rate of usage of a communications channel and are used extensively in all areas of communications.

Multi-tasking: Computer hardware (processor) and software that will permit more than one program to run (actively) at the same time.

Multiple Virtual Storage (MVS): IBM's standard mainframe operating system, similar to VM (Virtual Machine).

multiplex (adj): Using a single transmission medium to transmit over multiple logical channels at once, such as when an Internet site maintains HTTP. FTP, SMTP, telnet, and other channels.

multitasking (n) The simultaneous execution of two or more programs by a single computer.

MUSE: A multiuser simulation environment (for role-playing games).

Mylar: A polyester film, often used in the manufacture of magnetic tape and floppy disks. Mylar is light, easy to produce and has a high resistance to wear and tear, making it very suitable for tape and disk manufacture.

nagware: Shareware that reminds the user, automatically and frequently, to register the software and pay for it.

NAK (rhymes with *pack)*: A *negative acknowledgment* from a computer that a packet of data has not been received successfully, i.e., the *checksum* figure does not match that of the sent packet.

Name Binding Protocol (NBP): AppleTalk's transport layer protocol. It resolves numeric AppleTalk addresses into names and vice versa.

name server: 1. Also *domain name server,* an application that maintains a table of domain names and corresponding IP addresses in order to resolve the domain names of messages; 2. Also *CSO name server,* a searchable white pages listing of real names and associated e- mail addresses, usually reached gopher

NAND (rhymes with *hand)*: [Boolean operator] Not *and.* A text search with NAND between two words will match any documents that fail to contain both words.

NAND Gate: A logic gate that has two or more inputs and one output A NAND gate detects when less than two inputs are present. If more than one input reads 1 then the gate makes no output (the reverse of an AND Gate, hence the name NAND, short for NOT AND). The truth table for a NAND gate is shown below,

Input A	Input B	Output
0	0	1
0	1	1
1	0	1
1	1	0

The symbol for a NAND Gate is

Nanosecond: A unit of time equal to 1110^ 9 seconds (one thousand millionth of a second), usually abbreviated to ns. Nanoseconds are often used to measure the switching time of transistors and RAM.

Nassi-Schncidermann Chart: A form of flowchart developed by Isaac Nassi and Ben Schneidermann in the early 1970s. A NassiSchneidermann Chart uses different shaped boxes and shapes to indicate the varying processes involved in manufacturing goods or the provision of services. NS Charts are also useful for constructing flowcharts of computer programs.

nastygram: 1. An e-mail chastisement from a net.god for violating netiquette;. 2. A particularly vicious flame; 3. A letterbomb.

National Information Infrastructure (NII) The U.S. government's name for the Internet and other public networks. More information about the government's plans for the NII is available via anonymous FTP from ftp.ntia.doc.gov in the /pub directory in a file called NIIAGENDA.ASC.

National Information Standards Organization (NISO): A U.S. organization for standards in information, technology, and computing, most specifically as related to the Internet and WAIS, author of the revised WAIS standard.

National Institute for Standards and Technology (NIST): An organization of the U.S. government that promotes national standards of measurement, technology, computing, and networking (formerly the National Bureau of Standards).

National Public Telecommunications Network (NPTN): program, A nonprofit network that promotes free-nets and public networking in general.

National Research and Education Network (NREN): The network established by the High Performance Computing Act of 1991, intended to link government agencies, research organizations, and schools.

National Science Foundation (NSF): The U.S. government agency that funds and runs NSFnet, and consequently many university links to the Internet. Besides its involvement with the Net, NSF promotes science and research.

Natural Language: A programming language that relies on everyday words to generate commands. Whereas most software applications require knowledge of a particular command structure, natural languages (abbreviation NL) let the application user enter commands in a free-form, personal manner. Natural Languages are also called Fifth Generation Language although many computer gurus say that they are Fourth Generation.

natural language query: A query written in natural language (for example, plain English) seeking information from a database.

navigate: A computer jargon term meaning to get mound a program, find commands, move through a document, or hunt around the Internet.

Navigator CompuServe's graphical soft ware for browsing its online service.

Nazis: Mention them, or Hitler specifically, and you've officially ended a thread on Usenet.

ncftp: A sophisticated UNIX FTP program (a cut above ftp) that helps to automate and streamline FTP operations.

NCSA telnet: A free telnet client for Macintosh or Windows, available via anonymous FTP from ftp.ncsa.uiuc.edu.

Near Letter Quality: High resolution output from a printer. Many printers have low and high resolution settings on their control panels. In low resolution settings the print characters are not precisely formed, however for a draft copy this is usually acceptable and saves ink and time. High resolution settings are often labelled NLQ, an abbreviation for "Near Letter Quality". Low resolution settings are often labelled "Draft".net. 1. The original Usenet hierarchical distinction, superseded by the big seven hierarchies (comp., news., misc., rec., sci., soc., and talk.) in the Great Renaming; 2. A prefix added to a lot of common words to suggest their counterparts on the Internet.

net: An Internet domain, corresponding to constituent networks.

Net: *Also net* and *net,* often used as an abbreviation for the Internet or for Usenet, really a more general term for the lump sum of interconnected computers on the planet.

net address An Internet address.

net.celebrity: Someone famous on the Net (usually meaning on Usenet).

net.citizen: A responsible member of an online community.

net.cop: A derogatory term for someone who tries to censor or control the posts of others on Usenet.

NetCruiser Windows: software for CSLIP access to the Internet, distributed by Netcom Online Communication Services (it only connects via Netcom).

netdead (adj): Said of someone who has signed off IRC and can no longer be reached.

Netfind: An Internet resource for finding e-mail addresses, reachable by telnet (the exact address depends on where you are).

nethack: A popular text-adventure dungeon game, similar to Rogue.

nethead: 1. A Dead Head (fan of the Grateful Dead) who participates in the rec.music. gdead newsgroup (which is gated to the dead-flames mailing list) or any of the many Dead discussion groups on online services; 2. Any obsessed Internet user (a more recent definition of the term).

net.heavy: A person who knows a lot about how the Internet and Usenet work and whose opinions carry a lot of weight.

netiquette: Accepted proper behavior on Net. especially in regard to e-mail and Usenet Violate netiquette at your peril. Although the Internet and Usenet are effectively anarchies, they still have strong social cultures, and most of the rules and regulations of the Net are enforced by peer pressure.

net.kook: Any frequent Usenet poster whose posts reveal a strange and possibly obsessive personality.

netlag: An excessive delay on IRC that causes messages to bunch up.

net.legend A net.celebrity: net.kook, or other famous Internet/Usenet figure, many are discussed in the Net.Legends FAQ.

Net.Legends FAQ: A FAQ document that praises and excoriates various net. legends, available via gopher from dixie port 6969.

NetManage Chameleon: TCP/IP software for Windows and DOS.

netnews: *Also news* another name for Usenet.

net.personality: A somewhat well-known person on the Net.

netrc: A setup file for the UNIX ftp and ncftp programs.

Netscape: The state-of-the-art Web browser for Microsoft Windows,

Macintosh, and X Window, which, on top of allowing point-and-click Internet access and integration of text, pictures, sound, and movies, also provides security features and the ability to interact with documents before they're fully loaded. It's available for free to individual users via anonymous FTP from ftp. mcom.com.

netter: Someone who explores the Net.

Network: An interconnection of more than one computer and associated peripheral devices.

Network Database: A database in which the relationship of different data elements to one another is shown in a hierarchical manner but with horizontal links between subordinate entities.

network address: 1. The unique name of a node on a network; 2. An e-mail address.

Network File System (NFS): Not to be confused with *NSF* the National Science Foundation), a UNIX presentation layer protocol developed by Sun Microsystems: that makes it possible for a user to access files elsewhere: on the network just as if they: on the user's own computer.

Network Information Center (NIC): An organization that provides information and help to users of a network, as the InterNIC does Internet.

network layer: The third layer of the OSI Model. (IP governs the network layer in the TCP/IP protocol suite.)

Network management: *Open systems interconnection* (OSI) standards have been ten years in development, yet the subject of network management has become a significant part of this activity only relatively recently. It is not that the need has only just been realized. That was foreseen at the outset. Rather, the delay has been caused by the difficulty in agreeing: 1 What the scope of network management is, 2 Why it is needed. 3 Where its requirements can be supported through open management standards.

By seeking answers to these questions we shall obtain an overview ot, where OSI management standards are today and identify where further research and development is needed. To be a viable facility, network management must be as appropriate for inter-connected international networks to which many businesses are attached as it is for local area networks. In this context a business may be a national or multinational enterprise operating over one or several industrial/commercial sites, it can be government, an academic or similar research community. At each site we may postulate the existence of one or more local area networks, connected to each other and to networks at remote sites as dictated by local technical needs and management policies. This scenario helps to bring out the key features of network management: 1. There are many independent management domains which have to be able to interact meaningfully yet safely. 2. There are many areas which, while not truly independent have a measure of local autonomy. 3. There will be different communication technologies involved in the networking. 4. The networks can be large and they are a strategic component of many industries. 5. The networks will evolve over time, Although much of this chapter concerns OSI management, currently the subject of standards' activity, communications is but one of the services to be managed when information processing is distributed. Other information processing resources and activities need to be managed too, e.g. data storage, peripheral devices and processors. 'Network management' should properly include all these within its scope.

Business is dynamic. Consequently there is matching growth and decay of the networks that support the business. New requirements may lead to different types of equipment being connected to the network, or different networking technologies, with different behavioural characteristics may be introduced to meet changing workloads. As old equipment becomes obsolete and harder to maintain, it will be phased out to be replaced by newer technology. A network makes such evolution possible. Network management assists the evolutionary process and ensures that it is controllable. Management concerns the *planning, organizing, monitoring, accounting* and *control* of resources and activities. Business enterprises establish policies and provide human structures to carry out the planning and organizational activities to effect a particular management policy. Although computers will probably be used to plan and organize, this use of information technology is usually regarded as lying outside the scope of network management. Rather, network management is more concerned with the day-to-day, operational aspects of maintaining a viable network environment; that is it is concerned with the accounting, monitoring and control functions of management. A particular aspect of management policy in many systems concerns the availability and effective use of resources. The policy may also influence the security of information and its processing in the distributed processing environment. Where the policy demands availability, it is the task of network administrators to achieve this, for example by providing duplicate resources. Where the policy also demands economy, they will find cost effective ways of providing backup. Where security is important they will ensure that the network is operated in such a manner as not to compromise user and management data.

Whereas these tasks can in principle be carried out by people, the responsiveness demanded for monitoring and the complexity of management information is such that many of the tasks are handled by the distributed information processing system itself. The network management team interacts with the processing environment to effect management policies and to provide feedback to policy makers on network behaviour. In short, network management can be implemented as an interactive, distributed processing application where the application task is that of managing the distributed processing environment.

Not all parts of a large network need the same degree of management control, not all will be subject to precisely the same policies. The network environment is therefore composed of many domains of management. We define a *domain* as: A set of managed objects that are grouped together, for the purpose of management organization, to support a particular aspect of management.

At the outermost level, domains are determined by the boundaries of different organizations. Within organizations there can be a hierarchy of subdomains, each responsible for a given subset of resources and activities. Domains may also be established on the grounds of delegated responsibility, security, operational reporting, resource naming, etc.

Modelling concepts in network management A model for network management must cover three main aspects. The sphere of management responsibility. The delegation of management responsibility.

The principles of management authority and responsibility require that managers exercise control within their own management domain but that they cannot exercise control outside them. Yet, to provide effective management, managers will need information about activities in other domains which may influence their own domains. They will seek to access that information and even request the delegated authority to effect controlling actions on behalf of particular distributed applications. Management responsibility may be delegated within the management domain. A management entity lying within a domain and carrying out particular management activities is termed an *agent.* These requirements lead to the following dialogue types: Manager to manager: to obtain information or authority for control. Manager to manager: to request control be exercised on a manager's behalf. Manager to management agent: to invoke a management operation. Management agent to manager: to report the occurrence of a situation.

When a domain is distributed, the interaction between managers and agents becomes explicit. At the operations level there are no peer information flows but at higher levels there can be both peer communication and manager-to-agent communication.

At each level, control is exercised over managed objects and data values are obtained from them. Objects may be passive having values assigned to them or data read from them. Some objects may be active, i.e. changed by agencies external to management activity. Such objects may 'spontaneously' report changes in the values of their attributes to their managers.

Functional areas of management It is generally accepted that network management covers five areas: Fault handling; Performance monitoring; Accounting; Security management; Configuration management.

Analysis of these areas identifies the management requirements, specific management functions and the types of managed objects involved.

Fault handling is concerned with responding to situations when a system no longer meets its specification. For example, comparing a count of the successful number of transactions with a count of failed transactions will show if the error rate for a system has risen to unacceptable levels. A fault-reporting algorithm may contain a threshold to identify the level at which a fault report will be generated.

Performance monitoring records the actual behaviour of systems. For example, operations could monitor the values of the same two counters identified above to see what grade of service was being provided and if the system was meeting its management objectives. Alternatively, the rate at which transactions occur could be monitored to determine throughput.

Accounting management establishes the use that is made of the networked resources, essentially for the purpose of making a charge. Again, counters will be read that total the 'cost' of using a resource. Accounting management can also be used to exercise control over the use of resources by sanctioning only a given amount of resource to be used before warning that an accounting threshold has been reached. A further use of accounting management concerns the maintenance and communication of account records.

Because management operations influence system and network wide behaviour, it is essential that they be properly controlled. Like many other distributed applications, network management will have to demonstrate that authority exists before certain operations can be performed. The need for access control and the authentication of management actions are not of themselves aspects of network management. Rather, *security management* is the set of activities that maintain the security of the environment by controlling the way access permissions are communicated and exercised. Security management also includes activities that monitor the success with which security policies are enforced by, for example, maintaining security audit trails.

Configuration management is needed because the network and the activities within it change. As the network evolves new resources are added and old ones are discarded. The detection and rectification of faults also affects the availability of networking components. Configuration management monitors and controls the following: The state of resources and activities; The relationships between resources; The introduction and removal of resources.

Status is characterized both by administrative and operational attributes. Administratively a resource can be *available, unavailable* or *under test.* Operationally it may be *active* or *inactive.* Relationships characterize resource alternatives and the interconnectivity of resources. In the networking environment, configuration management controls and reports upon the path or route taken to communicate between resources. These aspects of configuration management and the need to create or delete references to both types and instances of managed objects may involve passing considerable amounts of information between systems, for example to update control tables or specify revised management algorithms.

These examples show that individual managed objects do not necessarily belong uniquely to a particular management functional area. Managed objects and their attributes, as typified by counters, gauges, reports, etc., are found in all aspects of management, and although some policy objectives may be satisfied by simple operations of the type described, many will require these simple operations to be compounded into more complex management procedures.

Users investing in distributed information technology want an open market for equipment in order to avoid being tied into a single vendor situation. They therefore welcome standardization which also brings the benefit of defined functionality and provides a yardstick against which to judge claims of conformance. These benefits of standardization apply equally to management standards though, because of the diversity of management requirement, the standards are both harder to define and to apply. Standards apply to interfaces and functions, not to the way systems are implemented. Having identified management functions, what are the interfaces? Network management is a distributed processing activity which requires a symbiosis between people and their computing systems. We identify three interfaces of concern to network management: User-system; System-system; Application program-system.

The first two require some form of command and response language. Although the semantic requirements of such languages are similar, the syntax of the first interface is oriented towards human expression. The second interface can be optimized for efficient communication between computer systems. The third interface also concerns language but this time it is the binding between conventional programming languages and the objects of concern to management. These allow systems programmers to write programs to carry out monitoring and controlling operations. All three interfaces provide mechanisms to express the activities which a system is required to perform but, whereas the first and third are handled locally, the second interface involves the communication of the management information between systems. Thus, system-system interfaces require us to consider two aspects of standardization: (1) the end system activity and (2) the open communications between systems. The latter are expressed through open systems interconnection standards.

This distinction between the standards needed to specify the management objects and their associated operations, on the one hand, and the communication standards, on the other, is being developed in a standard document which gives an *overview* of the set of OSI management services. This standard is essentially concerned with the services to manage the OSI environment, that is the communications environment. However, research suggests that the principles it embodies are applicable to the wider aspects of management which are the subject of this chapter. An analysis of the requirements of the open communications environment shows that the OSI basic reference model has to be augmented to handle management. This extension to the reference model is specified in the OSI management framework.

The OSI management framework: The purpose of this standard is twofold. It augments the protocol architecture of the OSI basic reference model by describing the principles of communication in the OSI environment when applied to communication management activities; It is prescriptive of some of the management standards that will be needed.

The basic reference model encapsulates the concept of protocol exchange between peer entities at seven layers. The service provided by each layer adds value to the communication service provided by lower layers and so provides an enhanced service to a higher layer. The highest layer specifies the application specific protocol. Network management is a distributed processing application so it is not surprising that the system-system communications discussed above should be conveyed by application layer protocol exchanges. This aspect of OSI management is defined as *systems management.* However, some management information is of necessity communicated also in lower layer protocols. This may occur during failure conditions, during system boot-strap or re-configuration. To handle these management communications, the OSI management framework defines the concept of *layer management.* It specifies the circumstances when layer management is appropriate and the constraints upon its use. Alternatively, in a local area network that offers a broadcast facility, it is appropriate to use data link layer protocols to identify which of the attached systems is acting as manager to control the operation of the network at that level. Systems management is however specified as the norm. Whereas normal protocol exchanges ultimately serve inter-application communications, layer management exchanges are only between the systems connected at that level of protocol. However, the information being transmitted may be destined for a further system or may be transmitted as a result of a request from a distant system. Consider the example of system A requesting system B to place a remote modem into the loop-back test mode. The communication between A and B is a systems management exchange, that between B and the modem occurs through layer management protocol. How the information is handled within system B is an implementation matter.

However, the OSI management frame-work provides an important modelling concept, the *management information base* to cover this type of communication. The management information base is a conceptual repository of information which is accessible for management purposes.

Management information services: OSI management standards encompass the following: Those parts of layer protocol standards that help to maintain layer activity on behalf of all users of the layer service; Specifications of managed objects that are the subject of systems and layer management communications; A naming structure to identify managed objects; Abstract definitions of management information together with the specification of operations on the information; Procedures that may be invoked to carry out management activities; Operations to perform management tasks for a specific management functional area; The definition of a common application layer service for communicating management operations between open systems; A protocol specification for that communication service; Mappings between the definition of managed objects and their operations onto their representation in protocol exchanges.

Of these standards, those for the common management information service and protocol are the most advanced. These standards set out the rules for open communication between a manager and a management activity operating as a management agent. The standards are independent of specific management procedures and are applicable to all management functional areas. They distinguish between communications that notify managers of event reports in the agent system and operations that the manager requests of the agent. The general form of the latter is

< operation type > < managed object identifier > < access right token > < value >

where the operation type is currently defined as one of the following: *Get* the value of the identified object; *Set* the value of the identified object; Perform a given *action* on the identified object; *Create* a managed object of a specified type; *Delete* the identified object. Other operations, now being appended to the above list, are those to *cancel* a get operation and to *add* and *remove* members from a set of managed objects. The *cancel get* operation has been introduced to deal specifically with the prospect that a large amount of data may be returned to a manager who has requested a *get* operation of an agent. When network traffic is particularly heavy or the manager does not wish to be overburdened, this operation allows the original *get* to be terminated. The operation may be cancelled at any time. The protocol will ensure that the manager will know, unambiguously, whether the *get* finished normally or prematurely. Because a *get* operation leaves the agent system unchanged, there is no uncertainty concerning the state of the agent system after an early cancellation. There are also proposals to be able to cancel *set* and *action* operations, but these are meeting with resistance because they would leave the state of the agent undefined. Although the common management information protocol is seen as the principal mechanism for the transfer of management information, there is no reason in principle why file transfer protocols should not be invoked for the transfer of very large volumes of information.

All operations and notifications may require the agent system to respond to the communication to acknowledge that the operation has been performed or the notification has been dealt with. However, these standards are not concerned with the consequences of the semantics of the end system operation; these are defined by the specific management information services for each functional area and by the definitions of managed objects.

Some of the standards relating to the fault and configuration management functional areas are well advanced and draft proposals for international standards have recently been registered. One of the difficulties of standardization in this highly integrated area of OSI management standards is establishing an effective structure for the standards documents and meaningful crossreferences between standards. It would be impractical to publish the whole of OSI management as a single standard since management is a potentially open-ended activity and new aspects of the standards could be added continually. Even if a reasonable subset were to be identified, publishing all those together represents a major editorial task which would delay stable parts of the standard while the less developed parts were refined.

Two sets of documents help to maintain the coherence of this set of standards. One, the management information services overview, has already been mentioned. The other set recognizes that many objects and operations are common to several different management functions. A group of documents defines the structure of management information, the common information types, their attributes and the operations upon them, The documents provide a prescriptive method for specifying new managed object types. For each type the following information is needed The individual *items* of information that can be invoked by management; The *permitted* operations on those items; The *inherent* properties of the object; The *implicit* relations with other information elements; The *specific* properties for each instance of an object type.

The documents define such objects and attributes as status, counter, gauge, threshold, event and log. One aspect of OSI management not included in this figure is the way conformance to management standards is defined. This area still needs further exploration since not only must implementations of the standard conform to the rules of the protocol exchanges but they must also conform to the definitions of the semantics of operations that take place in the end systems where management operations are performed. This presents an interesting problem since tests for conformance cannot expect common implementations of particular management operations. Therefore, indirect methods are needed to test for conformance to a distributed management algorithm and demonstrate that the desired operations have been performed correctly. The difficulties of testing for conformance are further compounded by the nature of the management operations themselves. For example, when testing for conformance to standards related to fault reporting, it is necessary to cause a system to simulate faults to carry out the specified procedure. However, responses may be generated spuriously when the system under test is itself faulty. Also, how may one test for performance without compromising the performance one is seeking to test? Even more significantly, how does one test security management functions without compromising system security? Finally, will it be possible to check re-configuration procedures in such a way that recovery is still possible even if the implementation of the standard under test fails to conform to requirements?

Further developments in open management: Those developing OSI management standards are well aware of the above issues and that they are only scratching the surface of the possible set of management activities that may need to be expressed as standards. So far, most operations and most objects are very simple as are their mappings onto management protocol. Also, they represent only those objects of concern to the open communications environment. It is the author's contention that, in the long run, all aspects of management have to be handled in a coherent manner whether they relate to communications objects, processing resources and activities or to data storage. It will not be possible for managers to monitor and control their distributed processing environments effectively if these areas of their responsibility are handled separately.

Research into distributed systems is now sufficiently mature as to show the appropriate architectures for distributed systems. This is now being complemented by the development of standards for open distributed processing (ODP). More recent work has extended these architectural approaches to encompass management by implementing distributed systems management activities in a wide area networked test bed. As a result, there is growing confidence that the current approach to OSI management is capable of handling all aspects of management. This requires that the current standards are developed with an eye to their eventual extension. Failure to do so runs the risk of constraining the development of open distributed management standards or, worse, of developing mutually incompatible sets of standards requiring different implementation approaches. The consequences for manufacturers would be increased development cost and this would be reflected to users in the costs of products.

What then must be done to extend OSI management? Firstly, the set of objects of concern to all of management and the operations upon them must be defined. Secondly, an extended set of management procedures is needed, though these are still likely to fall within the five functional areas of management that have been established. Then the objects, their operations and the procedures have to be mapped onto the services needed to communicate the management requirement between systems. This will call for extensions to the set of common management information services and protocol. One type of extension will allow for typical control structures to be communicated, for example to express conditional constructs or to request that a set of operations be repeated. Since these constructs can be nested, the syntax of information transfer will take on some of the aspects of a block structured language. A second type of extension will concern the conditions under which groups of activities will be performed. It will define relative priorities for remote operations and whether a group of operations shall be processed as an atomic action or whether a more relaxed processing regime is permitted. Many of these extensions will add to the functionality of the local operating system enabling its functionality to be extended over the distributed processing environment. This will assist in realizing the concept of a distributed operating system when interworking between existing systems with conventional operating systems.

One further benefit which is implicit in this approach to the development of open distributed management is that it handles the open endedness of management requirements and the need to allow managers to manage their systems according to their own policies; that is there is HU requirement to specify a standard way in which management is performed. Drawing upon the analogy of a programming language we see that, by adopting a language structured approach to management communications with a well-defined syntax and semantics we can generate any management procedure *in a standard way* and have it communicated and interpreted *according to a standard* so that it is understood, without having to standardize the procedure itself. With such a language, procedures for remote operation can be specified for immediate action or transferred as named procedures to be invoked by a subsequent *action* primitive.

Although progress towards management standards has been slow and there are, as yet, only proposed functional standards for OSI management, manufacturers have recognized the need for some management tools to handle their proprietary networking products. These provide facilities for gathering performance related data, carrying out tests and performing re-configuration of network resources. The products are largely related to managing the communications infrastructure though some local area networking products for personal computer and workstation systems do permit their users to manipulate remote processing and storage resources. Space does not permit a full analysis of existing products. However, the current ranges of products tend not to integrate their management functions into a single package. Rather, management is performed by a loosely coordinated group of software packages. Nor is communications management co-ordinated with distributed processing or distributed data management. Many of the current products are concerned solely with the local area communications network on which they reside. They are frequently installed within an IBM personal computer and observe network traffic as it passes; that is on a CSMA/CD network the interface would be instructed to operate in a 'promiscuous' mode, listening to all packets on the network cable. A similar operation is possible on token ring networks and though the packet is not processed by the management computer, it is able to monitor all traffic. Such management devices are well able to produce network traffic statistics, report packet collisions and detect ring failures. They are essentially monitoring devices. Some control can be exercised where such systems are used as filtering bridges between network segments. Also, where networks provide mechanisms for terminal multiplexing, some manufacturers offer proprietary products that restrict the services that may be accessed from a given terminal or by a given user at a terminal.

In some manufacturer's offerings the different aspects of management may have to be performed from different network management devices. For example, some of the products that support the interconnection of local area networks through fibre optic cable only allow the cable environment to be managed from a special management terminal. Management of the attached local networks must be done from other terminals while management of attachments must be done from yet another control system.

These are implementation matters, for even if there is a coherent set of management standards, manufacturers will not be obliged to place all their management functionality into one box. However, offering a coherent set of standards increases the likelihood of their doing so and, having a compatible set of management standards, allows the users to purchase networking products knowing them to be accessible, for management purposes, in a common way.

Network management has become a critical issue, especially in heterogeneous and multivendor computer net-works. Also, for the success of client-server computing, effective and proper implementation of network management is essential. Client-servers with a large number of workstations need network management to manage and control the networks and the components of networks with their associated hardware and software. Like other areas of the computer industry, network management has been undergoing rapid technological advances to meet ever increasing challenges.

It is worth mentioning that, these days, the *computer* has expanded to include desktop computers popularly known as personal computers, work-stations, laptops, palm-held computers, and other computing devices, which have the intelligence to do computation and also to communicate with each other. With computer technology growing at an incredibly fast pace, it may not be proper to place limitations on what a "computer" can be. Computers can connect to one another to form a *local area network* (LAN). In LANs, there are two important computer networking scenarios. The most popular scenario is known as *client-server* computing. In client-server computing, a client requests a service from a server and the server provides the service to the client. As an example, compiling a computer program in a client can be done by the compiler located in a server. On the other hand, in *peer-to-peer* computer networking, there are no fixed roles such as that of client or server, and any computer in the network can be a client or server. For our discussion purposes, we include both computer networking scenarios under LANs.

The evolution from hostcentric computer networks to heterogeneous LAN networks has been gradual. This transformation to LAN computing and networking is further complicated by existing applications and protocols from different standards bodies and vendors. However, the limitations of technology, protocols, and topology impose restrictions on the number of computers that can be connected to form LANs. Therefore, clusters of networks have become the trend. Once these islands of networks come into existence, the issue of connecting and managing networks becomes important.

To get a better appreciation of the problems involved in the present-day network management of LANs, let us look at some of the possible LAN environments. Some networks can be connected by *bridges* with similar LAN protocols. Here, networks A and B use similar protocols, and they are connected by bridges. Sometimes, network A and network B are known as *segments.* Here one network is using a token ring and the other network is using Ethernet. *Routers* are used to connect these networks to the backbone network. There are also cases where dissimilar networks have to be interconnected. In this case, *gateways* are used for connecting the networks. Here one network may be using TCP/IP, and another one may be using Open Systems Inter-connection (OSI) or System Network Architecture (SNA). Also, these LANs may span buildings and cities to form a *metropolitan area network* (MAN). An extension of the MAN can be found in the *wide area network* (WAN), which covers a larger area than a MAN does.

After having discussed some of the LAN scenarios, let us take some simple examples of problems involved in managing different components of a network. Suppose we have to apply a software fix to all the computers in a network. How do we do it? We cannot take a diskette and apply the fix to all the computers, especially if there are thousands of them. Or what about isolating a fault in one computer? How can we say with certainty that a problem has occurred in X computer? And we need to be sure what caused the problem, and how it can be rectified.

These sets of problems assume serious proportions if computers are from different vendors. These computers may be using different software and hardware architectures. There are various ways of reporting the problems and different ways to rectify them. In some cases, these architectures may be such that the computers attached to different LANs may not communicate with each other. In some cases, it may be necessary to connect these networks to a centralized computer. How do we connect these LANs from different vendors and then manage them from a single, central point?

All of these factors make the network management of computer networks and their components, which may be widely dispersed with multivendor origins and multiprotocol operation, a highly challenging task. How we meet it is the topic of this book.

Network management uses distinctions described by *open systems interconnection* (OSI) seven-layer architecture, it is imperative that we look into it right up front. The International Standards Organization (ISO) brought out the OSI architecture of seven layers for computer networking. The main idea behind partitioning computer networking functions into separate, independent sub-functions is to standardize each layer of activity more easily and expeditiously. Each layer is expected to carry out a set of functions and provide services to the layer above it.

As defined in OSI, a *system* includes computer hardware and peripherals, software, and applications, including those used for communications. *Open system* has different interpretations and connotations. We prefer the following definition: A system is said to be *open* if it supports a widely accepted and well-published set of standards. Openness is not concerned with the system technology, implementation, or how the systems are connected to one another.

The seven layers are as follows: The *physical layer* deals with physical interfaces and details of the physical medium used to connect two open systems. It is concerned with mechanical, electrical, optical, functional, and procedural characteristics of the links used in data transfer. The *data link layer is* responsible for reliable data transfer between two linked open systems. This may require flow control, error control and recovery, and synchronization. The *network layer* provides a path for data transfer between end systems. In this layer, routing of data through a network of intermediate systems may be required. As a consequence, this layer is responsible for making connections when required, maintaining them, and terminating the connections when they are no longer needed; The *transport layer* is concerned with data transfer from one end to another end. For this purpose, end-to-end error recovery and flow control may be required. Note that the network layer is concerned with data transfer from one system to another, whereas, in the transport layer, we are talking about end-to-end data transfer; The *session layer* is responsible for sessions between applications. This layer also provides services for establishing, maintaining, and terminating these sessions; The *presentation layer* is primarily responsible for resolving differences in the way data is represented between two applications on either end. As an example, ASCII to EBCDIC translation, or vice versa, may be done in this layer. This layer also may provide services such as encryption and data compression; The *application layer* provides services and functions required by user applications. In other words, this layer provides applications and services which are not provided by lower layers to support communication between the systems. In this layer, we may include *commitment, concurrency, and recovery (CCR)*. Applications such as electronic mail and network management belong to this layer. Network management applications, which use network management, also form part of this layer.

Network management, systems management, and *enterprise management* have been variously defined. This can lead to a lot of confusion and we will therefore clearly define what these terms will mean in this book. We define *management* as monitoring and controlling the resources in computers, the resources used in the connection and communication of computers, and the applications used in the computers. There are, broadly, two models for *network management,* based on how the management activities are accomplished. This, in turn, is dependent on the computing environment. A LAN is a typical *distributed-computing environment*. Management of LAN environments can be done by peer-to-peer network management. Sometimes, this is also known as *distributed-network management*. Here managers, which undertake the network management activities, act more as peers, and there is no one central manager.

The other model is *hierarchical,* or *centralized, network manageinent.* In this model, the network management is controlled from a single point, known as a *manager.* This manager may manage network resources from a centralized computing environment. This may cover the cases where one super-manager or one centralized controlling manager may manage devices via some intermediate managers. This supermanager is also known as the *manager of manager* (MOM). All these cases are grouped under *hostcentric network management.* Sometimes, this can also be termed *enterprise management.*

Many definitions are in vogue for network management. We use the one provided by IEEE Standard 802.6-1990. "Network management provides mechanisms for the monitoring, control, and coordination of all managed objects within the Physical Layer and Data Link Layer of a node." The same document also defines systems management as follows: "Systems management provides mechanisms for the monitoring, control, and coordination of all managed objects within open systems. Systems management is effected through application layer protocol." Here we have to note that *skinny stacks* or trivial upper layers can also be used. From the definitions provided by the IEEE, it is apparent that network management is a subset of the activities in systems management.

In the preceding definitions, we have to be clear on the terms *monitoring, control,* and *coordination.* This is central to the concept of systems management. Let us examine the term *monitoring* first. Resources used in computer networks have to be continuously watched, and any untoward behavior leading to the deterioration of functioning of a resource, resources, or network has to be rectified. This is more a proactive action than a reactive one.

The resources have to be controlled. This means that we should be able to control how the resources behave so that they function properly. When resources have to be monitored and controlled, there is a necessary factor coordination. If there is no coordination, the situation is a free-for-all, and chaos ensues. Not only do the activities of the managed resources have to be coordinated, but so do the facilities that monitor and control them.

Unfortunately, *systems management is* a very generic term. Readers can confuse it with management of systems used in other disciplines. This confusion is compounded by the use of different terms in the computer industry.

While treating the topics of OSI and SNA, especially in the peer-to-peer arena, *systems management* is the popularly used term; thus, it is better to use this term when dealing with these protocols. In Internet, *network management* is the prevalent term; hence, this term will be used when discussing this topic. While discussing IEEE-related management of resources and layer management, we will also use the term *network management.* In other places, where it is not specifically required to make distinctions between network management and systems management, the term *network management* has been used, as well.

The goals of network management are: *Higher network availability:* This involves improving the operational efficiency, which means reducing system and network downtime and improving response times. Problems in a network should be responded to as quickly as possible. In many cases, it should be possible to rectify the problems unattended. But the access and transfer of management information will require processing power and involve network traffic. Therefore, performance must be considered in the design and installation of network management.

Reduce network operational cost: Ultimately, cost reduction is one of the primary motives behind network management. Because the technology changes rapidly, management of heterogeneous systems and multiple protocols is desirable.

Reduce network bottlenecks: In some cases, network administration can be performed from a central site. Under these circumstances, it may be preferable to centrally monitor and control the activity of a network. In other cases, this activity may be distributed.

Increase flexibility of operation and integration: Networking technologies are changing at a fast rate to cater to changing requirements and needs. As new applications are used, protocols used in networking are also changing. It should be possible to absorb new technologies with the least cost. As an example, in LANs, data communication is common, but there may also be a need to integrate graphics, voice, and video capabilities as the application base expands. In addition, computer networks could be used to manage copiers and faxes.

It should be possible to add new technology and equipment without much difficulty. Also, there should not be major problems in migrating from one release of network management software to another version. Network management applications should not be overly platform-dependent for their function.

Higher efficiency: In some cases, some of the goals of network management overlap. If we reduce the network operational cost and improve the network availability, overall efficiency will increase. Here, factors such as utilization, operational cost, migration cost, and flexibility must also be considered.

Ease of use: End-user interfaces are critical for the success of any product. The use of network management applications should not involve a major learning curve. User interfaces based on object-oriented principles and technology are helpful for network management applications.

Security: Some network management functions may need security features. If some critical accounting data has to be secure, then there should be provisions for providing selective security. Here we are making the distinction between computer system and network and network management-related security. Our focus will be on the security of network management functions.

Network management systems architecture: This division is based on different functions performed at different levels. To avoid confusion with OSI layers, we have used the term *level* instead of *layer*, It may be noted that this division of functions is made to explain the concepts of overall network management systems. At the lowest level, we have the *operating system and hardware.* The operating system may be DOS, Windows NT, OS/2 Warp, Windows 95, or a combination of these. Network operating systems, such as Novell NetWare or OS/2 LAN server, are also part of this level. These resources may be on the same workstation as the operating system or they may be separate components, such as a bridge or a router. Over the operating system and hardware, we need *protocol support.* Protocol support provides distinct services; hence, it must be treated as a separate level. Protocol support includes the following: Layers below the application layer in OSI, UDP/IP in Internet, or layers which have similar functionality; Management protocols such as SNMP, CMIP, or CMOL; Conversion of different protocols and multiprotocols which may also be needed for supporting heterogeneous and multivendor protocols.

The level above protocol support is the *network management framework,* which provides the base for various network management applications. In the computer industry, it is becoming a trend to enable and open up this level such that different vendors and alliance partners can write network management applications. The network management frame-work provides for the following: Manager and agent functions; Database support such as relational databases and object-oriented databases for storing data for many network management functions and applications support. We prefer to include database support in the network management framework, because network management applications sometimes need close access to the database for topology, status, inventory of resources, logs, and other data; View and user interface support, which are important for the success of software applications. The base for these functions is provided in this layer; Network management functions, such as configuration management and fault management.

The *network management applications* area is a growing market and has the potential to produce very innovative applications. Some examples include the following: The business management applications area is still largely untapped. With the growing client-server market, this area has challenges and potential, especially regarding the dispersal of computing equipment and environment; Easy-to-use view applications can ease the tasks of system administrators. The use of multimedia and artificial intelligence has wide possibilities in this area; Fault identification and fault diagnostic applications such as automation applications will be in greater demand to cater to the highly decentralized nature of networks.

Performance-tuning applications are very important. Even though processor power is increasing at a rapid pace and constraints such as memory are becoming cheaper, demands on them are also increasing at a fast pace. Demands on processing power will increase as graphics, image, video, and audio applications become more prevalent.

The major emphasis is on the resources being managed, protocol support, and the network management framework. It is beyond the scope of this book to either discuss in much detail the operating system and hardware or examine in depth the network management applications area. Management of computer networks involves monitoring and controlling the different hardware, microcode, and software components of networks. Some hardware components that need to be managed are: *Physical media and connections:* These include physical and data link layer--related equipment. Many LAN products are coming out for these layers. The protocols used vary from IEEE 802--related products, including FDDI, frame relay, B-Integrated Services Digital Networks (BISDN), asynchronous transfer mode (ATM), Synchronous Optical Network (SONET), and other emerging protocols. Also included are products such as adapters of different protocols, concentrators, and switches; *Computer components:* These include storage devices, processors, printers, and others. Though Ethernet, token-ring, and token-bus adapters are considered part of the computer components, they have not been included here. We prefer to lump them under the aforementioned physical media and connections category; *Connectivity and interconnection components:* This refers to hardware components such as repeaters, bridges, routers, gateways, hubs, and modems; *Telecommunication hardware:* These are modems, multiplexers, and switches, such as, for example, an ATM switch.

Typical software to be managed includes *Operating system software:* This is the bare-bones system software provided on any computer. Some examples are DOS, Windows 95, and OS/2 Warp; *Application software and software tools:* The application software makes computers more popular and productive. With increasing integration of video, voice, text, and imaging, applications need to be managed. As the base of multimedia applications grows, multimedia applications need to be managed, too; *System software in client-server computing:* Some examples are NetWare servers and OS/2 LAN servers; *Interconnection software:* This includes software used in repeaters, bridges, routers, gateways, and hubs. In many applications, extra functionality is provided by adding software functions on the underlying hardware. These software applications are becoming complex, and are as important as the hardware; *Application software in client-server computing:* This includes the database server, file server, and print server; *Data communication and telecommunication software:* Management of software related to data communication and telecommunication protocols such as FDDI, ATM, and frame relay is necessary. We have specifically included this in the software section, because these protocols rely heavily on software; *Backbone telecommunication software:* This is increasingly used to connect different LANs. Though it is included in our earlier categories, we have added backbone telecommunication software here as well to account for the emerging backbone communication protocols.

The above mentioned wide variety of hardware and software to be managed is complicated by various protocols and differences among them. In addition, many proprietary protocols are popular and have a wide application base. Therefore, multiprotocol and multi-vendor products make connectivity and management daunting tasks. Broadly, the scope of network management is to manage both hardware and/or software products, which may be heterogeneous, multivendor, multiprotocol, and geographically dispersed, as well as managing the people who oversee these products.

Having introduced the topic of network management, we will examine different concepts and standards, including architectures, in the rest of the book. In some cases, to provide a better understanding and appreciation of the important concepts and methodologies involved in network management, lower-layer concepts are also briefly discussed.

As discussed earlier, there is a paradigm shift in the computing scenario. LANs and WANs are becoming increasingly popular. Also, with the introduction of fiber optics, telephone tariffs are coming down. At the same time, more applications, such as voice, video, text, graphics, and images, are being added to the computing environment. Simultaneously, these applications require bandwidth beyond what we have observed in the traditional transmission of voice or data. This changing scenario is slowly bringing about the integration of data communication and telecommunications, which adds complexity to network management. The management of equipment must include switches and different components used in the telephone industry. In addition, computing and data transmission environments are becoming increasingly heterogeneous. The different types of equipment use a variety of protocols, from standards to the proprietary ones. This adds another dimension to the management of heterogeneous, as well as multiprotocol, environments.

As one guides through the maze of protocols, standards are being advanced by vendors belonging to the telephone industry, computer industry, and government agencies. There are basically two types of standards. *De facto industry standards* become established when a target segment of the user population accepts them or when a majority of vendors uses them. In some cases, such industry standards are the result of prominent players in an industry forming cooperative bodies and introducing products that conform to the guidelines developed by these bodies.

Formal standards are mostly brought out by international, regional, or national standards bodies. In many cases, there is close cooperation among these standards bodies. Governments and their agencies, by and large, prefer formal standards. The ISO is one such body, which, as the name suggests, is an important international standards organization primarily comprising governmental agencies. At the national level, most countries have their own standards organizations. Standardization is becoming important in facilitating the compatibility of hardware and software from different vendors. From this angle, concepts of *portability*, *connectivity*, and *interoperability* should be emphasized. Let us examine what each term means. For portability, an application in one computer platform must be able to work with identical functions in another platform, or no modifications should be required to make an application work in different platforms. For portability purposes, application interfaces and functions provided to interact with lower-layer software should be similar. By connectivity, we mean that a system from one vendor attaches to a similar system from a different vendor, and these systems must be able to work together. For example, two computers manufactured by different vendors must work together when connected as LANs.

Interoperability, which is closely related to connectivity, goes a step further. For interoperability, the protocols, formatting of data, and application environments must be similar, such that applications developed on two different platforms must work together. An application developed by one vendor must work with a similar application from another vendor. Let us look at an example. Electronic mail and electronic data exchange applications are quite common. For interoperability, two electronic mail systems must work together regardless of which vendors developed these systems,

Having examined some terms relevant to standardization, let us return to the topic of standards bodies. In the United States and elsewhere, computer networks connected to the Internet follow their own set of standards and have well-established procedures for bringing out standards. In addition, the Institute of Electrical and Electronics Engineers (IEEE) in the United States formulates standards for LANs and in other areas where there is a need for them. Usually, the IEEE concentrates on the standardization of lower layers such as the physical and data link layers. Most standards bodies work closely with one another and adopt each other's standards, where they are available, to avoid duplication of efforts and standards. As software applications become more sophisticated and are developed by many vendors, there is a trend toward open systems. For open systems, conformance testing to find out whether applications really conform to the standards is becoming a norm. Many variations of standards are available; therefore, it is possible to have a set of implementations with different sets of standards at different layers. To facilitate smooth operation, some standard sets, known as *profiles,* have been developed by standards bodies. This reduces incompatibility and ensures that applications using the same profiles have interoperability.

Standards provide sufficient flexibility in implementation, which may create its own set of interoperability problems. To overcome this, many leading vendors are developing a set of profiles for network management. This effort is being pioneered by the Network Management Forum (NMF), which provides guidelines on how OSI standards must be implemented. In addition to the NMF, there are also vendor consortiums such as the Open Software Foundation (OSF), Unix International, and X/Open. Many applications are being brought out based on the work done by these groups. These consortiums also active in the network management area.

A common pitfall of standards is that they take a long time to produce. Once a problem is identified, some standards bodies take years before they bring out widely accepted standards. This presents problems in some cases. People in the industry with problems needing immediate solutions cannot wait for many years for standards to resolve these problems. Still, standards are generally useful and good for everyone in the industry.

Another common complaint is that the OSI standards are too complex, and it is difficult to implement them. This may be one reason for the slow implementation of standards. Because standards bodies work on the basis of consensus, there are influences in different directions, leading to frequent changes. As a consequence, it is becoming a practice to wait for standards to stabilize and become international before implementing them.

Network management standard functional model: Different network management standards are prevalent. Some are closely related to one another and, in some cases, they extend earlier protocols, taking migration aspects into consideration. Extensibility is an important part of every standard. General standards must be applicable to specialized cases and applications. In network management standards, we are interested in the following key areas:

Management functional area: This covers how network management functions are organized, how they interact with each other, and how they behave with the external components. The management functional area should also clearly delineate the scope of each network management function.

Informational area: This deals with how resources are represented from the standpoint of management actions. This has to be done in a consistent manner to facilitate smooth and easy definition of new resources. Representation of resources should also cover the scope of the management operations that can be performed on these resources. We stress the scope, because it is very important to precisely define the boundaries of these resources from the management point of view and the interactions possible with external components. There should not be any room for ambiguity, because this leads to confusion during implementation and problems of interoperability.

Communications area: This primarily covers management protocols. As we will notice, in network management, we use entirely different management protocols for communicating management information. The communications area should also include the communication stacks or profiles which are used to support the management protocols.

Conformance area: This is a key area for interoperability. A set of guidelines should be clearly stated for checking whether an implementation has adhered to the standards outlined. During implementation, taking too much liberty may result in incompatible implementations. This can be checked only if there are precise and clear guidelines on how implementations are to be done.

Network News Transfer Protocol (NNTP) The protocol used to distribute Usenet newsgroups.

network operating system (NOS A set of programs that enables networked computers to share files devices.

Network Operations Center (NOC): An organization that oversees network, monitoring its traffic and solving problems.

network peripheral: A device, such as a printer, that is directly connected to a network and not to one of the computers or workstations.

Network Time Protocol (NTP): A protocol that synchronizes time information on the Internet.

newbie (n): A beginner on the Internet or especially Usenet (not as derogatory as clueless newbie)

newgroup: A special kind of control message that creates a new newsgroup.

newgroup wars: Competing newgroup and rmgroup messages repeatedly posted by people, who alternately want and don't want a new newsgroup to be propagated.

The New Hacker's Dictionary: The printed-book version of the jargon file, published by MIT Press and well worth owning in book form. The contents of the jargon file are also available via the Web at http:// www.ccil. org/ jargon/j argon. html.

newline: Any character or group of characters used to indicate the start of a new line in an ASCII text file. The newline characters vary from system to system. An ASCII file that is mistakenly transmitted as a binary file to an incompatible system can end with garbage characters such as ^M at the end of each line.

news: Usenet articles, posted to newsgroups.

news: A Usenet hierarchy devoted to Usenet policy, guidelines, and administrative issues.

newsfeed: The packet of new's articles passed along from one computer to the next or. Usenet.

newsfroup: A common typo for newsgroup, now accepted (facetiously) as an alternative spelling.

newsgroup: A Usenet discussion group.

newsgroup creation: In the big seven Usenet newsgroup hierarchies, new newsgroups can be created only after a formal RFD (Request for Discussion) and a subsequent CFV. In the alternative newsgroup hierarchies, it is much easier to create a new newsgroup, which accounts for the proliferation of abandoned silly groups.

newsgroup name: The hierarchical name of a Usenet newsgroup, starting with the first-level hierarchical distinction, followed by a dot, then one or more further qualifying names, none of which may be longer than 15 characters, each of which is separated by a dot. In proper newsgroup naming, hyphens or underscores rather than dots should be used to break up compound words, For example, alt.fan.jimj.hendrix is incorrect, but alt.fan.jimi-hendrix is correct

newsgroup: A common type for newsgroup which, unlike newsgroup, has not been accepted as a humorous alternative spelling.

.newsrc: A setup file for newsreaders on UNIX systems that keeps track of which Usenet newsgroups the user is subscribed to and which articles have been read.

newsreader: A program used to read Usenet articles, and usually also to save, respond to, and post follow-ups to articles, as well as to post new articles.

news server: A program or computer that a supplies a newsfeed.

NewsWatcher: A newsreader for the Macintosh, available via anonymous FTP from sumex-aim.stanford.edu.

newsweeding: A pun on *newsreading,* meaning the process of killing or ignoring uninteresting threads and zeroing in on the worthwhile content of a high-volume newsgroup.

Nexis: An information service of Mead Data giving access to a searchable database of news and magazine articles and abstracts.

Nextstep: An operating system for UNIX hat offers a graphical user interface.

nick: A nickname used on IRC, not necessarily the same as your username.

nickname: An alias or address book in some e-mail programs.

Nightmare File System: A derogatory term for Network File System.

NISO: National Information Standards Organization

NIST: National Institute for Standards and Technology.

nixpub: A list of Internet service providers, posted, regularly to comp.bbs.misc and alt.bbs, also available via anoymous FTP from vfl.paramax.com in the /pub/ pubnetc: directory.

nn: A UNIX newsreaader (it stands for no news, as it tries to hide everything you don't want to see)

NNTP: Network News Transfer Protocol.

NO CARRIER: The message a modem displays when it detects no carrier signal from the phone line.

Nodal Switching System (NSS): The routing method of the NSFnet backbone.

Node: A hardware device that forms part of a computer or data communications network. Each one of these devices is a node.

Non-Breaking Hyphen: This is a term used in word processing, where a hyphenated word should not be split at the end of a line. For example it might be considered confusing to split the phrase "flip-flop" between two lines. The insertion of a nonbreaking hyphen will ensure that the two words are kept together.

NOR Gate: A logic gate that has two or more inputs and one output. A NOR gate detects when either or both inputs are absent, that is if either (or both) input reads 1 then the gate makes no output.

Normal Distribution: There is a tendency for all naturally occurring phenomena to clump uniformly around a mean value. Examples include the height of children in a particular grade at school, the length of life of a particular hard disk, the amount of petrol used per year per head of population. This tendency produces what is known as a "Normal Distribution". Graphically a normal distribution produces a characteristic bell-shaped curve.

Norton Index: One of several methods by which computer hardware/software processing speed may be evaluated. Abbreviation NI.

NOS: Network Operating System,

NOT [Boolean operator]: used to reverse the logical relationship to one of the: search elements. A text search for x AND NOT y will match only documents that contain x and do not contain y.

Not gate: A logic gate that has one input and one output. A NOT gate is used to reverse a logic signal (changes 1 to 0 and 0 to 1).

NSFnet: A major Internet backbone, operated by the National Science Foundation.

NSTL: Abbreviation for National Software Testing Laboratory, an American independent software testing and evaluation organisation.

O

oak.oakland.edu A huge FTP archive at Oakland University.

Ob- A prefix for an obligatory addendum to an off-topic Usenet or list post. Say you get into a political debate in the rec.music.dylan newsgroup.

Object File: Lines of code that are to be linked into machine code, or into a standalone executable file.

object-oriented Said of an operating system, programming language, or application that makes use of self-contained objects that can contain both programming code and data, and which function as modular program pieces.

Object Oriented Programming. A programming technique that concentrates on the data that is to be processed rather than the means of processing. Object Oriented Programming (abbreviation OOP) has become more widely used in recent years as in many cases it offers the optimum solution to many programming tasks.

obligatory * content Something added to a mailing list or Usenet post to make it relevant to the charter of the list or newsgroup (replacing the * with the subject of the group, as in obligatory Amiga content or obligatory cat content, and so on).

Obsolescence: Used to describe the premature replacement of products (hardware or software), not because of normal wear and tear or deterioration, but because technological advancements have necessitated their replacement by more up-to-date items.

Octal Numbering: A numbering system that uses a base of eight numbers and therefore has a range of digits from 07. Since the largest digit is 7, a digit is incremented once it reaches 7.

The main advantage of the octal numbering system is the ease with which conversions can be made between binary and octal. For this reason the octal system has become a useful shorthand method of binary notation. However computers still work in binary, the octal system is only for the convenience of computer operators/ programmers.

octet: Eight bits, especially on a system in which eight bits do not equal a byte.

odd parity: A method of verifying the correctness of transmitted data by summing each byte, adding a parity bit of 1 if necessary to make t h e sum odd, before sending the data, and then repeating the summation on the receiving end.

OEM: Abbreviation for Original Equipment Manufacturer. Many hardware devices are manufactured under licence by companies other than the hardware designer, these licencees may quote stock or part numbers which refer back to the OEM (Original Equipment Manufacturer) design specification or part numbers.

offline 1. Not currently connected to the Net; 2. Not responding to network requests; 3. Said of a person no longer involved in a chat.

offfine mail reader: A program that connects to the Net, downloads your e-mail, and then disconnects, allowing you to read, reply to, and send mail without being service charged for connect time.

offline newsreader: A news-reader that connects to the Net, downloads all unread articles in all subscribed newsgroups, and then disconnects, allowing you to read, reply to, and post articles without being charged for connect time.

Ohnosecond: The elapsed time between giving a wrong command and the realisation that this command will have disastrous consequences. A remarkably short period, of time!

OHP: Abbreviation for Overhead Panel, this is a liquid crystal display that can be connected to a computer (PC) and then placed on an overhead projector for projection on a large screen. A useful teaching/ training aid.

oldbie: A longtime user of the Net, coined by analogy to newbie.

Oldie: A text editor available in the Delphi Information Service.

127.0.0.1: The Internet loopback address, it is always the address of your localhost the computer you are currently logged in to.

On-Board: A reference to the inclusion of a particular hardware device as part of a "standard" model of computer. An advertisement may state, '1MB RAM on-board" indicating that this amount of RAM is included as standard in this particular model of computer. The phrase on-board is also used to indicate that a particular circuit is located on the motherboard.

One's Complement: The number obtained by changing each bit of a binary number to the opposite value (that is zero become ones and ones become zeros).

On-Line: This phrase describes a hardware device, for example, a printer, that is ready to receive data. A printer can be taken "Off-Line" manually, and automatically if, for example it runs out of paper or toner. A status panel on the hardware device will normally indicate whether the device is On-Line or Off-Line. Devices such as printers should always be taken Off-Line before doing any work on them, such as replacing a ribbon or fixing a paper jam.

Online Book Initiative (OBI): An organization that publishes uncopyrighted (or no longer copyrighted) books via the Internet, reachable via anonymous FTP at world.std. com.

Online Career Center: A nonprofit, organization that maintains a searchable database of employment information. It offers free access to job listings and resumes to both employers and job-seekers. For more information, gopher to gopher.msen.com or send e-mail to occ@msen.com.

Online community: Also *virtual community*, a group of people with shared interests who meet, communicate, and interact via a network, BBS, Internet discussion group, or any other form of electronic common space. Online communities have many of the properties of real-world communities.

Online Computer Library Center (OCLC): A nonprofit organization providing computer services (such as cataloging and interlibrary loans) for over ten thousand libraries and educational institutions. OCIC maintains the FirstSearch Catalog.

online service: A company that maintains a proprietary network and provides e-mail, forums, chats, games, databases of information, downloadable files, and information services (stocks, airlines, and so on), such as America Online, CompuServe, Delphi, eWorld, GEnie, Prodigy, Microsoft Network, and so on.

Most online services have e-mail connections to the Internet (though some charge extra for that e-mail). More and more are adding other Internet facilities, such as FTP, gopher, and soon the Web, blurring the distinction further between online and Internet service providers.

Open: To load a file into a software application or into a program. The word "OPEN' is a programming statement in several high level languages.

Open Plan: An office layout where there are few or no internal walls creating separate offices. Instead partitions and office furniture used to create separate work areas.

open protocol: A protocol that may be utilized by a variey of developers, not just the organization that formulated the protocol.

Open Software Foundation (OSF): An alliance of DEC, IBM, and Hewlett-Packard.

Open Systems Interconnection (OSI): An international organization sponsored by the **ISO** with a mission to create international computer communications standards, such as the OS1 Model, specifically to facilitate internetworking among incompatible systems.

operating environment: A front end for an operating system, a set of tools and a consistent look and feel that allow the user to interact with the computer. For instance, Microsoft Windows is an operating environment that runs on top of the MS-DOS operating system.

Operations Research: The development of, and research into, mathematical models for various business and scientific applications. Operations Research is usually computer based. Abbreviation OR.

Operating System: A collection of programs and utilities that provide a basic working environment for other software applications and the computer user. Typically the operating system controls input/output events, memory and file allocation.

option: A command or selection available on a menu or list.

OR [Boolean operator] Or. A text search with OR between two words matches any documents containing either word.

.org An Internet domain corresponding to (nonprofit) organizations.

OS/2: An IBM operating system for PCs and compatibles.

OSI: *Open Systems Interconnection*, an international organization sponsored by the ISO with a mission to create international computer communications standards, such as the OSI Model, specifically to facilitate internetworking among incompatible systems.

OSI Model: The seven-layer networking reference model (sometimes called the *seven-layer cake)* defined by the ISO's OSI to facilitate the internetworking of incompatible computers and networks.

Outernet: A collective name for all the networks, BBSs, and online services that have e-mail gateways with the Internet but no full connection.

overhead (n): The accumulation of protocol information wrapped around data transmitted over networks.

P

packet: Any unit of data (the size varies) sent cross a network. Besides the data a packet also includes the addresses of the sender and the recipient, as well as error-control information. On the Internet, a packet is the same thing as a datagram. A large piece of data will be split into several packets, each of which may take an independent route to the destination, where they will be reassembled.

Packetized Ensemble Protocol (PEP): A proprietary feature of Telebit brand modems that allows two moderns to be connected directly.

packet sniffer: 1. A person who tries to "listen in" on Internet traffic in search of information to steal; 2. The program that such a person employs to "sniff out" interesting packets.

packet-switched network: A network made up of interconnected circuits that route packets over a variety of alternative paths, as opposed to a circuit-switched network, in which packets are routed over dedicated lines.

packet switching: A method of transmitting data in which packets for many unconnected operations are routed simultaneously over a communications channel (often a telephone line) to make best use of the line. Related packets are reassembled at the destination.

packet switch node (PSN): The computer that the handles the routing of packets in a packet-switched network.

page (v): To display a document one screenful at a time in a character-based interface.
(n) A document published on the Web.

paging program A program (sometimes called a *pager)* that displays documents one screenful at a time, such as the UNIX utility more.

parallel (adj) Said of a connection in which bits are transmitted simultaneously.

parallel port A port in the back of a PC that can connect via cable to a parallel device.

parent directory 1. In a hierarchical file system, the directory for which the current directory is a subdirectory, symbolized in UNIX, DOS, and OS/2 by two dots (..); 2. Any directory which contains other directories.

parity An error-checking method in data transmission in which an extra bit is added to each byte (between the data bit and the stop bit) to round off bit-total values to even or odd numbers. The parity bit must match at both ends of the transmission.

Parity is therefore one of the settings you have to specify on your modem to make a connection. It's usually set to None, or Even, but it depends on the modem calling.

parity bit: A redundant bit added to a byte in data transmission as part of an error-checking technique.

parity error: An error caused by mismatched parity bits in a byte of transmitted data.

parse (v): To interpret an instruction by breaking it down and analyzing its parts.

Pascal: A beginner's programming language, often used as a stepping stone to C.

passive star: A network design with a central hub that connects all the branches but does not retransmit signals that pass through it.

password: A secret code used to restrict access to an account, channel, file, and so on to only authorized users who know the password. A bad password is one that is a real word or is otherwise easily guessable (a birth date, a pet's name, and so on). A good password contains upper and lowercase letters and numerals, and the longer it is, the better.

passwd: The UNIX command to change an account's password.

patch (n) A quick-and-dirty correction that fixes a bug, or at least works around it.

(v) To fix a problem with a temporary work around or kluge.

path: 1. A bang path, the route an e-mail message takes between its sender and receiver;

2. The channel through which a signal passes;

3. A completely specified location of a directory or file, starting from the root directory.

PC: A *personal computer*, generally a microcomputer, usually either an IBM PC or compatible, a Macintosh, or perhaps an Amiga.

PC-compatible Said of a computer that emulates the functionality of an IBM PC.

PC Eudora: A Windows mail program (a port of Eudora for the Macintosh) that PC uses Post Office Protocol (POP) and can function as an offline mail reader. It is available via anonymous FTP from ftp.qualcomm.com.

PC Gopher for DOS: A gopher client for the IBM PC or compatible running any flavor of DOS, available via anonymous FTP from sunsite.unc.edu.

PC Pursuit: A SprintNet service that allows users to connect directly to another computer.

PC/TCP Plus for DOS: DOS software that enables an IBM PC or compatible to connect via modem to a computer connected to the Internet for FTP and telnet.

PC-Xware: Windows software that includes TCP/IP, NFS, FTP, and server access for X Window applications, developed by Network Computing Devices. Inc.

PDIAL: *Public Dial Up Internet Access List,* Peter Kaminski's excellent list of Internet service providers, 'complete with cost information, posted regularly to alt.internet.access.wanted and alt.bbs.lists, and available via anonymous FTP from rtfm.mit.edu in the /pub/usenet/news.answers directory, with the file name pdial.

PDP-11 A series of DEC computers now largely superseded by VAXen. PDP stands for *programmed data processor.* The PDP-11 series was preceded by PDP-10, according to hacker lore the first real timesharing machine.

PeaceNet A BBS for nonprofit organizations, religious organizations, and people concerned with peace and justice. For more information, anonymous FTP to igc.org in the /pub directory.

peer A network device that communicates directly with other devices on the network.

peer-to-peer (adj) A network architecture in which each computer on the network can communicate directly with other nodes and function as both a client and a server

Pegasus Mail Also known as *p-mail,* a freeware e-mail program for IBM PCs and compatibles and Macintoshes, available via FTP from risc.ua.edu.

PENpages A database and information service covering every imaginable aspect of rural life in general and agriculture in particular, administrated by Pennsylvania State University. It is updated daily and the latest additions are always available on the main menu.

To connect, telnet to psupen.psu.edu and log in as your two-letter state abbreviation (no password).

Pentium A 64-bit micro-processor, Intel's successor to the 80486 chip (named Pentium after the courts decided that Intel could not defend as a trademark the number 586 or 80586).

The discovery of an error in the muchvaunted chip has spun off a long series of jokes about rounding errors (for example, "Q" How many Pentiums does it take to screw in a lightbulb? A: 1.9999965786.

peon: An ordinary user with no special privileges.

peripheral (adj): Said of a device that is not essential to the computer or physically a part of it (as opposed to the processor or hard-disk drive), such as a printer or modem.

Perl: A programming language (it stands for practical *extraction and report language)* distributed over Usenet, favored by UNIX system administrators.

permissions: Settings associated with an account on a network or multiuser system that define a level of access (to certain system resources) permitted to the user of the account.

PGP: A shareware public-key encryption program (it stands for *pretty good privacy),* developed by Phillip Zimmerman. For more information see the Web page at http:// www. mantis. co. uk/pgp/pgp.html.

phage: (n) A program that modifies other programs or databases in unauthorized ways.

phreak (v): To crack (break into) a network or phone system.

physical: Said of hardware and mechanical connections, as opposed to logical.

physical layer: Layer 1 (the bottom layer) of the OSI Model; it defines protocols for connecting cables and other hardware.

pico: A full-screen, modeless text editor for UNIX machines based on the built-in editor in the pine e-mail program.

pile-on (n): A flame war in which many participants take turns attacking a single victim, creating long posts of polymorphous abuse.

pine: A UNIX e-mail program whose name is a recursive acronym (pine stands for *pine is* 'not elm). Pine has a built-in full-screen, modeless editor, MIME support, and the ability to attach files.

.pinerc: *(dot-pine-are-see)* A setup file for pine.

ping (v) 1. To check the presence of a host with PING; 2. To send e-mail to an entire mailing list, requesting a response, in order to check which addresses are still valid.

PING Said to stand for *Packet Internet* a protocol for sending a signal to Whether another network host or other device is online and responding. (It's probably actually named for the sound made by submarine sonar/depth equipment.)

pipe (v): To send the output of a process or dump the contents of a file to a device (such as a printer), program (such as one that will the data), or another file.

(n) The character used in the piping process.

Pipeline for Windows: Windows front end software for a connection to a service provider, developed by Pipeline.

.pit: The file extension for Macintosh PackIt files. (PackIt has largely been superseded as a Macintosh compression standard by StuffIt.)

pixel: A single dot on a monitor or in a bit mapped image.

.pkg: The file extension for an Applelink Package file.

pkunzip: The uncompression program for pkzipped files.

pkzip: A DOS file compression program.

plain ASCII: Said of an ASCII text file (a document with no word-processor formatting).

.plan: A text file that is displayed when your username is fingered. Originally intended to alert people to your whereabouts or immediate plans, .plan files have evolved into personalized files sometimes filled with information or absurdities.

platform: A computer operating system type.

plokta: *Press lots of keys to abort.* Many newbie posts end with a pathetic series of attempts to a quit while still in insert mode, like so

***Plonk*:** A follow-up post that means I just put you in my kill file." (It's supposed to be the sound of the bozo falling into the kill file.)

p-mail: 1. Pegasus Mail; 2. Physical mail, as opposed to e-mail.

point at: To start a client program, such as a Web browser, by supplying it with an address, as in "Point your Web browser at http:/ /enterzone. berkeley.edu/enterzone. html to see the latest episode of Entorzone."

point of presence (POP): A local phone number connected to a modem connected to the network of a service provider., to enable users to log in to the network without paying long distance charges.

Point-to-Point Protocol (PPP): A TCP/IP protocol, similar to SLIP, for transmitting IP datagrams over serial lines such as phone lines. With PPP, PC users can connect to the Internet and still function in their native environment (instead of having to deal with a character-based UNIX environment).

poll (v): 1. To check a port to see whether a device is connected and available for network or communications activity; 2. To connect to another system to check for new mail or news.

port (n): 1, A socket on the back of a computer for connecting cables and hence modems, printers, etc.; 2. On Internet hosts, a channel dedicated to a specific program, so that a multiplexing host can run telnet sessions on one port, FTP connections on another, logins on another, etc.; 3. The interface between a router and a network; 4. A version of a program that was originally designed for a different platform.
(v) To translate software designed for one platform so that it will run on another.

post (v): 1. To send a message to a mailing list or an article to a newsgroup;
2. To publish information in any medium on the Internet. (The word *post* comes from the bulletin-board metaphor, in which scraps of paper are posted to the board to be read by anyone who comes by, as opposed to the British usage, which means to send mail.)
(n) A message sent to a mailing list or newsgroup.

postcardware: Shareware that's almost free, except the programmer requests that satisfied users send a postcard

postmaster A person who oversees a network's e-mail connection to the internet. Questions about users at a host or problems with e-mail to or from that host can often be addressed to postmasuer@host name.dimain.

Post Office Protocol (POP) A protocol that specifies how a personal computer can connect to a mail server on the Internet and download e-mail.

PostScript A proprietary "page-description" computer language developed by Adobe Systems It describes pages (text, graphics, layout) in mathematical terms. Post Script files generally have a .ps or .eps extension.

Pot.Kettle. Black: A shorthand newsgroup or mailing list follow-up, criticizing the previous poster for exhibiting the same foibles she was faulting another for. (It's short for the aphorism "That's like the pot calling the kettle black.")

pour (v): To pipe the output from a process or file to a device or other file.

power cycling: Turning the hardware off, waiting, and then turning it on again.

PPP: *Point-to-Point Protocol,* a TCP/IP protocol similar to SLIP for transmitting IP datagrams over serial lines such as phone lines. With PPP, PC users can connect to, the Internet and still function in their native environment (instead of having to deal with a character-based UNIX environment).

presentation layer: Layer 6 of the OSI Model, it defines how data is formed, encoded, converted, and presented.

prime time: The period of heaviest usage of a network, usually 9-to-5 the work week.

Principia Discordia: An underground track that elucidates the worship of Eris, ancient goddess of discord.

printed circuit: A computer chip with microcircuits literally printed (via a photographic process) onto it.

Printer Access Protocol (PAP): The AppleTalk protocol that defines how a workstation and a printer communicate.

privacy: Because the Internet is not inherently secure, users are cautioned to e-mail and post only information that they don't mind being public, or take steps to increase the privacy of their communication, either via encryption, through anonymity, or by using other communications channels entirely.

privacy-enhanced mail (PEM): E-mail-handling systems that incorporate encryption techniques to secure privacy and verification of message integrity.

private key: In public-key encryption, the secret key the user reveals to no one and uses to sign outgoing messages and to decrypt incoming messages that were encrypted with the public key.

private virtual circuit (PVC) Software circuits that maintain a private line between hosts.

privatization: On the Internet, generally refers to the U.S. government's process of placing maintenance of backbone networks in the hands of private organizations. So far this has not significantly changed the pricing structure for individual users.

privilages: Also called access privileges, a set of system resource and directory actions that a user is permitted to perform.

process: A program or part of a program being executed in a multitasking operating system. More generally, one task of many that a computer is doing.

ProComm Plus: A popular communications package for IBM PCs and compatibles, sold by Datastorm Technologies.

.profile: A startup file in some flavors of UNIX.

programmer: A person who writes computer programs.

programming: The process of writing programs.

.project: On some systems, a file similar to a plan that is displayed when a user is fingered, intended to discuss the project the user is currently working on.

project Gutenberg: An organization that publishes uncopyrighted books on the Internet, reachable via anonymous FTP at mrcnext.cso. uiuc.edu.

prompt (n): Also *command-line prompt*, a string of text that a character-based operating system displays on the screen to tell a user that it is ready to accept input (such as a command or the name of a program to run).

propagation: The process of dissemination for packets in general, and Usenet newsfeeds in particular, as they are passed from computer to computer. Propagation delays are responsible for the sometimes confusing situation that occurs when you read a follow-up to a post that hasn't yet appeared at your site.

proprietary: Said of a technology, architecture, or set of protocols whose design is the property of the company that developed it.

Prospero: A distributed directory system, file system, and index service (and the protocol that underlies it) that allows users to access both local and remote directories in the same way. For more information, connect via anonymous FTP to prospero.isi. edu and go to the /pub/ prospero directory.

protocol: An agreed-upon set of rules that allows otherwise incompatible machines or software to communicate. Protocols can govern a wide range of the aspects of communications, from the order in which bits are transmitted to the rules for opening and maintaining a connection to the format of an electronic mail message.

protocol layer: One portion of a set of protocols that handles one aspect of the transmission of data.

protocol stack: A set of protocol layers that work together to provide reliable communication between a computer and a network or another computer, also called a Protocol family or protocol suite. The TCP/IP protocol stack includes such protocols as TCP, IP, FTP, SMTP, telnet, and so on.

.ps The file extension for PostScript files.

pseudo (n) A new identity assumed on Usenet in order that the user might act (provocatively or otherwise) without those actions being associated with the user's real (or better-known) name.

/pub A UNIX directory often found on FTP hosts, where public information is stored and made available.

pubic directory Slang for an FTP public *directory*.

public data network (PDN) A type of commercial packet-switched network offering wide-area services to customers, with sophisticated error-checking, buffering, and handling of *protocols*. Tymnet, SprintNet, and the CompuServe Packet Network are all PDNs.

Public Dial-Up Internet Access List (PDIAL) Peter Kaminski's excellent list of Internet service providers, complete with cost information, posted regularly to alt. internet.access.wanted and alt.bbs.lists, and available via anonymous FTP from rtfm. mit.edu in the /pub/usenet/ news. answers directory, with the file name pdial.

public domain (adj): Available for free to the public, uncopyrighted, as are much of the information, system software, and applications available on the Internet.

public key: In public-key encryption, the key a user distributes freely and which correspondents use to encrypt messages to the user and decrypt the user's signature (encrypted with the user's private key) on messages from the user.

public-key encryption: A form of key encryption which uses two keys, a public key (for encrypting messages) and a private key (for decrypting messages) to enable users to verify each other's messages without having to securely exchange secret keys.

public libraries: Many libraries have made their card catalogs available and searchable via the Internet, often telnet addresses. The easiest to many libraries is with Hytelnet.

publishing: posting on the Net (to newsgroups, the Web, gopher. etc.) is considered equivalent to publishing, though the paradigm is different—the readers comes to you and you do not distribute the information.

put (v): To copy a file from your host computer to a remote site, particularly via FTP. (n) The FTP command to put a file.

Q

q: The quit command in many UNIX programs. (Often a capital Q will mean quick *quit* and will allow you to quit without any questions.)

qotd: (written only, also QOTD) *Quotation of the day.* Some systems display a quotation when you log in. Some Usenet posters change the quotations in their sig block daily.

query (n): 1. A search request submitted to a database to find a particular record (piece of information) or all records that meet certain criteria, such as an archie query;
2. A question mark.

question mark ?: 1. A wildcard character in UNIX (and hence in many Internet applications), it stands for any single character., 2. A help command in some character-based applications.

questionnaires: Usenet news-groups are often bombarded by purveyors of questionnaires hoping to exploit a ready made audience. That the responders are self-selecting doesn't seem to bother the questioneers, but to regular readers of the newsgroups, these posts and the ubiquitous surveys get tiresome awfully fast.

queue *(cue,* n): A list of items (such as print jobs or messages) waiting to be sent from one device to another.

QuickTime: An Apple technology that debuted with Macintosh System 7. It compresses, Stores, and plays back files combining text, sound, animation, and video, Many QuickTime clips are distributed via the Internet and the Web.

quit: To stop running an application and (usually) return to the operating system.

quoting: Including a relevant portion of a preceding article when posting a follow-up. Most newsreaders precede quoted text with a symbol, such as >, and try to indicate who said what, though multiple embedded quotations often require that the latest author untangle the attributions. It is bad netiquette to quote no text (unless the follow-up makes it absolutely clear what it is responding to), and it's both bad netiquette and an unmistakable marker of a clueless newbie to quote an entire article merely to add "I agree" or "Right on, dOOd" at the end.

QWERTY (n): The standard typewriter and computer-keyboard layout, so named for the first six characters of the first alphabetical row.

R

RAM (ram) *Random access memory,* memory that any application or process can read or write to. It's frequently confused with storage, because both resources are often measured in megabytes.

ranking: The order in which a WAIS program displays the results of a database search—from most likely to least likely.

rb: The Ymodem command for receiving (uploading) a file.

rc file: A UNIX text file with a file name of the form, *rc, containing command line instructions or other startup information for an application or for the operating system itself. Examples include newsrc, pinerc, and so on.

rcp: The UNIX remote copy command.

read: To copy data from a disk into memory.

README file: An information file describing the contents of an FIT directory or the files associated with an application.

readme.txt: Typical name for a README file.

read notification: A feature of some e-mail programs that lets you know when the recipient of your e-mail has received and opened the message.

read-only (adj): Said of a file that can be read but not altered.

read-write (adj): Said of a file that can be both read and written to (altered).

real life: The offline world, as in the question "What do you do in real life".

real name: Also called a full name, a user's full name as it appears on e-mail messages and Usenet posts., as opposed to their username (the real name can also be a pseudonym). On UNIX systems, the user's real name is a variable that can be set with the chfn command. Many Windows and Macintosh Internet applications allow the user to enter or change a real name on the fly.

Real Soon Now Also *RSN,* similar to *as soon as possible* but with a subtext that it ain't really gonna happen any time soon.

real time: Also *realtime,* the time used for synchronous communication, in which both participants must be available. Also, taking place at me present time, live, not delayed or recorded.

reboot: To restart a crashed operating system, either through a designated key combination (a warm boot), or by turning it off and on again (power cycling).

rec.: A Usenet hierarchy devoted *to* recreation.

receipt notification: A proof of delivery feature provided by sonic e-mail programs (similar to the idea of registered mail in the real world).

record (n): A set of related data from a database.

recursive acronym: An acronym that contains the acronym itself in its spelled out form, such as GNU, which stands for *GNU's not UNIX,* and pine, which stands for pine is not elm.

redirection: Sending output from one device or file to another device or file.

refresh: To redraw the screen, usually either to reflect changes to the data or to restore the screen when something has marred its intended appearance.

redundant path: A secondary path that a router can assign to a packet when the normal route is not available.

register (v): To sign up and pay for shareware.
(n) A designated area of memory.

registered jack (RJ): Any of a series of specialized jacks used tor connecting wires, such as RJ-11 and RJ-45.

rehi *(ree-high)*: *Hi again,* typed on IRC when you rejoin a channel.

relevance feedback: A system used by WAIS applications to rank documents retrieved in a search in order of relevance to the search criteria. Documents are ranked based on the number of times that key words from the query appear in them.

reliable: Said of networks with dedicated connections.

religious issues: Neverending debates (such as those that go on in some of the talk. newsgroups) on subjects such as abortion, gun control, or IBM PC vs. Mac.

remailer: A program that receives e-mail and then resends it, with different information attached.

remote: Said of a host or other network resource that is locate d on a computer or network elsewhere, as opposed to a local host or resource.

remote access: The process of accessing another computer's resources, such as files or printers. Dial-up accounts and telnet are both forms of remote access.

remote login: To connect to a remote computer over a network, usually done on the Internet with telnet or rlogin.

Remote network monitoring: *Network monitors,* also known as network analyzers or probes, are quite useful for network management. They basically collect and analyze the packets going through them. These data may be statistics, such as packet sizes, number of collisions, and number of packets per second. In relation to management stations, these network monitors are remote; hence, they are known as *remote network monitors* (RMON). These network monitors, by using the RMON MIB, can be extended to collect data for network management and to communicate with management stations. Note that the RMON MIB extends MIB-II RFC 1271 defined MIB objects primarily for the Ethernet protocol. RFC 1513 is an extension of RFC 1271 and defines the MIB objects required for monitoring networks running on tokenring protocols. RFC 1757 makes RFC 1271 obsolete. RFC 1757 is basically the same as RFC 1271, except it corrects and clarifies some of the terms, such as channel and captureBuffer, used in RFC 1271. Management data collected by a network monitor is sent to management stations. This can be on an exception basis, that is, when changes happen. The location of the network monitors is implementation-dependent. One network monitor can be placed per segment, per subnetwork, or per token-ring network.

As an example, in which there is one network monitor for each subnetwork. FDDI rings have management stations M1 and M2.

Remote network monitors are placed in RMON agents Al, A2, A3, and A4, which provide functions such as protocol support for communication with management stations and error recovery for the remote network monitors. RMON agents act as intermediaries between remote network monitors and management stations. For transfer of data to management stations, these RMON agents can use SNMPvl or SNMPv2 protocols. However, if RMON agents are to be implemented, SNMPv2 is preferable because SNMPvl agents must ultimately migrate to SNMPv2 agents. We have made the assumption that RMON agents communicate with only one management station. It is not necessary to have this restriction; an RMON agent carrying a remote network monitor may send data to one or more management stations. Also, these RMON agents can be placed in hosts, routers, and bridges, and there are no set rules prescribed in RFC 1757 or RFC 1513 on the placement of remote network monitors.

This particular approach of having a network monitor exclusively for the purpose of network management has its own advantages. The network monitor can continuously collect data and selectively send it to the management stations. Also, when thresholds are crossed, events may be formed and alarms can be sent to the management stations. This action can help reduce network traffic, because the data collected is logged in agents with network monitors instead of transmitting every piece of data to the management stations. When the management stations need further details, they can access and collect the information required from the agents with remote network monitors.

RFC 1757 covers some of the scenarios where remote networking monitoring may be used. These include:

Offline operation: Primarily relates to cases in which the network monitor operates as a stand-alone monitoring device. These cases can arise due to communication failure between the remote network monitor and a management station, or due to selective collection of data by a management station.

Because a remote network monitor can operate independently of the management station, it can continue to perform its operation of continuously collecting and storing data. The management station, in turn, can retrieve these data stored whenever required.

Communication with management stations on an exception basis: Because the remote network monitor can function independently of management stations, it can collect data on the network and log data for analysis at a later time. When problems are observed in the network due to crossing thresholds or failures, notifications can be sent to management stations. Management stations can retrieve the logged data for problem analysis and diagnostics.

Relevant data collection: A monitor can also concentrate on the hosts in its portion of the network that have maximum traffic or errors and can log the data required for management stations. This will help in zeroing in on a portion of the network, as well as with the collection of data on the critical hosts in a network.

Multiple management stations: Management stations may be organized on the basis of actions performed. Under these circumstances, it may be necessary to concurrently deal with more than one management station to which a network monitor is reporting. Also, a breakdown by function, such as accounting, will help reduce the workload in management stations and makes it easy to focus on each of the functions. This can help to centralize the data required for certain network management functions such as configuration management. In many cases, configuration management activities need to be centralized in one management station. Similarly, under certain circumstances, it may be necessary to have centralized fault management, including monitoring, in another management station. So, a scenario where a remote network monitor may have to communicate with more than one management station becomes quite common, especially in large networks with thousands of workstations.

RMON for Ethernet (RFC 1757) Objects defined in the remote network monitoring MIB are primarily for the Ethernet protocol. They can be expanded to cover token-ring and FDDI protocols. RMON objects are defined using the guidelines furnished in SMI (RFC 1155). However, in addition to the ASN.1 data types mentioned in SMI, RMON defines the following two data types:

OwnerString (DisplayString): Contains information such as IP address, management station name, network manager's name, location, and phone number. This data type is used for identifying the owner of a resource, and helps in resolving conflicts when more than one management station is the owner of a resource. For example, if an instance of a resource is to be deleted by a management station, then there is the possibility that one management station may delete the instance created by another management station. But, by identifying the owner, a rule may be made that only the management station that created an object instance can delete that object instance. Thus, the data type OwnerString is useful when resources are shared by more than one management station.

EntryStatus (INTEGER): Useful when a resource is shared by more than one owner. Suppose that an object instance is created by,, one owner. At the same time or later, another management station' creates an object instance with conflicting values to the one that has been already created. In such a case, there can be major problems regarding the validity of values. The major question is which are the correct values? Under such circumstances, EntryStatus is quite useful because it helps to determine whether an object instance exists.

EntryStatus has these values: valid = 1, createRequest = 2, underCreation = 3, and invalid = 4. As we have seen previously, creating an object instance is equivalent to creating a row entry in a MIB table. So, when an object instance is created, we have the value createRequest. Creating an instance may lead to supplementary actions such as creation of more objects by an agent. During this operation, the value is set to underCreation. When this operation is completed, the value is set to valid, abort, or invalid, depending on the results of the object creation operation. Another management station that wants to create the same entry will get a result of error. Thus, it is prudent for a management station to check whether an object instance has already been created by checking EntryStatus.

After examining the new data types OwnerString and OwnerStatus, we can conclude that their primary objective is for facilitating resource sharing. This is due to the fact that network monitors can send monitored data to more than one management station, which is one of the salient points of RMON. These objects are transmitted across the wires using the BER, which was discussed in earlier chapters. Under the subtree {mib-2 16}, new groups for RMON are defined. Nine main groups are defined in RFC 1757. The tokenRing group, {rmon 10}, has been added in RFC 1513 specifically for monitoring networks working with the token-ring protocol.

Ethernet statistics group Objects in the statistics group are used to collect statistics on each of the monitored devices. The statistics group has one table, etherStatsTable, which is formed as shown in Figure 9.5. etherStatsTable will have a row for each Ethernet interface. Thus, there are etherStatsEntryl to etherStatsEntryN in the etherStatsTable, and each etherStatsEntry has columns from etherStatsIndex and etherStatsDataSource up to etherStatsStatus. Data types for the statistics group are mainly counters, and they are created with a value of zero. In the statistics group, objects are:

etherStatsIndex (INTEGER): Provides the row position in the etherStatsTable.

etherStatsDataSource (OBJECT IDENTIFIER): Relates to the Ethernet interface from which a remote network monitor is receiving the data.

etherStatsDropEuents (Counter): Provides the number of times packets were dropped in network monitors for limitations of resources, such as lack of storage space.

etherStatsOctets (Counter): Provides the total number of octets received on the network monitor from an Ethernet interface. This includes the total number of data octets and FCS octets. However, these octets do not include the framing bits.

etherStatsPkts (Counter): Includes the total number of packets received, including those packets which had errors.

etherStatsBroadcastPkts (Counter): Furnishes the total number of good broadcast packets received in an Ethernet interface.

etherStatsMulticastPkts (Counter): While in etherStats-BroadcastPkts, the concern is good broadcast packets; in etherStatsMulticastPkts, a count of good multicast packets is kept.

etherStatsCRCAlignErrors (Counter): Provides the number of packets which were between length 64 and 1518 octets or had FCS errors. While counting the length, the FCS octets are included but the framing bits are excluded.

etherStatsUndersizePkts (Counter): Relates to the total number of good packets which had lengths less than 64 octets.

etherStatsOversizePkts (Counter): Refers to the well-formed packets which had lengths greater than 1518 octets.

etherStatsFragments (Counter): Provides data on packets which had bad lengths or FCS errors, and were of lengths less than 64 octets.

etherStatsJabbers (Counter): etherStatsFragments provides details on the bad packets which are of lengths less than 64 octets. We need to have data on bad packets which are over the Ethernet length limit of 1518 octets. etherStatsJabbers provides this data.

etherStatsCollisions (Counter): Provides the number of collisions in a subnetwork.

etherStatsPkts64Octets through *etherStatsPkts1024to-1518Octets*: Provide granularity for counters by breaking them into different counters for lengths of packets ranging from 64 to 1518 octets. Note that these packets also include the error packets.

etherStatsOwner (OwnerString): Identifies the owner that created this row in the etherStatsTable. As we have seen earlier, OwnerString furnishes many details.

etherStatsStatus (EntryStatus): Provides the status of the etherStats entry.

Objects in the statistics group are basically very useful for performance management, but some of them, such as etherStatsDropEvents, etherStatsCRCAlignErrors, and etherStatsUndersizePkts, will be useful for fault management, too. If corrective action is to be taken before a failure occurs, then it may be useful to have thresholds set for objects such as etherStatsDrop Events, ether StatsCRCAlign Errors, and etherStats Collisions.

History group In the history group, samples at fixed time intervals are collected and stored. This data can be used for analysis in fault and performance management. As is apparent from the figure, there are two tables: historyControl Table and etherHistoryTable. history ControlTable provides information on how data are to be collected. Corresponding to a row in the historyControlTable there are one or more rows of data in etherHistoryTable. etherHistoryTable has the actual data which is useful for analysis purposes. This pattern is followed by some tables in RMON MIB. RFC 1757 recommends that while collecting data, it is better to start data collection at the beginning of the next hour of the day. If data is collected for different stations in a network uniformly at the same time, data will be useful and meaningful for comparison purposes. Objects of thehistory Control Table are:

historyControlIndex (INTEGER): *A* unique identifier of an entry in the historyControlTable. Each entry defines a set of entries in the etherHistoryTable on an Ethernet interface.

historyControlDataSource (OBJECT IDENTIFIER): Relates to the Ethernet interface on which a remote network monitor is collecting data.

historyControlBuckersRequested (INTEGER): Porovides the requested number of sampling intervals.

historyControlBucketsGranted (INTEGER): In a network monitor there may be limitations on resources, so naturally, a network monitor cannot always provide the numbers of sampling intervals as requested inhistoryControlBuckets Requested. As a result, history-ControlBucketsGranted furnishes the feasible number of sampling intervals, and, as is obvious, the historyControl BucketsGranted value is kept as close to the value requested by history Control Buckets Requested.

historyControlInterval (INTEGER): Refers to the sampling interval in seconds for each bucket. The value can be set from 1 to 3600 seconds.

history ControlOwner (OwnerString): Identifies the owner which created this row in the historyControlTable. Because management stations will be using the data collected, history Control Owner refers to a management station.

historyControlStatus (EntryStatus): Provides the status of historyControlEntry.

etherHistoryTable has the data which have been collected over an Ethernet interface. Parameters for data collection are guided by history ControlEntry. The columns in etherHistoryTable starting from etherHistoryDropEvents up to etherHistoryCollisions are similar to those in the etherStatsTable, and mean almost the same thing, therefore, we will discuss those objects which are unique to the etherHistoryTable. These objects are:

etherHistoryIndex (INTEGER): Has the same value as historyControlIndex. This entry links the historyControl-Table and etherHistoryTable.

etherHistorySampleIndex (INTEGER): Each etherHistory-Index has one or more entries for etherHistorySample Index. This entry starts from 1, and each sample has a unique value increasing by 1.

etherHistoryIntervalStart (YYrnencks): Refers to the sysUpTime when data collection was started.

etherHistoryUtilization (INTEGER): Provides the best estimate of the mean physical layer network utilization in percentage over the time interval during which data collection was done etherHistoryUtilization refers to the utilization over one Ethernet interface.

Alarm: roup Implementation of the alarm group is optional. If it is implemented, then the event group must also be implemented because they are interrelated. In the alarm group periodic samples are collected and then compared with the threshold values. If the value of a monitored variable crosses the threshold, then an event is generated. Objects in this group are useful for performance management. Events generated are useful for fault management. The alarm group uses an alarmTable which has entries stating how samples are to be taken and how the alarms are to be generated. The objects in the alarmTable are:

alarmIndex (INTEGER): A unique identifier which identifies a row in the alarmTable. alarmIndex refers to a sample for an object at a particular interval of time.

alarmInterval (INTEGER): States the time interval during which samples are taken from an object being observed.

alarmVariable (OBJECT IDENTIFIER): Refers to the identifier of the object being sampled. The object being sampled should have a data type of INTEGER, Counter, Gauge, or TimeTicks.

alarmSampleType (INTEGER): States how sample values are interpreted. It has two values: absoluteValue = 1 and deltaValue= 2. If the sample value is the absoluteValue, then it is compared against the threshold value for generating alarms. However, if it is a deltaValue, then the previous sample value is subtracted from the current value and this difference is compared with the threshold values.

alarmValue (INTEGER): Provides the last valid sample value. A sample value is complete and available only at the end of a sampling period.

alarmStartupAlarm (INTEGER): Has three values: rising-Alarm 1, fallingAlarm = 2, and risingOrFalling-Alarm = 3. This states what type of alarm will be generated. When a sample value is greater than or equal to alarmRisingThreshold, and, alarmStartupAlarm is equal to risingAlarm or risingOrFalling Alarm, then a single rising alarm will be generated. Similarly, when a sample value is less than or equal to alarm. FallingThreshold and the alarmStartupAlarm is equal to fallingAlarm or risingOrFallingAlarm, then a falling alarm will be generated. These conditions can result in events being generated and sent to network monitors or management stations.

alarmRisingThreshold (INTEGER): Represents a threshold value for a monitored object. A rising event can be generated when the sample value of a monitored object is greater than or equal to alarmRisingThreshold. The previous value should not have crossed the alarmRisingThres hold value. A rising event can also be generated if the first value of this entry is greater than or equal to the alarmRisingThres hold value and the associated alarmStartupAlarm is equal to risingAlarm or risingOrFalling Alarm.

alarmFallingThreshold (INTEGER): Similar to the alarmRisingThreshold, but it represents a threshold value in the opposite direction. When a sampled value is less than or equal to this alarmFallingThres hold and when the value of the previous sampling interval was greater than the alarmFalling Threshold, a falling event is generated. A falling event is also generated if the value of the first entry is less than or equal to this threshold value and the associated alarmStartupAlarm is equal to fallingAlarm or risingOrFallingAlarm.

alarmRisingEventIndex (INTEGER): Used to identify the event generated when a rising threshold is crossed. The value in this entry corresponds to the eventIndex in an eventTable. If there is n corresponding entry in eventIndex, then there is no relationship this alarm entry with the event entry in eventTable. If this value zero, then there is no valid entry in eventTable.

alarmFallingEuentIndex (INTEGER): While alarmRising-EventIndex is used when crossing rising thresholds, alarmFallingEventIndex is used when a falling thresholds is crossed.

alarmOwner (OwnerString): Refers to one or more management stations which configured this entry in alarmTable.

alarmStatus (EntryStatus): Refers to the status of the entry in alarmTable.

Host group: The host group contains statistics on each of the hosts discovered in the network. These are derived by noting good packets received on the network. Each host is identified by the MAC address.

hostControl Table: The entries in this table determine how the statistics on hosts are to be maintained. Based on the parameters' of this table, data is collected and entered in hostTable and hostTimeTable.

hostTable: Has entries on each host based on the MAC addresses. These MAC addresses are used to index into hostTable.

hostimeTable: The rows in this table are arranged in order of hostTimeCreationOrder. The hostTimeCreationOrder column of the table starts from 1, and this is used for indexing into hostTimeTable. There is a subtle difference between hostTable and hostTimeTable. In hostTable, we index into the table using MAC addresses, while in hostTimeTable, we index into the table using hostTimeCreationOrder.

The format of the data collected is the same for both tables. By indexing in the order in which the entries are created in hostTimeTable, it is easier to download these tables by means of management stations using SNMP. Also, it is easy to break the packets into manageable SNMP PDUs. The other advantage is that to get details of new hosts added after a download of data from hostTimeTable, entries must be downloaded after a particular value of *N* instead of downloading hostTimeTable all over again.

The entries in hostTable and hostTimeTable are useful for configuration, performance, and fault management. Knowing the addresses of hosts in a network by frequently downloading the entries in hostTimeTable helps in keeping track of the active hosts in the network. When entries are deleted from hostTimeTable, the configuration of the network on the hosts can be accordingly modified. The different objects of the host group are:

hostControlIndex (INTEGER): Each discovered host in a network has an entry in hostControlTable. hostControl Index is a unique identifier for a row and a host.

hostControlDataSource (OBJECT IDENTIFIER): Identifies t source for data. This source can be any interface on a host and h a corresponding entry in ifIndex.

hostControlTableSize (INTEGER): Corresponds to the number of entries in hostTable for a host. As the entries in hostTable and hostTimeTable have one-to-one correspondence, this number also refers to the number of entries in hostTimeTable.

hostControlLastDeleteTime (TimeTicks): Relates to the time when an entry was last deleted from hostTable. A zero value indicates that no deletions were made in hostTable.

hostControlOwner and *hostControlStatus*: have the same significance as described earlier in other RMON MIB groups. In both hostTable and hostTimeTable, only the objects which need explanation will be examined, and we will avoid discussing those objects which are similar in meaning to the ones already explained. Some of the objects which need explanation are:

hostAddress (OCTET STRING): Refers to the MAC address of the host.

hostCreationOrder (INTEGER): A number from I to *N* and having a corresponding row in hostControlEntry. The numbers in hostCreationOrder are increased by one as a new entry is created.

hostIndex (INTEGER): The value in this column is the same as the value in hostControlIndex.

hostInPkts (Counter): Provides the number of good packets received through this host address, furnished by hostAddress, after adding this host to hostTable.

hostOutPkts (Counter): Identifies the total number of packets transmitted by the host, including the error packets.

hostInOctets (Counter): Contains the total number of octets received by this host after it was added to hostTable. hostInOctets does not include error octets and framing bits.

hostOutOctets (Counter): Furnishes the total number of octets transmitted by this host. It includes error octets, but does not include framing bits in the count of octets.

hostOutErrors (Counter): Relates to the number of error packets transmitted by a host after being added to the host table. This object is very useful for performance and fault management. hostOutErrors along with hostOutOctets can furnish solid information on how a host is behaving.

hostOutBroadcastPkts (Counter): A counter for the number of good broadcast packets transmitted by this host after this entry was added to hostTable.

hostOutMulticastPkts (Counter): Counter contains only the packets transmitted to multicast addresses after being added to the host table. Because the distinction has been made between multicast and broadcast, this counter naturally does not include the number of packets broadcast by this host.

The entries in hostTimeTable are:

hostTimeAddress (OCTET STRING): Pertains to the MAC address of the host.

hostTime Creation Order (INTEGER): The index used for hostTimeTable. The entries are arranged sequentially from one to N. This entry has the same value as hostControlTableSize of hostControlTable.

hostTimeIndex (INTEGER): Has the same value as hostControl Index of hostControlTable.

In hostTimeTable, other entries, from *hostInPkts* up to and including *hostOutMulticast Pkts,* have the same significance as described in host Table.

HostTopN group: The HostTopN group can be used to report the statistics on a group of hosts over a period of time. These statistics on selected hosts over a sampling interval is known as a report and is sent to one or more management stations. These statistics are derived from the host group. The interval for collecting data and start and stop times from the host group is determined by management stations. Once the data is collected in hostTop NTable, then it is available for management stations. The implementation of the Host TopN group is optional. However, if this group is implemented, then the Host group must also be implemented. Data collected from the HostTopN group are useful for performance and fault management. The objects in the HostTopN group are:

hostToPNControlIndex (INTE-GER): *A* unique entry which identifies a top *N* report for one interface.

hostTopNHostIndex (INTEGER): The value of this entry and the value of hostIndex in hostTable are the same.

hostTopNRateBase (INTEGER): Identifies an object in hostTable on which data is collected. The values of the objects in hostTopNRateBase are: hostTopNInPkts = 1, hostTopNOutPkts = 2, hostTopNInOctets = 3, hostTopN-OutOctets = 4, hostTopNOutErrors = 5, hostTopNOut-BroadcastPkts = 6, and hostTopNOutMulticast Pkts = 7. The significance of these variables is as explained in the host group.

hostTopTimeRemaining (INTE-GER): Provides the time remaining in the sampling interval to complete the data collection for hostTopNTable. Only when the value becomes zero will hostTopNEntry be available. If the value is nonzero, then host top N entries cannot be retrieved.

hostTopNDuration (INTEGER): Provides information on the sampling interval in seconds for the previous report, or, if the data is being collected, then this furnishes elapsed time since data collection started. The value of hostTopNDuration is set along with the value of hostTopN-TimeRemaining.

hostTopNRequestedSize (INTEGER): Identifies the maximum number of hosts requested for hostTopNTable. Here, the default value is 10.

hostTopNGrantedSize (INTE-GER): Furnishes the number of hosts on which data can be collected in hostTopNTable. Because there can be limitations on resources, sometimes this value cannot be equal to the value of hostTopNRequested-Size. This value should be set as close to hostTopNRequested-Size as possible.

hostTopNStartTime (TimeTicks): Provides sysUpTime at which hostTopNReport was started.

hostTopNOwner and *hostTopNStatus* have the same meaning as described previously for corresponding entries in other RMON groups. HostTopN group also has hostTopNTable, which includes the following objects:

hostTopNReport (INTEGER): Identifies a report. Its value is the same as the value of hostToPNControlIndex.

hostTopNIndex (INTEGER): Identifies a row in the hostTopNTable. hostTopN Index starts from 1 and increases by a value of 1.

hostToPNAddress (OCTET STRING): Refers to the MAC address of a host.

hostTopNRate (INTEGER): Provides the amount of change in the selected object, which is selected by hostTopNRateBase.

Matrix group: In the Matrix group the statistics on conversations between two sets of MAC addresses are maintained in two tables: matrixSDTable and matrixDSTable. Entries in these tables are controlled by the objects in matrixControlTable. In all these tables, when there are shortages of resources, the least recently used entries are deleted. Implementation of the matrix group is optional. matrixSDTable is primarily indexed on the basis of source and destination addresses. However, in matrixDSTable, the statistics on a conversation are indexed on the basis of destination and source addresses. So the major difference between these two tables is in the manner in which the tables are accessed for processing. These tables are useful for configuration, performance, and fault management. In configuration management, granularity may be depicted to the conversation levels, in which case, it is easy to collect data on active conversations from the matrix group. The explanations of objects in the matrix group are:

matrixControlIndex (INTEGER): Uniquely identifies an entry in matrixControlTable. For each matrixControlIndex entry, statistics are stored in matrixSDTable and matrixDSTable.

matrixControlDataSource (OBJECT IDENTIFIER): Represents the identifier of the source device on which conversation statistics are collected.

Other objects, from *matrixControlTableSize* through *matrixControl Status,* have the same meaning as corresponding objects in other *groups.*

matrixSDSourceAddress (OCTET STRING): Refers to the source MAC address for the conversation on which statistics are being collected. Note that the MAC address identifies a host.

matrixSDDestAddress (OCTET STRING): Refers to the destination MAC address.

matrixSDIndex (INTEGER): Has the same value as matrix ControlIndex in matrix ControlEntry. This entry helps to associate matrixControl Entry with a row in matrixSD Table.

matrixSDPkts (Counter): Provides the total number of packets transmitted from a source to the destination. It also includes error packets.

matrixSDOctets (Counter): Refers to the total number of good octets transmitted from a source to the destination address. It does not include framing bits but does include error octets.

matrixSDErrors (Counter): Includes error packets transmitted from a source to the destination address. By subtracting matrixSDErrors from matrixSDPkts, statistics on the number of good packets can be recovered.

The objects of matrix DSTable have similar meaning to those in matrixSDTable.

Filter group: The filter group helps in matching the conditions for capturing data or generating events. The concept of channels is used here. Input data is subjected to a set of filter rules stated in different variables in the filter group. Filter rules are applied to packet data and packet status. From the filter operation, a channel is obtained. The channel data can be stored with the aid of captureBuffer Table. Note that *channel is* a technical concept and not a physical component. If the channel is enabled, then *events* are generated. An event can also enable the channel on or off. From a channel, we can generate SNMP trap messages and log the events.

The filter group has two tables: filterTable and channelTable. The objects provided are:

filterIndex (INTEGER): A unique index which identifies an entry in filterTable.

filterChannelIndex (INTEGER): Identifies a channel and matches the channelIndex in channelTable.

filterPktData Offset (INTEGER): Points to the starting point in data after which a filter will be applied. The offset is measured after framing bits in a physical layer frame.

filterPktData (OCTET STRING): Provides the data for filtering. It is used along with filterPktDataMask and filterPktDataNotMask.

filterPktDataMask (OCTET STRING): Bits with Is are relevant. filterPktDataMask is extended with Is if it is shorter than filterPktData.

filterktDataNotMask (OCTET STRING): The inverse of the filterPktDataMask. If the filterPktDataNotMask is shorter than the filterPktData, then this mask is extended with 0s.

filterPktStatus (INTEGER): Matched with the input packet, and the input bits relevant here are those corresponding to Is in the filterPktStatusMask.

filterPktStatusMask (INTEGER): Applied to the filterPktStatus, and only those bits which have Is are relevant. Here, as with filterPktDataMask, if filterPktStatus is shorter than the filterPktStatusMask, then filterPktStatus is extended by adding Is.

filterPktStatusNotMask (INTE-GER): Operates inversely to filterPktStatusMask.

filterOwner and *filterStatus* have the same meanings as described for corresponding objects in other groups.

The objects in the channelTable are:

channelIndex (INTEGER): Identifies a unique entry in the channel table.

channelIfIndex (INTEGER): Uniquely identifies an interface on the RMON device (just like IfIndex).

channelAcceptType (INTEGER): Controls the actions of the filters associated with the channel. It has values of acceptMatched = 1 and acceptFailed = 2. In accept-Matched, packets will be accepted if there is a match of packet data and packet status. In acceptFailed, for a packet to be accepted, the packet data match or packet status match must fail.

channelDataControl (INTEGER): Controls the flow of data, status, and events through the channel. It has two values: on = 1 an~ off = 2. If the value is on, then data, status, and events can flow through the channel. If the status is off, then data, status, and events do not pass through the channel.

channel TurnOnEventIndex (INTEGER): Controls the generation of events. If an event is generated, then this value has a corresponding value in the eventIndex entry in eventTable.

channelTurnOffEventIndex (INTEGER): Will turn channel-DataControl to off from on, after an event is generated. It also has an entry in the eventIndex entry in eventTable.

channelEventIndex (INTEGER): Will identify the event to be generated when there is a packet match and channelDataControl is on.

channelEventStatus (INTEGER): Used for controlling the flow of events. It has three values: eventReady = 1, eventFired = 2, and eventAlwaysReady = 3. When this object is set to eventReady, an event will be generated and the object will change to the eventFired state. The eventAlwaysReady state will disable flow control, and events will be generated freely.

channelMatches (Counter): States the number of times there has been a packet match, including those cases where channelDataControl is off.

channelDescription (DisplayString): Describes the channel.

channelOwner and *channelStatus* have the same significance as described for corresponding objects in other groups.

Packet capture group On the basis of filters, packets are captured and stored in, capture Buffer Table of the packet capture group tables. A channel is associated with captureBuffer Table. bufferControlTable determines how filtered data are stored in captureBufferTable. One row of captureBuffer-Table is used to store data on packets from a channel. The implementation of the packet capture group is optional. If the Filter group is implemented, then this group must be implemented. The objects in the packet capture group are:

bufferControlIndex (INTEGER): A unique index that identifies a entry in bufferControlTable.

bufferControlChannelIndex (INTEGER): Identifies the channel Its value is the same as the value in channelIndex.

bufferControlFullStatus (INTEGER): Shows the status of the buffer which is used to store data received from filters. It has two values: spaceAvailable = 1 and full = 2.

bufferControlFullAction (INTEGER): *Will* indicate the action to be taken when the buffer becomes full. It has two values: lockWhenFull = 1 and wrapWhenFull = 2.

bufferControlCaptureSliceSize (INTEGER): Furnishes the maximum number of octets of each packet which will be stored in the capture buffer. If it is set to zero, then as many octets as possible will be saved in the capture buffer.

bufferControlDownloadSliceSize (INTEGER): States the maximum number of octets that will be retrieved from a management station by an SNMP GetRequest or GetNextRequest PDUs. The default value is 100 octets.

bufferControlDownloadOffset (INTEGER): States the offset after which data in the buffer will be retrieved by a management station with an SNMP GetRequest or GetNextRequest PDU. The default offset value is 0.

bufferControlMaxOctetsRequested (INTEGER): Furnishes the maximum number of octets which a management station desires a capture buffer to save. *A* default value of -1 indicates that the request by the management station to the monitoring device is to save as many octets as possible.

bufferControlMaxOctetsGranted (INTEGER): We have noted earlier that a monitoring device may have resource limitations. Under those circumstances, it is not possible to furnish the buffer space requested by a management station. buffer ControlMaxOctets Granted supplies the actual number of octets that can be saved, and if the default value is 1, then the capture buffer" will save as many octets as possible.

bufferControlCapturedPackets (INTEGER): Furnishes the nu ber of packets actually stored at present in a capture buffer.

bufferControlTurnOnTime (INTEGER): Provides sysUp Time when the capture buffer started functioning.

bufferControlOwner and *bufferControlStatus* have the same significance described for corresponding objects in other groups.

The captureBufferTable has the following entries:

captureBufferControlIndex (INTEGER): Provides the index of an entry in captureBufferTable.

captureBufferIndex (INTEGER): Increases in value by 1 from 1, and uniquely identifies an entry in captureBufferTable.

captureBufferPakcetID (INTEGER): An index, in ascending order, describing the order of the packets received on an interface. These packets may be stored in one or more capture buffers, hence aiding in identifying the packets.

captureBufferPacketData (OCTET STRING): Contains the captured data of a packet.

capture BufferPacketLength (INTEGER): Furnishes the length of the captured packet and includes the FCS octets.

captureBufferPacketnme (INTEGER): Furnishes the relative time in milliseconds when a packet was captured since the capture buffer was turned on.

captureBufferPacketStatus (INTEGER): Provides the error status of a packet. The values defined are: packet length greater than 1518 octets = 0, packet length less than 64 octets = 1, packet had CRC or alignment error = 2, first packet in the capture buffer after an error was discovered = 3 and packet's order in buffer is only approximate = 4. The fourth bit definition is an addition in RFC 1757.

Event group The event group helps in the generation and notification of events. These events might have been generated due to conditions elsewhere in the MIB. It may be determined that when a certain threshold is reached an event is generated. Parameters of events are described in eventTable. When an event is generated, it may be necessary to log the event. Events are logged in logTable. Here an SNMP trap may be generated and used to notify a managing station. The objects are:

eventIndex (INTEGER): Identifies an entry in eventTable.

eventDescription (DisplayString): Provides the description of the event.

eventType (INTEGER): Describes the type of event. The values are: none = 1, log = 2, snmp-trap = 3, and log-and-trap = 4. If an event is logged, then a value of 3 is used and there is a corresponding entry in logTable. If an SNMP trap is sent to one or more management stations, then the value is 3. When the SNMP trap is logged the value is 4.

euentCommunity (OCTET STRING): Names the SNMP community to which the SNMP trap must be sent.

eventLastTimeSent (TimeTicks): Furnishes sysUpTime when an event was last generated. If it is set to 0, then no event was generated.

eventOwner and *eventStatus* have the same significance as described for corresponding entries in other groups.

logEventIndex (INTEGER): Has the value of eventIndex for which a log was generated.

logIndex (INTEGER): Identifies an entry in the log table.

logTime(TimeTicks): Furnishes sysUpTime when an event that has been logged in logTable was created.

logDescription (DisplayString): Presents the description of the event.

RMON for Token Ring (RFC 1513) RFC 1513 extends the RMON MIB for the tokenring protocol by adding a new group for tokenRing under RMON.

We discuss RFC 1513 separately, because it neatly describes extensions for the tokenring protocol. Because RFC 1271 is specifically tailored for collecting data on Ethernet protocols, new groups are exclusively added to statistics and history groups for the tokenring protocol. Error counters in a hostEntry for token ring will be incremented for isolating errors such as LineErrors, BurstErrors, ACErrors, InternalErrors, and AbortErrors. In token ring, matrix group error counters are not incremented. For bit mask interpretations for the filter group, refer to RFC 1513. The following new object groups have been added to the token-ring protocol.

Token-ring station
Token-ring station order
Token-ring station configuration
Source routing statistics

New data types in RFC 1513 are:

MacAddress (OCTET STRING (SIZE (6)): Defines the MAC address used in IEEE Standard 802. 1. When MacAddress is used, the source routing bit is stripped off.

TimeInterual (INTEGER): Refers to a period of time, and is measured in intervals of 0.01 seconds.

Token-ring MAC-layer statistics group The token-ring MAC-layer statistics group consists of one table: tokenRingMLStatsTable. This table has statistics on the MAC layer for one token-ring interface, so the objects defined have significance to the MAC layer. We will discuss only those objects which are unique to this group and will not repeat the explanations of those objects which are similar to the ones we discussed with RFC 1757. As we have seen with RFC 1757, these statistics are useful for performance and fault management. In the following discussion, ML stands for MAC layer. The objects in the group are:

tokenRingMLStatsMacPkts (Counter): Refers to the total number of octets in good MAC packets received. It does not include the packets which had errors. A good frame refers to a token-ring frame defined by IEEE 802.5 standards.

tokenRingMLStatsRingPurgeEvents (Counter): Specifies the number of times the ring purge state has been reached from a normal state. In token ring, data is received when a station is in a *normal repeat mode.* In this mode, a station will receive a frame and transmit it. A ring purge MAC frame must be sent before an active monitor originates a new token. When a ring purge frame is received, timers in stations are reset, and stations enter the normal repeat mode.

tokenRingMLStatsRingPurgePkts (Counter): Refers to the total number of ring purge MAC packets.

tokenRingMLStatsBeaconEvents (Counter): Refers to the number of times a beacon state has been entered. To understand this counter, the concept of *beacoming* must be understood. In token ring, a ring can become nonoperational due to faults in stations, which are known as *hard errors.* A hard error in a station is usually detected by its immediate downstream neighbor. On receiving this frame, the downstream neighbor sends a *beacon frame,* which contains the address of its upstream neighbor and the information on the type of error. By knowing the address of the upstream neighbor, the ring station that has a failure can be pinpointed.

tokenRingMLStatsBeaconTime (TimeInterval): Furnishes the duration of the beaconing state.

tokenRingMLStatsBeaconPkts (Counter): Provides the total number of MAC beacon packets.

tokenRingMLStatsClaimTokenEvents (Counter): Separates the entry to the claim token state into three states: from the normal ring state, from the ring purge state, and from the beacon state. In this counter, only the first two cases are taken, and the total number of times a token enters the claim token state is furnished. Note that the claim token process is done to elect a new active monitor.

tokenRingMLStatsC1aimTokenPkts (Counter): Refers to the total number of claim token MAC packets.

tokenRingMLStatsNAUNChanges (Counter): Has the total number of *nearest active upstream neighbor* (NAUN) changes. Note that when an active monitor broadcasts an active monitor present MAC frame, the first ring station that receives this frame saves the source address of the active monitor present frame as the NAUN address. These NAUN addresses are useful for isolating errors in a segment.

tokenRingMLStatsLineErrors (Counter): Provides the total number of line errors.

tokenRingMLStatsInternalErrors (Counter): Refers to the total number of adapter internal errors.

tokenRingMLStatsBurstErrors (Counter): Provides the total number of burst errors.

tokenRingMLStatsACErrors (Counter): Refers to the total number of address copied errors.

tokenRingMLStatsAbortErrors (Counter): A counter of the total number of abort delimiters in error-reporting packets.

tokenRingMLStatsLostFrameErrors (Counter): Refers to the total number of lost frames.

tokenRingMLStatsCongestionErrors (Counter): Provides the total number of receive congestion errors.

tokenRingMLStatsFrameCopiedErrors (Counter): For counting frame copied errors.

tokenRingMLStatsFrequencyErrors (Counter): Provides the total number of frequency errors.

tokenRingMLStatsTokenErrors (Counter): For counting the total number of token errors.

tokenRingMLStatsSoftErrorReports (Counter): Refers to the total number of *soft error* frames. Soft errors mean errors which temporarily make the rings nonoperational, although it is possible to recover from them. These soft errors can pose major problems if there are too many of them.

tokenRingMLStatsRingPollEvents (Counter): Relates to the total number of ring polls initiated by an active monitor.

The other group in the token ring statistics group is the token ring promiscuous statistics group. According to *Webster's New Collegiate Dictionary,* one meaning of *promiscuous is* "composed of all sorts of persons or things." In the MAC layer statistics group data was collected on just the MAC layer. It is necessary to know data about the physical and link layers too. Hence, there is the tokenring promiscuous statistics group. Data on this group is also useful for performance and fault management. The objects in this group are similar to the data collected in etherStats Table, thus, we will not discuss each of the objects in the group. Because there is no Ethernet restriction that the packets must be between 64 and 1518 octets, the range of packet length in token ring is greater.

Token-ring history group Similar to the statistics group, the token-ring history group extends the history group described for RFC 1271. Here, too, history on a token-ring interface is collected and data are saved in tokenRingMLHistoryTable for the MAC layer and in tokenRingPHistoryTable for the non-MAC layer data. Data collected in these tables is useful for performance and fault management. The implementation of the token-ring history group is optional, but it requires the implementation of history groups mentioned in RFC 1757. The meanings of objects are similar to the corresponding ones in RFC 1757 and the token-ring statistics group, so we will not provide individual explanations.

Token-ring ring station group The token-ring ring station group contains the statistics and status of each station attached to a token-ring network. When there are resource limitations on the network monitor, the resources which have been inactive for the longest time must be freed. The implementation of this group is also optional. The data collected for, this station are useful for configuration, performance, and fault management. RingStation ControlEntry has parameters for collecting data on stations in the ring which have been discovered. ringStationEntry has the actual data on the stations. For this group, we will discus those objects that have new meanings.

ringStationControlActiveStations (INTEGER): Furnishes the number of active ringStationEntry in the ringStation-Table.

ringStationControlRingState (INTEGER): Presents the current status of the ring. The values are: normalOperation = 1, ringPurgeState = 2, claimToken-State = 3, beaconFrameStreamingState = 4, beaconBit-StreamingState = 5, beaconRingSignalLossState = 6, and beaconSetRecoveryMode State = 7. These status values can be useful for depicting status in appropriate colors, while showing the configuration and status of the token-ring network.

ringStationControlOrderChanges (Counter): Contains the number of add and delete events in ringStationOrderTable.

ringStationControlBeacon Sender, ringStationControl-BeaconNAUN, and ringStation ControlActive Monitor refer to the address of the sender of the beacon frame, the address of the NAUN in the beacon frame, and the address of the active monitor, respectively.

ringStationTable furnishes statistics on a particular station in the ring. Here, ringStation StationStatus, which can have values of active = 1, inactive = 2, and forced Removal = 3, respectively, is very useful for depicting the status of a station in a ring in configuration management. These states of a station may be represented by different colors. In addition, ringStation-LastEnterTime and ring StationLastExitTime indicate when a station entered and exited a ring and are also useful for configuration management. The value unknown, indicated by a value of 0 in these variables, can be shown by a specific color when depicting these stations in a ring.

Tokenring ring station order group The token-ring ring station order group has ringStation OrderTable, in which stations are identified from the station on which the network monitor is placed. The order of a station relative to the station with the network monitor is furnished by ringStationOrder-OrderIndex, and the address of the station is furnished by ringStationOrder MacAddress.

Token-ring ring station config group The token-ring ring station config group manages token-ring nodes. Another popular term to describe managing token-ring nodes is the *configuration of nodes.* The following describes the nonobvious objects in ringStationConfigControlTable:

ringStationConfigControlRemove (INTEGER): Has two values: stable = I and removing = 2. When RMON agents set the value of this variable to removing, it results in the remove station MAC frame. After this frame is processed, the RMON agent sets this variable to stable.

ringStationConfigControlUpdateStats (INTEGER): Also has two values: stable = I and updating = 2. The behavior of this object is similar to the behavior of ringStationConfigControlRemove. When this object is set to updating, then the configuration information associated with this entry is updated. After this update is over, the RMON agent will set this object to stable.

ringStationConfigTable provides the configuration, entries after a query by the ringStationConfig-ControlUpdateStats',, variable. These data are also useful for configuration management. Some of the associated variables needing explanations are:

ringStationConfigLocation (OCTET STRING(SIZEW): Refers to the actual physical location of the station.

ringStationConfigMicrocode (OCTET STRING(SIZE(10)): Indicates the microcode level of the station.

ringStationConfigGroupAddress (OCTET STRING (SIZE (4)): Pertains to the low-order four octets of the group address recognized by the station.

Token-ring source routing group The implementation of the token-ring source routing group is optional. Data in this group are collected in source routing bridges and are valid in source routing environments. In transparent bridging or mixed source and transparent bridge environments, the data are not accurate. sourceRoutingStats Table provides a list of entries with statistics on source routing for tokenring interfaces. Some of the variables in this group are:

sourceRoutingStatsRingNumber (INTEGER): In an internetwork, there may be many rings, which are assigned numbers by management stations. It is this ring number that is entered here.

sourceRoutingStatsInFrames (Counter): Provides the total number of frames sent to a token-ring station from another ring.

sourceRoutingStatsOutFrames (Counter): Refers to the number of frames sent out from a ring.

sourceRoutingStatsThroughFrames (Counter): Provides the total number of frames which went through a ring. Here, frames are received by a ring and they are transmitted to the next ring.

sourceRoutingStatsAllRoutes Broad cast Frames (Counter): Refers to the total number of good all routes broadcast frames that were received.

sourceRoutingStatsSingleRoute BroadcastFrames (Counter): Has the count of good frames received which had single route broad, cast.

sourceRoutingStatsInOctets, *sourceRoutingStatsOut-Octets*, *sourceRoutingStats Through Octets*, *sourceRouting-StatsAllRoutes BroadcastOctets*, and *sourceRouting Single-RoutesBroadcastOctets* have counts of octets instead of frames, which we saw earlier. The counts refer to good octets only.

sourceRoutingStatsLocalLLC Frames (Counter): Provides the total number of frames received which had no RIF field. All route broadcast frames are not counted here.

sourceRoutingStats1HopFrames through *sourceRouting-StatsMore Than8HopsFrames* provide the frames for the hops mentioned. The all route broadcast frames are not counted. The source and destination stations are expected to be in the same ring.

remove To kill or erase a file or directory.

rename To change the name (or path) of a file or directory.

repeater A device that connects two stretches of cable and boosts the power of the signal it passes, to reduce line noise and the risk of errors.

reply (v): To respond to an e-mail message or Usenet post.
(n) 1. A message sent in response to a previous message or pcst; 2. An e-mail command that takes the return path from the current message and makes that address the recipient of a new message, possibly quoting the previous message as well.

repost (n) An article posted again in full. (Many news-groups expect that reposts be labeled as such in their subject lines.)
(v) To post the same information again.

Request for Discussion (RFD) The first stage in the formal process of Usenet newsgroup creation.

-request: A suffix appended to the user name of a human-administered mailing list to form the username of the administrative address for the list. (So a human administered mailing list called atoz@ netcom.com would have an administrative address called atoz-request@netcom.com associated with it.) It is a Bad Thing to post administrative requests (generally to subscribe or unsubscribe) to the actual mailing list rather than to the request address.

Research Libraries Information Network (RLIN) An online catalog of catalogs with information from most major research libraries in the United States, reachable by telnet at rlg.stanford. edu (it's not free).

Reseaux Associes pour la Recherche Europeenne (RARE) A European group of research networks. For more information, connect via anonymous FTP to ftp.rare.nl.

Reseaux IP Europeenne (RIPE) A group of European TCP/IP networks.

resolution 1. Conversion of a physical address into a logical address *(address resolution);* 2. The degree of detail, sharpness, or fineness of an image.

resolve (v): To convert a physical address to a logical address or vice versa.

return from the dead (v): To be reconnected to the Internet after a hiatus.

return path: An address in the header of an e-mail program that tells the recipient's mail program where to send a reply message.

Reverse Address Resolution Protocol (RARP) A TCP/IP protocol for converting logical addresses to physical addresses.

RFC: *Request for Comments,* one of a set of documents that contain Internet protocols, standards, and information, and together more or less define the Internet, in ai) open way. The standards contained in them ire followed carefully by software developers. The name Request for Comments can be confusing, since the contents are settled, but they arrived from free and open discussion on the Net.

RFCs can be found via anonymous FTP at the ftp.internic.net site among others.

rib site: A computer with a high-speed link to a backbone site that distributes traffic to smaller networks.

rights: Another name for privileges.

Right Thing: Something which is absolutely, the right thing to do.

ring topology: A network architecture in which the nodes are arranged in a circle.

RINGO: An experimental service at MIT that allows you to rate a list of musicians and bands and receive back some suggestions about other music you might like. To participate, send e-mail to ringo@ media.mit.edu..

RJ-45: A modular jack that can hold up to four pairs of wires, used most often to connect unshielded twisted-pair wiring in LANs. An RJ-45 looks like a phone jack (Rj 11) except bigger.

rlogin: A protocol (and program) for remote login from one UNIX machine to another. It automatically supplies the username and password given when the user first logged in.

rm: The UNIX *remove* command, for deleting a file. (Be very careful not to type *rm* and press Enter by mistake—there's no "undelete" in UNIX)

rmdir: The UNIX *remove directory* command, for deleting a directory.

rmgroup: A special kind of control message that removes a newsgroup.

rn: The most common UNIX newsreader. It's not a threaded newsreader.

robocancel (v): To automatically cancel articles. A controversial (because it's a form of censorship) method for dealing with spammers and roboposters.

robopost (v): To post automatically, usually done by a 'bot that is programmed to post reams of articles and responses to Usenet.

roboposter: 1. A 'bot that automatically posts and reposts huge numbers of articles to Usenet; 2. The programmer behind the roboposting 'bot. A reputed roboposter using the name of Serdar Argic singlehandedly rendered soc.history (and a number of other newsgroups) unreadable without a kill file to screen him out. His howling through the wires (ranting Holocaust revisionism about the Turks and the "xSoviet" Armenians) came to an unexpected but welcome halt in the spring of 1994.

robot: A user on IRC or in a MUD (or, less commonly, on Usenet) that is actually a program. Some perform useful functions while others are merely annoying.

robust: Said of software that doesn't crash often and recovers well when it does.

Rogue: A widely circulated text-adventure role-playing game, with a dungeon/ swords-and-sorcery motif.

role-playing game: A game or activity, such as a MUD, in which participants take on fictional identities and strive to remain in character.

ROM (rhymes with prom): *Read-only memory.* Fixed memory that can't be altered.

root (n): 1. In a hierchical file system, the first directory, to which all other directories are subdirectories; 2. On UNIX machines, a superuser account with unlimited permissions.

rot13 *(rot-thirteen)*: A simple cipher in which each letter is replaced with the one 13 letters away from it in the alphabet, traditionally used to hide spoilers and offcolor jokes from sensitive eyes. (Because the alphabet has 26 letters, the same rotation will both encode and decode.)

rotfl: (written only, also *ROTFL) Rolling on the floor laughing.*

route (n): The path a packet takes from sender to destination. (v) To send a packet along a path.

router: A device that physically connects two networks or a network to the Internet, converting addresses and sending on only the messages that need to pass to the other network.

routing information protocol (RIP) A TCP/IP protocol that specifies how routers exchange information.

routing table: A list used by a router to determine the best route for a packet.

RS-232C: A 25-pin connector, such as the one used to connect a computer to an external modem.

RTBM (written only, also *rtbm)*: *Read the bloody manual!*

RTFAQ (written only, also *rtfaq) Read the* FAQ Typical reply to a newbie who posts a frequently asked question.

RTFM (written only, also *rtfm)*: *Read the fucking manual!* An impatient reply to someone asking questions about a program that could be answered by reading the documentation.

samizdat *(sam-is-dot)*: Also *samizdata,* from the Russian word for self-published underground pamphlets, a word used to describe the flow of unofficial information on the Internet, particularly e-zines.

save: Literally, to copy a file or some from memory (RAM) to a disk (or other storage medium). More loosely, to preserve the work you're doing by storing it on a disk.

sb: The Ymodem command for sending (downloading) a file.

sci: A Usenet hierarchy devoted to science.

screen dump: A copy of the contents of a screen, saved to a file or sent to a printer.

screen name: An America Online term for a user's real name or one of several allowable pseudonyms.

screen-oriented: Said of applications that permit the user to move the cursor around the screen.

script: A sequence of commands to be executed by an application or operating system, often saved as a text file.

scroll (v): To browse through a document, moving the text up the screen as if on a continuous parchment. Usually suggests being able to move as little as a line at a time, as opposed to the display of a paging program, which always moves through a document one screenful at a time.

scroll-back: The ability to scroll to an earlier part of a document, which in a terminal emulation program requires that it be saved in a buffer.

SCSI (scuzzy): Stands for *Small Computer Systems Interface,* a standard for connecting personal computers to certain peripheral devices including CD-ROM drives and external hard drives.

.sea: A file extension that indicates a Macintosh self-extracting archive.

search (v): To seek information from a database, document, or other source, usually by specifying key words to match.

(n) The process of seeking specific information from a source.

(adj) Said of programs, interfaces, or tools that facilitate the process of seeking specific information.

searchable (adj): Said of indexes, databases, and documents that are formatted to facilitate searches by standard Internet search tools, such as WAIS, gopher, and Web clients.

search criterion A set of keywords separated by Boolean operators (such as AND, OR, and NOT) specified in a query in order to find matching documents or entries in a database, such as an archie or WAIS server.

secondary service provider An organization that provides a direct Internet connection to a regional set of networks.

security The Internet is not inherently secure. For example, e-mail messages are in some ways more like postcards than like letters sealed in envelopes. Your mail generally passes through many sites on the way to its destination, and postmasters and other superusers can read your mail if they want, although it would be unethical for them to do so.

If you are interested in making your e-mail more private or secure, look into encryption software, such as PGP. New Web products such as Netscape are exploring methods of making private transactions over the Internet as well.

seed: In a tape tree, the original master tape from which the first set of copies is made.

See you on the Net: A farewell customarily uttered to net.friends whom you've happened to run into in real life.

segment: 1. A length of cable in a network; 2. A unit of data packaged by TCP for IP.

select articles (v) In a newsreader, to choose which articles to read (by their tides or authors).

self-extracting archive: An executable file, containing one or more compressed files, that will extract the files it contains when run.

sequenced packet exchange (SPX): A Novell NetWare transport layer protocol that coordinates mesages between workstations.

serial: Said of a connection, such as a phone line, in which bits are transmitted one at a time.

Serial Line Internet Protocol (SLIP): A TCP/IP protocol for transmitting IP datagrams over serial lines, such as phone lines. With SLIP, personal computer users can connect to the Internet and still function in their native environment.

serial port: A port in the back of a PC that can connect via a cable to a serial device, such as a modem or printer.

server: A network application or computer that supplies information or other resources to client applications that connect to it. In conventional networking, server usually refers to a computer, for Internet client/server applications, server usually refers to a program.

Many Internet features are provided by servers: file servers, mail servers, WAIS servers, Web servers, FIT servers, archie servers, name servers, finger servers, and so on.

service provider: A company that provides direct access to the Internet.

session: A period of connection and exchange of communications between hosts.

session layer: Layer 5 of the OSI Model, it specifies how computers make and maintain connections.

setext: A sophisticated text-formatting program for UNIX.

shareware: Software available for a free trial that must be registered and paid for if you decide to use it. Payment may also buy you manuals, support, and updates. Much shareware is distributed via the. Internet. A large FTP archive for Macintosh software can be found at sumex.aim.stanford. edu; another large FTP site for IBM PC and compatible software can be found at wuarchive.wustl.edu in the/systems/ibmpc directory.

shar file: Also called a *sharchive,* a UNIX archive file that contains one or more compressed files. It can be uncompressed in a UNIX shell without any special software.

shell: 1. An operating environment, that is, a program through which a user communicates with the operating system. There are many flavors of UNIX shells, such as Bourne, Korn, Bourne again (bash), C shell, and so on; 2. A command in many applications that allows you to enter shell commands without quitting the program.

shell account: An Internet account that provides access to a UNIX shell, usually via a modem and a terminal-emulation program.

shell command: An operating-system command entered at a command-line prompt or from within an application.

shell out (v) To temporarily escape an application and get access to a shell without quitting the program.

Shergold, Craig: If you get the chain mail telling you to send this poor kid a get well card, don't! He is the famous "dying boy" (no longer dying and no longer a little boy) who, according to a perennially circulating meme, is hoping to become the *Guinness Book of World Records* champion for postcards received. Due to the persistence of this story (it was true once, over 10 years ago), the hospital he stayed in still gets postcards.

shielded cable: A cable protected from electromagnetic interference by wire mesh and plastic, such as a coaxial cable. Shielded cable will not interfere with other electronic devices and is secure from wire tapping. *See* also shielded twisted-pair, unshielded cable, unshielded twisted-pair.

shielded twisted-pair (STP): A cable shielded with foil and a copper braid surrounding the wire in twisted pairs, suitable for high-speed transmission over long distances, often used in token ring networks.

shitogram: A particularly nasty flame.

shouting: On the Internet, TYPING IN ALL CAPS is frequently interpreted as shouting, and is one of the many signs of a newbie.

shovelware: A whole CD-ROM of freeware and shareware, easily obtainable from the Net and thrown together without rhyme or reason.

Shub-Internet: A mythical god or demon thought to be responsible for all slowdowns on die Net. It lives under the Pentagon and is worshipped by some MUD people. Its name is spoken aloud at great peril.

sig block: Also *sig,.sig, signature, signature, signature block, or signature file,* a text file containing a user's name and, optionally, e-mail address, other identifying information, aphorisms, ASCII graphics, etc., automatically attached to the ends of e-mail messages and Usenet posts.

It is generally considered a breach of netiquette to have a sig block over four lines long.

signal (n): An electronic impulse passing over a medium such as a wire, carrying data from one device to another; 2. More loosely, any useful information.

signal-to-noise ratio: 1. Literally, an electrical engineering measurement of the quality of a communication medium; 2. On the Internet, colloquially used as a metaphor for the proportion of useful information to junk on a list or in a newsgroup.

sig quote: A quotation contained in a sig block, not unlike a yearbook quotation and frequently about as interesting.

sig virus: A meme in sig blocks that became very popular around late 1991 to early 1992, usually some variation on "Hi! I'm a sig virus. Copy me into your signature file and join the fun."

silicon: The mineral that computer chips (and sand) are made from,

silly group: A newsgroup created simply for the sake of amusement, either because the name itself is silly or because the topic to be discussed in it is silly, many of which can be found in the alt-silly-group.hierarchy, Some silly groups have a *gag.gag.gag* ending, for instance, alt. tv. dinosaurs. barney die.die.die.

Simple Mail Transfer Protocol (SMTP) The TCP/IP protocol that specifies how computers exchange electronic mail. It works with Post Office Protocol, and is one of the reasons that Internet e-mail functions so well.

Simple Network Management Protocol (SNMP) A TCP/IP protocol that specifies how nodes are managed on a network, using agents to monitor network traffic and maintain a management information base.

Simple Wide Area Information Server (SWAIS) A WAIS interface for VT100 terminals that shows sources in numbered lists.

simplex: Transmission of a signal in one direction at a time.

.sit: The file extension of a Macintosh StuffIt file.

site: An Internet host that allows some kind of remote access, such as FTP, telnet, gopher, and so on.

site name: Also *sitename,* the portion of an Internet address that precedes the (subdomain, if any, and the) domain. In the address mang@garnet.blob. com, *garnet is* the site name.

64K line: A 64 kps telephone circuit, also called a DS0 line. A 64K line is called a clear channel when its entire 64 kps band width is available for transmission.

slack (n): 1. Unused storage space on a disk. 2. According to the teachings of the Church of the SubGenius, the prerequisite of all human happiness. For more information, see the newsgroup alt.slack.

slash /: In UNIX (and hence in gopher addresses and URLs), the separator character between directory levels.

SLIP: *Serial Line Internet Protocol,* a TCP/IP protocol for transmitting IP datagrams over serial lines, such as phone lines. With SLIP, personal computer users can connect to the Internet and still function in their native environment (instead of having to deal with a character-based UNIX environment).

SLIP emulator A UNIX program, such as TIA, that runs in a shell account and

mimics the behavior of a SLIP connection, enabling a shell user to run Internet applications on a personal computer.

slot: A rack inside a computer where an expansion card can be put.

smart terminal: A terminal that can handle some of the display processing, taking some of the load off the computer it's connected to (an obsolete term in the PC world).

smiley: A sideways smiley face, also called an emoticon, used to indicate an emotion. Here are some examples of smileys:

smurf (n): A sickly-sweet newsgroup participant (from the icky-cute little blue elf characters from Saturday morning television rot).

SNAFU: *Situation normal-all fucked up,* an old U.S. Army term used frequently on the Net.

snail (n): A snail mail address, especially labeled as such in a sig block. (v) To send snail mail.

snail mail: Internet slang for U.S. Postal Service mail, so called for its relative slowness compared to electronic mail,

snarf (v): To fetch a set of files across a network, as with FTP.

sneakernet: The kind of network in which you copy the file to a diskette, walk the diskette over to another computer (that's the sneaker part), and then copy the file onto the new computer. The lowest-tech LAN.

'Snooze: A derogatory term for Usenet News, commenting on the low signal-to-noise ratio.

SO *(ess-oh)*: *Significant other,* a genderless term for partner, spouse, lover, etc. common on Usenet.

soc: The Usenet hierarchy devoted to society (and usually sectarian groups in it).

socket: A subdivision of a network node reserved for a single application or process.

socket client: An application or process that reserves a socket for a specific purpose.

socket number: A unique number assigned to a socket by a network.

soda remailer: An anonymous remailer.

soft boot (v): To reboot only part of a system without restarting the whole thing.

software: 1. A program-either an application or operating system-that a computer can execute, as opposed to hardware (the computer itself). 2. A suite of related programs.

sorcererls apprentice mode: What happens when a program or process spins out of control, spawning more and more processes from itself until it eventually crashes its system, or worse, slows down or crashes parts of the Internet.

source: A remote database storing files available to WAIS searches.

source code: The original, uncompiled program instructions that make up a piece of software.

SPACEWAR: The original spaceship combat game, first created on DEC PDP machines, then ported to UNIX, and eventually inspiring one of the first video games.

spam (v): To post (or robopost) huge amounts of material to Usenet, or to post one article to huge numbers of inappropriate groups. (The term comes from the commercial meat product Spam and the Monty Python

Sturgeon's Law: "90% of everything is crap," attributed to science-fiction author Theodore Sturgeon (though he reportedly' used the word crud in the original).

subdirectory: In a hierarchical file system, a directory that is the child of another directory.

subdomain: A named portion of an Internet domain, usually a network, university or company.

Subject says it all: What some people write as the contents of a post or e-mail message for which the entire question or comment is contained in the Subject line.

subnet: A subdivision of a network.

subscribe: To join a mailing list or start reading a newsgroup.

substring search: Air archie option that specifies that the text to be searched for may be contained within a longer file name and need not match the file name exactly

suite: 1. A group of related protocols; 2. A group of related programs that make up a software package.

summarize: To collect the results of a survey or voting process via c mail and *then* post the results to a newsgroup to prevent all the votes or opinions from being posted individually to the Net.

Sun Microsystems: A computer company that makes workstations.

supercomputer: The most powerful ,type of computer. Supercomputers cost tens: millions of dollars and are used for very complex calculations and modeling.

superuser: A special user account with unlimited permissions.

surf (v) To browse, following tangents (trendy slang). You can surf [illegible] the Web is best suited for surfing, since

Switched Multimegabit Data Service (SMDS) A new high-speed technology for data networks, developed by Bell Labs.

synchronous (adj) Said of communication that happens for both participants at the same time. IRC is a synchronous form of communication, while e-mail is asynchronous.

Synchronous Data Link Control (SDLC) A data link layer protocol used on IBM SNA networks.

synchronous transmission A transmission method that uses a clock signal to synchronize the sending and receiving computers in order to regulate the data flow, instead of using start bits and stop bits, as in asynchronous transmission Data is then sent at a fixed rate.

syntax Rules for properly formed commands.

system 1. A program that supervises a computer and coordinates all its functions, also called an operating system; 2. An entire computer taken together with all its devices. 3. A large program.

system administrator Someone who runs or maintains a network.

system file A file reserved for use by the system and not ordinarily killable by a user (at least not without a Warning)

Systems Application Architecture (SAA): A set standards that specify interfaces (user interfaces, programming interface, and communications) for IBM software.

Systems Network Architecture (SNA): A set of communications protocols for networks running on IBM mainframe computers , incompatible with the OSI Model.

T

table of services: A service provider's internal list of Internet services (such as FTP, finger, IRC, and so on) offered to users.

talk (n): 1. One-to-one synchronous chatting over the Net;
2. The UNIX command for initiating or accepting a talk request (the form of the command is talk *username@ address*).

talk: A Usenet hierarchy devoted to discussion, argument, and debate.

talk mode: A UNIX feature in which two or more users can participate in an online conversation in real time.

TANSTAAFL: (written only, also tanstaafl) *There ain't no such thing as a free lunch,* of ten pointed to as a general principal of the universe, probably taken from economist Milton Friedman's book *There's No Such Thing as Free Lunch.*

tape tree: A distributing mechanism for audio cassette tapes employed in some of the music-related newsgroups and mailing lists, in which a seed tape is copied by a root participant for a number of branches, each of which, in turn, dub copies for their children on the tree, until copies of the tapes reach leaf participants, who have parents but no children in the tree structure.

tar (n): A UNIX program (tape archiver) that concatenates a number of files into a single file (without compressing them).
(v) To create an archive file with the tar program.

.tar: A file extension indicating that the file is a tarred file, an archive consisting of several concatenated files.

tar file: A file containing several files, concatenated with the UNIX tar program.

.tar.Z: A file extension indicating that the file is tarred and compressed with the UNIX compress program.

TCP: Transmission Control Protocol, part of the TCP/IP stack. It functions on the transport layer of the OSI Model, establishing and verifying the data connection.

TCP Connect/II: A suite of Macintosh software comprising Internet tools such as e-mail, a Usenet newsreader, FTP, and telnet, developed by InterCon Systems Incorporated.

TCP/IP: A protocol stack, designed to connect different networks, on which the Internet is based. The suite includes protocols for remote login (telnet), file transfer (FTP), e-mail (SMTP), and so on. TCP/IP can work with any hardware or operating system. TCP/IP was developed by DARPA in the late 1970s as a set of robust internetworking protocols that could survive the partial destruction of constituent networks (as might occur in a nuclear war).

TECO: A once popular text editor with a powerful built-in programming language, now largely supplanted by emacs.

teledildonics: A trendy term for online sex, alluding to the mechanical "interface" devices that might evolve in the near future.

Telenet: The original name of SprintNet

telex: An international communications system made up of linked terminals that can send and receive data. Some online services offer telex access.

telnet: 1. A terminal-emulation protocol (defined in RFC 854) for remote login over the Internet, part of the TCP/IP suite;

2. The UNIX program that uses that protocol.

(v) To log in to a remote computer via the telnet protocol.

10BaseF: The Ethernet specification (802.3 standard) for fiber-optic cable.(10 for the 10 Mbps bandwidth, *base* for baseband, and E for fiber-optic.)

10Base5: The Ethernet specification (802.3 standard' using "thick" coaxial cable. (10 for 10 Mbps bandwidth, *base* for baseband, and 5 for 500-meter-long cable segments.)

10BaseT: The Ethernet specification (802.3 standard) using two pairs of unshielded twisted-pair (UTP) wire. (10 for 10 Mbps bandwidth, *base* for baseband, and *T* for twisted-pair cable.)

10Base2: The Ethernet specification (802.3 standard) using "thin" coaxial cable (A") also known as *thinnet, or cheapernet.* (10 for 10 Mbps bandwidth, *base* for baseband, and 2 for 200-meter-long cable segments.)

term: A DOS program that enables a personal computer to function as a UNIX terminal-emulation program over a dial-up connection.

terminal: A keyboard-and-monitor combination, one of many, connected to a computer. The terminal passes the user input from the keyboard to the computer and displays the computer's output on the monitor (screen).

Large, multiuser computers such as mainframes have traditionally been accessed via terminals, as have UN1X machines.

Terminal Access Controller (TAC): A device that provides and maintains a dial-up terminal connection to the Internet.

terminal emulation: Behaving like a specific type of terminal (such as a DEC VT100 or VT52 or an IBM 3270), passing keyboard input to a computer and displaying computer output on the screen (possibly in a window).

terminal-emulation program: Software a personal computer uses to imitate a specific type of terminal (such as a VT100, ANSI, or TTY terminal) and connect to a host.

terminal/host computing: The model of computing used by dumb terminals and host computers, in which the terminal is only a messenger and the host does all of the processing.

terminal server: A device that enables several modems (usually assembled on a modem bank) or terminals to connect to a host on one channel by sending a combined signal.

terminal window: A window in a graphical user interface in which a terminal-emulation program displays an terminal screen connected by network to a remote computer.

terminator: A device connected to the end of a LAN cable to prevent signals from being transmitted.

***.test:** Any of the newsgroups with names such as misc.test, alt.test, rec.test, and so on, designated for test posts. If you post to a '.test newsgroup, daemon's all over the Internet send you e-mail acknowledgments when your post reaches It is a breach of netiquette to post test messages to any newsgroup other than *.test newsgroups.

One trap often set for newbies is a post with its follow-up line set to a *.test newsgroup. Anyone who responds to the post without noticing and removing the *.test group will suffer a mailbox flooded by well-meaning daemons.

test post: A post with no meaningful content, posted to a newsgroup (preferably a *.test newsgroup) so that the user can determine if her newsreader software and Internet connection are working properly.

text editor: An application for editing text files, usually less fully featured than a word processor. The Notepad accessory in Windows is a text editor, as are the UNIX programs vi, pico, emacs, ee, and joe, among others.

text file: Also *ASCII file* or ASCII *text file,* a file containing only ASCII characters. This means no formatting—no bold or italics, no headers, footers, margin adjustments, non-breaking hyphens, and so on.

text file transfer: A form of file transfer, both with FTP and with uploading/downloading programs (kermit, zmodem, etc.) used to transfer files containing only ASCII characters. (Newline characters are automatically converted for the operating system being transferred to.)

text transfer: 1. A text file transfer; 2. A transfer of text directly from a local file to a remote computer, as if typed directly from the keyboard, or from the output of a remote program running on a remote host computer to the terminal window and/or to a text file on the local computer.

T4: A long-distance, digital, point-to-point communications circuit developed by AT&T that transmits a signal at 274.176 Mbps, with up to 168 T1 channels (4,032 channels of 64 Kbps), handling both voice and data.

TFTP: *Trivial File Transfer Protocol,* a simplified version of FTP that does not include password protection.

thanks in advance: Often abbreviated *TIA* or more whimsically as aTdHvAaNn KcSe, a common sign-off for requests made on the Internet.

The Internet Adapter (TIA): A UNIX, program that enables a dial-up shell account to emulate a SLIP connection, allowing the user to run Internet software native to his desktop environment without the full costs (or full functionality, either) of real SLIP. TIA is available from Cyberspace Development at http://marketplace.com/.

Thomas: U.S. Congressional archives on the Web, administered by the Library of Congress, named for Thomas Jefferson, at http://thomas.loc. cov/.)

thread (n): 1. A series of messages related to the same topic in a discussion group, such as an original post and related follow-ups. It is appropriate to read an entire thread before contributing to it to avoid repeating something that may already have been contributed one or more times; 2. A process that is part of a larger process or program.

threaded newsreader: A newsreader that organizes posts according to thread and allows you to read your way up or down a thread, such as trn, tin, and Newswatcher.

throughput: A measure of the rate of data transmitted, expressed as bits per second.

***thwap*:** A virtual slap, as on IRC, indicating that you've just smacked the recipient for writing something stupid or inappropriate.

TIA: 1. An abbreviation for thanks in advance; 2. The Internet Adapter, a SLIP-emulation program for UNIX.

TidBITS: A weekly newsletter about the Internet and Macintosh computers, dis-tributed via e-mail by Adam Engst.

tidy: Cool, stylish, and confident, from the idea of structured, well-organized and easy-to-read programming code.

tilde: The ~ character, used to issue commands in the UNIX mail program.

tilde escape: A command in the UNIX mail program that starts with a tilde character (~) and performs a function, rather than inserting text into the mail.

time out (v): To fail, as a network process, because the remote server or computer has not responded in time, to close a connection after waiting too long for acknowledgment.

timeout (n): The occasion when a remote computer times out.

tin: A threaded newsreader for UNIX.

TLA (written only): *Three-letter acronym,* many of which persist throughout the Internet.

tn3270: A program similar to telnet that emulates a 3270 terminal connected to an IBM mainframe.

toaster: A mildly pejorative name for a Macintosh or PC.

toggle (n): A logical or physical switch (or even a single bit) that can be set to two positions, usually on and off. A light switch is a toggle.

(v) To change a switch or bit from one state to the other (from 0 to 1 or back again).

token ring: A (typically IBM) type of network architecture in which nodes are connected in a closed circle. The nodes continually pass a token (a special message) around the circle. To transmit data, a node has to wait until it's "it." Then the data rides along with the token and gets off at the, right stop.

TokenTalk: An Apple product that, enables AppleTalk protocols to work on a token ring network,

T1: A longdistance, digital, point-to-point communications circuit, developed by AT&T, that transmits a DS1 signal at 1.544 Mbps, with 24 (voice) channels of 64 Kbps. If the circuit uses fewer than 24 channels, it's called ET1 or *fractional T1*.

tool: A utility program, a useful program that performs a set function.

topic drift: As threads wear on in discussion groups, they frequently stray from the original topic as listed in the Subject header. Some posters take the initiative of changing the Subject line to spawn new threads.

This same phenomenon is noticed in e-mail conversations, in which the original header, perhaps preceded by *Re: Re: Re:* outlasts its relevance.

topic group: Any electronic common space for people who share an interest.

topology: Any type of physical network layout, organizing the devices and the cables connecting them. Most LANs have bus topology, star topology, or ring topology.

toy: A computer or system less powerful than the one used by the speaker, not necessarily derogatory.

traditional newsgroup hierarchy: The seven newsgroup hierarchies in Usenet news proper: comp., misc., news., rec., sci., soc., and talk. New newsgroups in any of the traditional hierarchies can only be created after a formal process, including a request for discussion and a call for votes.

traffic: 1. Mailing list or newsgroup posts, taken as a whole. 2. Network activity, measured in bits per second, kilobits per second, or megabits per second.

trailer: Information following the data in a packet, signifying the end of the data and possibly including error-checking information.

transceiver: A device that both transmits and receives signals, exchanging frames between a node and a network

Transmission Control Protocol (TCP): Part of the TCP/IP stack. It functions on the transport layer (layer 4) of the OSI Model, establishing and verifying the data connection.

transmit network: A network that communicates with at least two other networks and transmits data among networks as well as among local nodes.

transport layer: Layer 4 of the OSI Model, controlling delivery and verification of messages.

tree administrator: In a tape tree, the person who designs the tree and administers the process, not necessarily the person who provides the seed (usually not, in fact).

trn: A threaded newsreader for UNIX based on rn.

troff: A UNIX text processor that can produce output for typesetting equipment, superseded largely by TEX.

Trojan horse: An attack program, hidden inside a seemingly benign program, that enables the program's creator to gain access to the user's system.

troll *(v)*: *1.* To deliberately post egregiously false information to a newsgroup in hopes of tricking dense know-it-alls into correcting you; 2. From the fishing term, to explore information sources or communication methods on the Net, looking for something specific, as in the *New Yorker* cartoon in which a boss tells his employee: "I hear you've been trolling for babes on the Internet."

Trumpet newsreader Windows newsreader: software that works with NNTP, available by anonymous FTP from biochemistry.cwru.edu.

Trumpet for Windows: Windows Internet software featuring a newsreader and a mail program, available by anonymous FTP from biochemistry.cwru.edu.

T3: A longdistance, digital, point-to-point communications circuit, developed by AT&T, that transmits a signal at 44.746 Mbps, with up to 28 T1 channels (762 voice channels of 64 Kbps), running over a leased line, usually fiber-optic cable.

T2: A longdistance, digital, point-to-point communications circuit, developed by AT&T, that transmits a signal at 6.3 Mbps, with up to four T1 channels (92 channels of 64 Kbps). T2 is used within telephone company networks, not commercially.

tunafish test: A series of posts in 1994 to a *.test newsgroup via the anon.penet.fi anonymous remailer service that may have compromised the identities of some of the remailer's users.

tunneling: Encapsulating a datagram of one protocol within that of a different protocol to transport the enclosed data across an intervening backbone that does not support the former protocol.

tuple *(toople)*: *A* pair of related values in a routing table (the network number and the number of hops to that network).

TurboGopher: 1. A gopher client for the Macintosh, available via anonymous FTP from sumex-aim.stanford.edu; 2. An improved version of the original gopher software developed at the University of Minnesota.

tweak: 1. To make small changes in order to get something just exactly perfect; 2. To tease someone in a minor way.

twilight zone: An imaginary place where only IRC channel ops may go.

twisted-pair cable: Cable comprising four or more copper wires, twisted in pairs (one grounded, one carrying a signal) to reduce interference, usually one pair for sending, one for receiving. There are two types of twisted-pair cable shielded twisted-pair (STP) and unshielded twisted-pair (UTP).

.txt: A file extension indicating a text file

Tymnet: A global public data network, offering local dial-up access in one hundred countries, including access to some online services and Internet service providers.

Typeface: A style of lettering, often designed for a specific purpose, for example, readability in small sizes, for display purposes in large sizes, to attract the reader's attention, to create a particular mood or impression etc. Many typeface designs are copyright. A design can be specified by profile, style, ornamentation, thickness of lines etc. A typeface is also known as font, however the two terms are not directly interchangeable.

(abbreviation WAN) would cross state borders and have computers in Perth, Adelaide, Brisbane, Townsville and Sydney. A less dispersed WAN may have computers in each provincial town of a large state such as New South Wales. Even smaller WANs may be restricted to metropolitan areas.

Wild Card: A character inserted into an operating system command that is interpreted as having several meanings. For example the MS-DOS command "Erase *.doc" will erase all files with the file extension doc. In another example the VAX command "Purge Prog26*" will delete all but the most up-to-date, versions of Prog26 files. Wild cards are useful productivity tools but can, create havoc if an erroneous command is given.

WIMP (adj): From *Window Icon, Menu, Pointing device,* said of a graphical user interface such as Macintosh. Windows, or X.

Winchester Disk: A particular type of hard disk technology which uses a high density of data storage tracks and a very low flying read/write head requiring a closely controlled operating environment. Winchester technology was developed by IBM and first introduced in 1973. A Winchester disk is hermetically sealed and provides an operating environment that is free of dust and moisture, an essential method of operation since the separation between read/ write head and platter is about 20 microns.

WinCIM: *CompuServe Information* manager for windows

Window: This is part of the on-screen display on a monitor. The display may use only one window, occupying most of the available space. However some software applications allow the user to split the screen into several windows in order to load more than one program or data file at the same time.

Windows: A proprietary adjunct to the MS-DOS operating system. Windows was developed by Microsoft and provides enhanced file handling features and the ability to load more than one program at once.

Windows 95: The version of Windows (formerly known as Chicago). It is rumored to include TCP/IP support as well as direct access to Microsoft Network, which itself will include full access to the Internet.

Windows NT: A 32-bit operating system based on the Windows operating environment with built-in networking capabilities and no remaining traces of DOS.

Windows socket: The conventional: method of configuring the Windows operating environment, for TCP/IP networking.

Windows for Workgroups: A version of Windows with built-in peer-to-peer networking capabilities.

Windoze: A derogatory term for Windows, referring to its legendary slowness.

Winqvt/Net: Combined mail, news, telnet, FTP for Windows.

Winsock: A type of Windows application that sets up a socket and works with TCP/IP protocols to establish an Internet connection.

WinVN: A newsreader for Windows based on the UNIX vn newsreader that communicates with Network News Transfer Protocol-based news servers, available via anonymous FTP from titan.ksc.nasa.gov.

WinWAIS: A Windows WAIS client program, available via anonymous FTP from ridgisd.er.usgs.gov.

WinWeb: A Web browser for Windows, created by EINET, and available via anonymous FTP from ftp.einet.net in the /einet/pc/winweb directory.

wizard: Someone who really understands how a piece of hardware or software works and is willing to help newbies; 2. By extension, any expert, as in the alt.sex.wizards newsgroup.

Word: The basic storage unit of a computer, typically one word occupies two or more bytes of memory.

Word Processor: A software package that is primarily concerned with the entry, manipulation and formatting of text.

Word Wrap: A feature of most word processors which ensures that a word that will not fit at the end of a line of text will automatically be placed at the start of the next (new) line.

workaround: A temporary patch for a bug that avoids but does not fix the underlying problem.

workgroup: A group of users, often on a LAN, working on the same project.

Working Directory: The directory currently being used for data transfers.

Workstation: This is essentially a PC (microcomputer), often in a network environment. Increasingly workstations are becoming synonymous with superior processing capabilities, however many workstations are fairly ordinary machines. A diskless workstation does not have floppy disk drives, data storage is provided by a centralised hard disk. This provides management control over data storage as it reduces the likelihood of data theft, the introduction of computer virus, and of employees running their own software.

world: The default distribution choice for newsgroup posts. Post distribution can also be limited to geographical areas (by their two-letter abbreviations) or to local.

World Wide Web: Also called the Web, WWW, W3, and w^3, an interlinked collection of hypertext documents (Web pages) residing on Web servers and other documents, menus, and databases, available via URLs (uniform resource locators). Web documents are marked for formatting and linking with HTML (hypertext markup language), and Web servers use HTTP (hypertext transport protocol) to deliver Web pages.

The Web was invented as an online documentation resource by physicists at the CERN European Particle Physics Laboratory in Switzerland,

worm: A program that duplicates itself repeatedly, potentially worming its way through an entire network.

WORM Drive: A Write-Once-Read-Many times optical disk drive which can be of varying size and which is an increasingly important form of secondary memory. A 30Omm diameter disk has a storage capacity of about 6GB, 5.25" (135mm) disks hold about 800MB.

WPO: Abbreviation for Word Processor Operator, a person who is trained to use a word processor.

:wq: The save *and quit* command in vi, often seen at the end of newbies' posts when they fail to switch back from insert mode to edit mode before typing the command.

Write: The process of entering data into primary memory or secondary memory.

Write Protection: A technique used to prevent accidental or intentional alteration/deletion of important data and/or programs, for example, the operating system. Write Protection can to provided by hardware, for example, by write-protect notches on a floppy disk, or by software. Hard disks can usually only be write protected by alteration of the control circuitry.

Wrong Thing: An action that's clearly incorrect, not the Right Thing.

WS_FTP: A Windows FTP client program made by John A. Junod, available via anoymous FTP from 129.29.64.246 in the /pub/msdos directory.

wumpus: A game, originally written in BASIC, in which the user hunts a monster called the Wumpus, in a sort of maze of rooms containing various hazards. Depending on how near the Wumpus is the user can hear, smell, or see it, and the user has "crooked" arrows with which to shoot through up to three connected rooms.

wustl archives: A huge FIT archive at wuarchive.wustl.edu.

www: The original text-based UNIX Web browser, developed at CERN European Particle Physics Laboratory. To try out www (if it's not installed on your system), telnet to info.cern.ch. Abbreviation for World Wide Web.

WWW Browser for the Macintosh: A Macintosh Web browser available via anonymous FTP from info.cern.ch.

WYSIAYG *(whizzy-egg)*: *What You see is all you get,* a pejorative phrase for the limitations and unhackability of some GUI software.

Xerox Network System (XNS): A suit of communications protocols, similar to TCP/IP, developed by Xerox Corporation and later used by Novell and other network developers.

Xerox PARC: Xerox's legendary Palo Alto Research Center, where the modem GUI (which combines the use of a mouse, windows, and icons) was invented, not to metion laser printers and LANs.

X.500: A CCITT and standard for electronic using a distributed database of X.400 information, including usernames, postal addresses, telephone numbers, fax numbers, and so on.

X.400: A CCITT and ISO standard for international e-mail handling. X.400 is different from Internet e-mail standards, but mail can be transferred from one system to the other via gateways.

XGopher: X Window gopher client ware, available via anonymous FTP from boom box.micro.umn.edu.

Xibo: The evil anti-Kibo. This unfortunate devil has many fewer adherents than his nemesis.

XLibrary for the Macintosh: software for designing SLIP front ends to network services, via anonymous FTP from sumex-aim. stanford.edu.

Xmodem: A file-transfer protocol sup ported by just about every program. Xmodem sends 128-byte blocks and is used for uploading and downloading to and from dial-up Internet accounts and BBSs.

Xmodem-CRC: An extension of Xmodern using more stringent errorchecking

XOFF: Ctrl-S (ASCII 19), a character that pauses data transmission.

XON: Ctrl-Q (ASCII 17) a character that pauses data transmission.

XON/XOFF: A form of flow control, using ASCII characters 17 and: 19 to control the flow of data over an asychronous connection, usually one of the choices for configuring a modern to connect to a dial-up service.

XOR [Boolean operator]: *Exclusive or. A* text search with XOR between two words matches any documents containing one word or the other, but not both.

X.25: 1 A CCITT-recommended standard for connecting computers to public packet-switched networks that specifies transmission and error correction protocols, now largely superseded by frame relay.

XWAIS: X Window WAIS client software available via anonymous FTP from sunsite.unc.edu

X Window: Also called X, an open, nonproprietary graphical user interface often used with UNIX, It was developed at MIT and is independent of the hardware or operating system it runs on. It's easy to find Internet client software for X Window.

YAFIYGI *(yaffy-yiggy,* also written yafiygi): *You asked for* it, you got it, applied to certain forms of word-processing and desktop publishing applications in which the user gets no preview of the eventual appearance of the document.

Yanoff's Intenet Services List: A thorough and frequently updated list of Internet services, maintained by Scott Yanoff of the University of Wisconsin. It's available via anonymous FTP from csd4.csd.uwm.edu in the /pub directory, with the file name inet. services. txt. It's also posted regularly to alt. bbs. internet.

YAUN *(yawn,* also written *yaun)*: *Yet another UNIX nerd.*

yellow pages: 1. An informal name for the database of machine names and addresses of the InterNIC Registration Service; 2. An informal name for the security and file-access database of a UNIX system.

YHBT: (written only) You *have been trolled.*

YHBT. YHL. HAND.: (written only) *You have been trolled. You have lost. Have a nice day.*

YMMV (written only, also *ymmv)*: *Your mileage may vary* (used metaphorically).

Ymodem: Also called *Xmodem 1K,* a file-transfer protocol supported by many communications programs. Ymodem sends 1024-byte blocks, is faster than Xmodem, and can send multiple files.

You misspelled: A form of silly follow-up post favored by kibologists 'followers of kibology), in which the original poster is accused of spelling some entirely different word from the one obviously intended, but perhaps what the poster meant or should have meant.

Z

.Z: A file extension indicating a file that has been compressed with the UNIX compress program.

Zen and the Art of the Internet: Brendan Kehoe's excellent Internet primer, available as a paper book from Prentice Hall and online from many FTP and gopher sites (try an archie or Veronica search), including via anonymous FTP from ftp.cs.widener.edu in the directory pub/zen.

zine: *Also zine,* a fanzine or other underground publication, possibly produced on company time or using office equipment. Most'zines are still produced on paper and mailed to subscribers, but many are archived on the Internet, and there are also some e-zines, electronic zines distributed by e-mail, by gopher, or on the Web.

zip (v.): To compress a file with pkzip or another program.

zip: A file extension indicating that the file has been compressed with the programs pkzip, zip, or WinZip.

zip codes: U.S. postal zip codes as of 1991 can be found via anonymous FTP from oes.orst.edu in the /pub/almanac/misc directory with the file name zipcode.txt.Z.

zip file: A compressed file.

zip up: To compress a file with pkzip or another program.

Zmodem: A batch file-transfer protocol supported by some communications programs. Zmodem is faster than Ymodem and Xmodem and recovers from disconnections more gracefully.

zone (n): A logical (as opposed to physical) group of users on a LAN, such as thin an AppleTalk network, within a larger group of interconnected networks.

Zone Information Protocol (ZIP): The protocol AppleTalk routers use to exchange zone names and network numbers.

Zone Information Table (ZIT): A list of zone names and corresponding network numbers used by AppleTalk routers.

zone fist: A list of AppleTalk zones in the Chooser.

zone name: 1. The text name of a zone, corresponding to a network number; 2. The name of an AppleTalk network zone.

.zoo: A file extension indicating a file compressed with the zoo210 program.

Zork: A text adventure first written in the late '70s and distributed with BSD UNIX, also ported as *Dungeon* Now sold in a commercial form as the Zork Trilogy.

zorkmid: A unit of currency used in many computer games, originally from Zork.

Z39.50: The ANSI information-retrieval service definition and protocol specification for library applications, a format by which all Internet database information could potentially be made available.